Homemade Money
Starting Smart

Also By Barbara Brabec

HOMEMADE MONEY
How to Select, Start, Manage, Market & Multiply
the Profits of a Business at Home

CREATIVE CASH
How to Profit from Your Special Artistry, Creativity,
Hand Skills, and Related Know-how

THE CRAFTS BUSINESS
ANSWER BOOK & RESOURCE GUIDE
Answers to Hundreds of Troublesome Questions About
Starting, Marketing & Managing aHomebased Business
Efficiently, Legally & Profitably

HANDMADE FOR PROFIT
Hundreds of Secrets to Success
in Selling Arts & Crafts

MAKE IT PROFITABLE
How to Make Your Art, Craft, Design, Writing or
Publishing Business More Efficient, More Satisfying,
and More Profitable

Homemade Money
Starting Smart

*How to Turn Your Talents,
Experience, and Know-How into
a Profitable Homebased Business
That's Perfect for You!*

By Barbara Brabec

**Featuring home-business idea charts
and checklists, success stories,
an encyclopedic A-to-Z "Crash Course"
in Home-Business Basics, and everything
else you need to successfully launch a
profitable homebased business**

M. Evans and Company, Inc.

New York

M. Evans and Company, Inc.
216 East 49th Street
New York, New York 10017

Library of Congress Cataloging-in-Publication Data

Brabec, Barbara.
  Homemade Money: starting smart : how to turn your talents, experience, and know-how into a profitable homebased business that's perfect for you! / by Barbara Brabec.—[Rev. ed.]
  p. cm.
  Includes bibliographical references and index.
  ISBN 0-87131-998-5
  1. Home-based business—Management. I. Title.
HD62.7.B684 2003
658'.041—dc21

Printed in the United States of America

Designed and typeset by Evan Johnston

10   9   8   7   6   5   4   3   2   1

Dedicated to the Memory of
William J. Schaumburg

Unlike his children, my father did not have the benefit of a good education. Yet he was smart enough to teach himself what he needed to know to make a living, first as a farmer and, later, as an auto mechanic and repairman who never met anything mechanical he couldn't figure out.

With little more than talent, determination, and a belief in himself, he built his own home and garage business in the small farming community of Buckley, Illinois, where he lived until he died in 1982.

As children, my two sisters and I did not realize that our father, by example, was quietly instilling in each of us his work ethic and entrepreneurial spirit, but as three entrepreneurial women, we certainly know it now.

All of the information in this book is presented to assist individuals in starting a business at home. Much of the material offered is in such professional service categories as legal, tax, and accounting. While the information provided has been carefully researched and checked for accuracy, it is not the business of either the author or the publisher to render such professional services. Readers are asked to exercise normal good judgment in determining when the services of a lawyer or other professional would be appropriate to their needs.

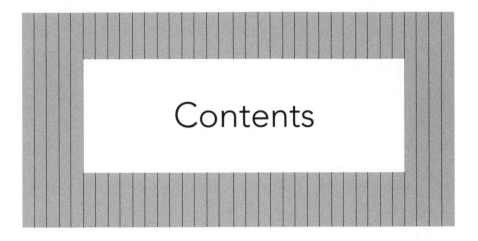

Contents

Section I

• Why People Avoid "Business" • Why People Fear Success • Is Something Holding You Back? • Home-Business Pros and Cons • "Self-Employed Individuals" vs. "Entrepreneurs" • Taking a Chance on Yourself • Why Businesses May Fail • Overcoming Your Fear of the Unknown

Section II

Acknowledgments

I am indebted to the many business professionals who, through the years, have made special contributions to *Homemade Money* and this new book as well. In particular, I wish to thank attorney Mary Helen Sears, specialist in copyrights, patents, and trademarks for her help in ensuring that all my information on these topics has always been accurate and up-to-date. I also owe special thanks to CPA Bernard Kamoroff for his help in checking the accuracy of my information on tax deductions, accounting, and other related business content. The time and talent of these professionals, so generously contributed, has benefited all of us.

My thanks, too, to the countless home-business owners and other business professionals in my network who have been sharing their experiences and expertise with me through the years so I could pass the information along to my readers.

Finally, a nod of gratitude to my husband, Harry (last on the list, as usual). Now retired, his help with my business for more than twenty years made all the difference in my ability to find extra time for writing books. Today, his support for my work and his sense of humor continue to make the difference between a good day and a bad one.

Introduction

Millions of Americans are generating income—I call it "homemade money"—from an incredible variety of homebased activities. This book is one of two Homemade Money guides that explain how to get in on the action and maximize profits from a business at home.

These two books—a dynamic duo!—are actually the second generation of my home-business bible, *Homemade Money*, published in 1984. Between 1984 and 1997, I updated or completely rewrote this book five times to ensure that readers had the best information possible, each time adding additional content until the book was practically bulging at the seams. (Weighing in at nearly two and a half pounds, the last edition was the heftiest home-business bible ever published, with more than 120,000 copies sold.)

By 2001, after my first intense year of writing for the Web and launching my own Web site, I finally understood how the Internet was dramatically changing both the home-business industry and the lives of those involved in it. Once again, I was ready to write a totally new edition of *Homemade Money*, but—surprise!—the publisher was no longer interested in the book. Frankly, I was stunned by this lack of interest at a time when people were losing jobs every day for one reason or another. (See "The Restructuring of the Workforce" in Chapter One). The failure of so many dot-com businesses in 2000, followed by the September 11 terrorist attack and the 2001 recession, convinced me and another publisher, M. Evans, that thousands of people needed a new edition of my home-business bible. Because of all the new Internet/Web-related content I now needed to add to the book, however, it was necessary to turn my old home- business bible into two new *Homemade Money* guides—one directed to home-business beginners, the other to established business owners needing help to grow their business and improve profitability.

In *HOMEMADE MONEY: Starting Smart*, you'll learn how to brainstorm and select a business that's right for you, and how to plan your moves, price your products and services, position yourself for success, and maintain control in your personal life once you've begun your business. You'll also get answers to hundreds of questions on how to legally start and operate a new business at home, whether it's a small, part-time endeavor for extra money or a full-time entrepreneurial venture. (In fact, the important tax, legal, and financial tips in Section II of this book are likely to keep you out of a peck of trouble and save you hundreds–if not thousands–of dollars.)

After you've used this book to get your business up and running, you'll be ready for its companion business management and marketing guide, *HOMEMADE MONEY: Bringing in the Bucks*. Picking up where this book leaves off, it offers information on how to find and keep customers or clients through better marketing and PR strategies; how to expand a product line, add new services, or diversify into new business areas; how to do business on the Web, improve business management skills, handle employee/independent contractor issues, maximize profits, and much more. (See inside back cover for more detailed content information.)

Both books are a reflection of my lifetime of business experience coupled with that of thousands of other professionals who have shared information with me through the years. Trial-and-error experience is a great way to learn, but it can be quite expensive in terms of both time and money. Fortunately, there is no need for you to learn everything the hard way, because so many people are willing to share the benefit of their experience with you. This book is but one example. In both of my *Homemade Money* guides, you'll find inspiration and ideas from many business owners, authors, and other experts in my network who have "been there, done that." Something that makes these books especially valuable is the fact that many of the business owners and experts quoted or featured in them are people whose businesses I have been tracking for twenty years or more. In fact, many of them launched their

Introduction

businesses with an early edition of *Homemade Money* or one of my other books, then went on to share information I added to later editions. How they grew and overcame obstacles, generated new business, changed directions, or went on to do other things entirely, is the kind of real home-business history you won't find in other books in this field.

Don't tackle this book with the idea that you need to absorb all of it in one sitting; rather, think of it as an idea stimulator and answer book you can turn to for help as you select, plan, and launch your homebased business. (The detailed index will be helpful in this regard.) Meanwhile, check my Web site at www.BarbaraBrabec.com to join my e-mail network and get additional support as you embark on what is likely to be the most interesting, frustrating, exciting, frightful, satisfying, and fulfilling thing you will ever do: *become your own boss!*

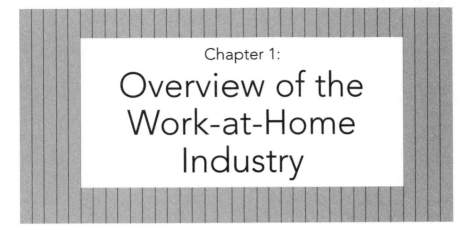

Chapter 1:
Overview of the Work-at-Home Industry

With fewer choices in the job market and no opportunity in the stock market, people will naturally start to consider a business launch. Just fifteen years ago, that meant renting office space or a storefront. Not any more. A homebased business is perfectly respectable now. It's even coveted.

—Rob Spiegel, author of *The Shoestring Entrepreneur's Guide to the Best Home-Based Businesses* (Griffin)

In 1984, three years after I had started my own publishing business, home businesses were still a novelty to most people. Those who did give consideration to the idea were likely to be thinking only in terms of doing something part time for extra money. Few of us could have imagined in the early 1980s that millions of people in the 1990s would be earning a living from some form of homebased work. And fewer still would have believed—even in the late 1990s—that they would be selling their products or services on the World Wide Web at the turn of the century.

As a speaker at many entrepreneurial events in both the U.S. and Canada between 1981 and 2000, I had a ringside seat in the home-business move-ment, and my contact with so many entrepreneurial-minded people through the years has given me unique perspective on the home-business industry. Before I get to the meat of this book—how to get started in a business at home—I want you to have an understanding of the BIG work-at-home pic-ture so you can see exactly how and where you fit into it.

Actually, homebased businesses are just one segment of today's huge and still-growing work-at-home industry, which also includes: (1) telecom-muters, (2) corporate employees who regularly bring work home from the office, (3) "moonlighters" (people who work full time and run a part-time business on the side), and (4) self-employed individuals who have a business base at home, yet do not think of themselves as home-business owners because they perform services away from home.

When computer technology began to fuel the work-at-home industry in the mid-1980s, market research firms began to gather statistics for clients interested in marketing to this diverse group of homeworkers. Their findings became news because this was the first time anyone had made an effort to count the steadily growing number of people who were working at home. As researchers predicted in the 1990s, the home-business industry continued to grow into the new century, moving gracefully onto the Web with millions of other businesses around the world.

Using data collected by the Bureau of the Census in 1996 and 1997, The Small Business Administration's (SBA) Office of Advocacy did a study (released in March 2000) that provided a detail-rich portrait of the home-based sector of the U.S. economy. It revealed that homebased businesses then represented 52 percent of all firms and provided 10 percent of the total receipts of the economy. The average receipts of all homebased firms was in the $40,000 range. Currently, the U.S. Small Business Administration reports that 53 percent of all small businesses are now homebased, and these businesses are pouring $450 billion into the American economy every year. According to the U.S. Department of Labor, some 60 percent of all busi-nesses are now being started at home. Swelling the ranks of the self-employed, reports *Home Business* magazine, are "recently dot-bombed Internet workers and professionals from other Nasdaq-ravaged technology sectors." (This magazine is online at HomeBusinessMag.com.)

In spite of all the statistics being bandied about today, no one really knows for sure how many people work at home for others versus how many actually own part- or full-time businesses of their own. Surveys by government agencies do not always agree with those of various market-research firms who are gathering data in different ways for different purposes. For example, one market research specialist told me that his company's statistics were based on an annual telephone survey of 2,500 consumer households, with telephone numbers generated randomly by computer. By comparison, the U.S. Labor Department gathers its data periodically from a changing database of 60,000 households. Karen Kosanovich of the Labor Department explains the process: "The work-at-home data are collected in a special supplement to the Current Population Survey (CPS)—a monthly survey of about 60,000 households that provides information on employment and unemployment in the US. The CPS collects data about all persons sixteen years and over in the selected households—over 100,000 in an average month. All employed persons in the survey were asked to complete the work-at-home supplement. Persons that identified themselves as self-employed (whether or not their business was incorporated) were asked if their businesses were run from home, some other location, or both. This is how home-based business data were derived in both 1997 and 2001."

In summary, depending on whose statistics you wish to believe, there are 16 to 27 million homebased businesses today, and they are not only an important economic revitalization tool in both urban and rural areas, but also the lifestyle of choice for millions of Americans.

What Will You Call Yourself?

One of the reasons it is so hard to obtain a definitive count of the number of people working at home is that different surveys of this population do not use the same definitions of homebased work, and homeworkers themselves aren't sure what they should be calling themselves. Are they "independent contractors," "consultants," "homebased entrepreneurs," "home office professionals," "teleworkers," "freelancers," "home-business owners," or "self-employed individuals"?

Some writers erroneously refer to businesses at home as "cottage industries." A true cottage industry, however, is a business that has its management and marketing operations in one location with production taking place in the homes of several individual workers.

Adding to the confusion is the fact that writers and media people have coined a variety of "preneur" words to describe the current generation of "work-at-homers," including:

Solopreneurs
Entrepreneurial Parent (see below)
SingleParentPreneur
Mompreneurs
Copreneur (couples who work together)
Countrypreneur (those who are earning a living in the country)
Agripreneur
Cyberpreneur
Netpreneur
Ecopreneur (those who are ecologically minded)
Homepreneur
Infopreneur (those who sell information)
Intrapreneur/Ideapreneur (see sidebar on this topic)
Kidpreneur
Lifepreneur (someone who wants to create a living in balance with his or her life)
Propreneur (corporate refugees and recent college graduates)
RVpreneur (for those who work from their recreational vehicle)

NOTE: Some of the "preneur" names above are now the domain names of established Web sites. Most of the other names have been claimed and registered by others, and at least two have been trademarked business names, (Entrepreneurial Parent and Mompreneurs), so be careful how you use these names in the future. Also, note that for some time now, Entrepreneur Media (publisher of *Entrepreneur* magazine) has taken a hostile, litigious stance toward the entrepreneurial community by attempting to prevent everyone but them from using the word "entrepreneur" as part of their business name. They have already sued several companies and forced other businesses and individuals to cease using this word. However, they have lost at least two cases with companies who had the legal and financial clout to wage a court battle.

EntrepreneurPR.com, which provides PR services to innovative small business entrepreneurs, emerged victorious after a long battle with Entrepreneur Media. As a result of Entrepreneur Media's aggressive legal efforts to monopolize the word "entrepreneur," EntrepreneurPR was forced to change its name to "BizStarz" in June 2000. However, in February 2002, the 9th U.S. Circuit Court of Appeals unanimously ruled that Entrepreneur Media's trademark is "weak" and they do not have exclusive rights to the word "entrepreneur."

At that point, EntrepreneurPR resumed use of its name. Scott Smith, president of this company, told me that many, if not most, of the businesses sued by Entrepreneur Media for using the word "entrepreneur" are homebased businesses. "It's important to make use of professionals when choosing the name of a company," he says, "because homebased businesses are some of the easiest targets for frivolous intellectual property disputes."

Entrepreneurs.com (owned by WebMagic, Inc.) is another company that won its suit with Entrepreneur Media, and you'll find some information about their story on its Web site.

Entrepreneurial Moms and Dads

The National Association of Entrepreneurial Parents, created by Lisa Roberts, serves as a vehicle for connecting local entrepreneurial parents. After writing and publishing *How to Raise a Family & A Career Under One Roof* (Bookhaven Press), Lisa relaunched her Web site, EN-Parent.com, for parents who work at home. By mid-2002, more than 1,200 members had registered on the site, and Lisa had co-authored a second book with Paul and Sarah Edwards titled *The Entrepreneurial Parent: How to Earn Your Living at Home & Still Enjoy Your Family, Your Work and Your Life* (Putnam/Tarcher, 2002).

Based on 2001 surveys by the market research firm IDC, Lisa estimates there are 10 million entrepreneurial parents. "IDC's 2001 survey estimated there were 12.1 million households that had one parent who had a child 17 years or younger generating income at home," she says, "while CyberDialog's survey turned up 8.5 million parents online who described themselves as being self-employed."

Lisa, mother of four, believes three-quarters of all parents now working at home came from the corporate world. "Some jump out of the workforce, but many more are pushed," she says. "Self-employment is a step up from unemployment, and most people use a home business to reposition themselves until the economy gets better and they're ready to enter the workforce. But many find they like being their own boss and never go back." Lisa adds that there are just as many dads running businesses at home as there are moms. "It's just that moms get all the PR, whereas dads feel uncomfortable saying they're home based. They want to stay off the radar."

In an online article at Bankrate.com, Dana Dratch reported on IDC statistics, saying, "They estimate that 38.7 million households have at least one home-based business, and U.S. Census data show that roughly half of all married dads are providing full- or part-time care of their pre-school children. The bottom line is that men are finally learning to do what women have done for years: juggle career, kids and home. Their conclusion: It isn't easy—but it is worth it."

At-Home Dads also have a network and informal online organization of their own, thanks to Peter Baylies. When he was laid off from work, he decided to stay at home with the children while his wife continued her job as a school teacher. To find support, and to give it to others, Peter started a newsletter that soon gained a large following. Now that his youngest son is in first grade, Peter has the time to turn the newsletter into a book, and he is now networking with dads through his Web site, AtHomeDad.com, which he calls a "loose-knit grassroots organization for at-home dads." It now sponsors the annual At-Home Dad Convention in Chicago.

Although there are no current definitive figures on the number of at-home dads, Peter believes there are at least two million out there. Many of these dads probably have businesses on the side, but there are no statistics as to their number. "Twenty years ago it was bizarre to be an at-home dad," says Peter, "but with the advances in technology and increased broadband access, more moms getting paid more, and the resistance to daycare, I think the at-home dads trend will increase, although slowly. I plan to stay at home as the kids go through elementary school and beyond," he says.

Comments from People Who
Yearn to Earn at Home
(from the author's mail)

"Our money is extremely tight and I would like to get a home business going to supplement our income and afford me the luxury of being at home where my children need me."

"My husband was forced to take an early retirement and nobody will hire him at his age of 54."

"I am a burned-out registered nurse who would like to start something on my own in the health care field."

"I am faced with that age-old question: what to do now that the kids are in school. I am frustrated with my present choices and wonder what I might do at home."

"I am a new widow who has been sewing for people for years on a limited basis. Now I'm ready to work full time in making a career that will be as profitable as it is enjoyable."

"Our financial situation is making it necessary for me to find employment. But because of my son's health, working outside my home is impossible."

"Daily I disguise myself as a legal secretary and put up with a multitude of egos and personalities. How I ache to join the ranks of homebased entrepreneurs!"

Home Businesses Then and Now

Technology has certainly been responsible for the tremendous growth in the work-at-home industry since the mid-1980s, but homebased enterprises have been part of the American culture since the days of the Early American Colonies when everyone worked at home—the baker, the silversmith, the candlestick maker, the weaver, the blacksmith, the doctor, and so on. Bit by bit, we seem to be coming full circle as more and more people look upon their homeplace as workplace, too.

My own home-business beginnings date back to the mid-1960s when, like thousands of others, I got caught up in America's arts and crafts revolution. After ten years as a secretary in Chicago's Loop, I had great fun for several years selling my handcrafts at local shops and fairs, an experience my husband, Harry, thought I should write about. At his urging, and in spite of knowing nothing about the craft of writing, I began to create quarterly issues of a magazine we later would laughingly refer to as "a literary success and a financial flop." This second little entrepreneurial venture of mine survived only five years, which was more than long enough to make my husband wish he'd never told me to "get a hobby" back in the 1960s. Those three little words ultimately changed not only my life, but his. After five years of working full time at home, we had gained a clear understanding of how a home business impacts one's personal life. It all came to a head the day Harry said, "It's me or the magazine, kiddo, take your pick."

I didn't know it at the time, but twenty years before "homebased businesses" would become watchwords of America, I was gaining experience and contacts that would neatly position me as a pioneer and leader in the industry. People who worked at home during the 1960s and 1970s didn't broadcast the fact, and "entrepreneur" was a word few individuals could identify with, let alone spell. Yet, just like today's self-employed individuals, we attached a Schedule C form to our annual income tax return to show income derived from sources other than a job. Common money-making activities of the day included mail order businesses, home sales of products such as Mary Kay and Tupperware, writing and publishing, consulting, and arts and crafts. The main difference between then and now is that now, thanks to technology and the Internet, we have many more work-at-home options and ways to earn self-employment income. People's perceptions about working at home have also changed dramatically in recent years. Now, working at home has become the "in thing" to do, and people at large have come to realize that it's a special kind of achievement to be able to live by one's wits and build a successful business at home.

In the past, a homebased business was likely to be viewed as a side business operated primarily as a hobby or a source of secondary income. But an SBA-sponsored study released in 2000 proves this assertion was inaccurate. "The researcher's findings demonstrate how the home has become a hub of business activity, entrepreneurship, and business creation," the report stated. "If anecdotal evidence is correct, the homebased business sector is growing in importance, driven by the revolution in information technology. This activity is much more significant than previously thought."

Like many others a couple of decades ago, I took notice of, but did fully comprehend, the concept Alvin Toffler advanced in his book, *The Third Wave*. He spoke about "commuting electronically between home and office," said there would be "new emphasis on home as the center of society," and predicted that technology would be the spark for a revolution in the way people viewed work and play. What vision! In recent years, computer technology has dramatically changed our business and personal lives in ways few of us would have believed possible, and even now it seems we're seeing only the tip of the technological iceberg. One new technological advance after another is automatically moving us and our homebased businesses forward at breakneck speed, and it's a challenge to stay abreast of it all.

Thanks to the Internet, however, the average person now has unlimited opportunities for earning money from home, and we all have access to more small business information online than we'll ever be able to use. In addition, today's would-be business owners can choose from a wide selection of small business courses in their community. Most of them are sponsored or supported by adult education centers, YMCAs, Chambers of Commerce, Cooperative Extension, SBA or SCORE, or small business development centers at community colleges where entrepreneurial courses are now common.

The Importance of Trends

"A trend is born when society makes a general movement toward or away from something," Erika Kotite once said in an article for *Entrepreneur* magazine (Entrepreneur.com). "A trend happens because of one big event, or as a result of many small events; it can happen overnight, or over a couple of centuries. Most trends are identified by marketing research experts who monitor the media, interview consumers, conduct surveys, look at past trends and then make predictions. Trends are tricky, and businesses had better pay attention to them because they are vital to maintaining a competitive edge."

"As homebased business owners, we need to lift up our eyes regularly to connect with the larger world," confirms consultant Patricia Katz. In addition to the business and marketing trends listed below, there is an important overall homestyle trend called "cocooning," a word coined by trend-master Faith Popcorn in the 1990s in her book, *The Popcorn Report* (Harperbusiness). She said the cocooning trend began when technology and the growing range of personal and business services available gave us less need to go out to do things—from shopping, to getting an education, to earning a living. After the September 11 terrorist attack and warnings of other attacks in the future, the idea of home as a fortress against the world only reinforced this trend. Popcorn predicted that, by the turn of the century, most homes would be as complete and self-sufficient as the Star Trek *Enterprise* ship, and we would hardly ever have to go out.

Recently, Popcorn identified another trend many of us can relate to, which she calls "99 Lives." "Too fast a pace, too little time, causes societal schizophrenia and forces us to assume multiple roles," she says. "Time is the new money: people would rather spend money than time. Eighty percent of Americans are looking for ways to simplify their lives; 78 percent want to reduce stress." (Important marketing considerations, to be sure.) See Popcorn's Web site at Brainreserve.com for the latest trends she has observed.

Smart Tip

Start now to be a "trend watcher." This will enable you to pick up on things that will give you ideas not only for new products and services you might sell, but new business and diversification ideas as well.

Trends of Interest to Home-Business Owners

- Corporate "downsizing" and company mergers continue to increase the demand for subcontractors (homebased entrepreneurs, moonlighters, and self-employed people who consider themselves independent contractors).

- Home has become an important center of life where people are entertaining themselves inexpensively. This suggests that people will buy more books, videos, software, music, games, personal care items, candles, gourmet food items, etc.

- People are increasingly concerned about their personal safety and financial security, so entrepreneurs who can offer products or services that will answer such needs will find a ready market.

- The environment remains a hot market niche. Because more health-conscious people now perceive the environment as a health issue, consumers are more interested in purchasing environmentally safe products for personal use, cleaning purposes, air filters, water purifiers, etc. This spells opportunity for entrepreneurs interested in selling such products—or information about them.

- There is an "I-control-my-life mindset" in the population today, especially among younger people, reports the *Herman Trend Alert* (HermanGroup.com). "As people assume greater responsibility for their own lives and their own destinies, we will see growth in the personal services industry," it reports. "This suggests new business opportunities for personal trainers, coaches, nutritionists and career counselors."

- Teens and "Tweens" are now a huge market being tapped by sellers everywhere because they have incredible spending power. (A recent news item on TV reported that many teens today spend a hundred dollars a week or more on clothes, cosmetics, and other personal items.

- America's population is aging at an amazing rate—some 35 million people are now 65 or older (compared to only 123,000 in 1990)—and business owners need to keep this older audience in mind as they develop new products and services. Nine million seniors are already online, and their

11

number is expected to explode over the next five years. Remember, too, that many older Americans hire self-employed individuals to do jobs they no longer have the time or energy to do, such as home decorating, home repairs, yard work, and shopping.

- More than 30 percent of American adults are now grandparents, and their number is rapidly growing, too. Since grandparents often have discretionary income and love to buy presents for their grandchildren, they represent a large niche market for craft and gift producers.

- There is an increasing number of dual-earner and single-parent families, all of whom have special needs. They desire hassle-free products and services and are often willing to pay more for something if its purchase will relieve stress or give them more free time.

- More dads are now becoming caregivers because Mom is the one with the greatest income potential. This growing "dads-at-home" audience, which includes some homebased business owners, needs a variety of personal and business services that can be delivered by other homebased entrepreneurs.

The Restructuring of the Workforce

The growth of homebased businesses in America has been greatly influenced not only by the economy but by technological advances that have totally eradicated millions of factory jobs and middle-management positions. During the last sixteen months of the 1991–1992 recession, Fortune 500 companies released over 600,000 people through early retirement or layoffs. At that time, a spokesperson at a small business development center reported an increase in the start-up of homebased consulting businesses by corporate VPs in their fifties who had taken cash benefit packages as early retirement bribes and went on to work for their former employers as independent consultants.

In mid-1996, one researcher stated that 33,000 employees were losing their jobs every day. (That's 12 million lost jobs in one year alone.) At that time, in a newsletter for entrepreneurs, futurist Watts Wacker stated that the upside of this economic upheaval was a growing entrepreneurial wave and way of thinking that he believed would continue to grow for at least the next quarter century. In an editorial in *Home Office Computing* (now out of print),

Nick Sullivan was right when he predicted that the restructuring of America's workforce in the 1990s would be more dramatic than the retooling of American industrial plans in the 1980s.

Although we enjoyed a boom period in the late 1990s, millions more lost jobs after the turn of the century because of corporate downsizing and bankruptcies, the dot-com failures of 2000, the aftermath of the September 11 terrorist attack, the Enron disaster, and the 2001–2002 recession, which was worsened by the midyear bankruptcy of WorldCom. According to a report by one outplacement agency, by January 2001, over 6,000 people were being laid off every day. Interestingly, a note in the June 2001 issue of *Home Business* magazine pointed to other studies showing that over 6,000 new homebased businesses were being launched each day, making homebased business the fastest-growing economic sector in the country.

Who's Working at Home and Why

With job security a thing of the past, millions of people who once thought they would have a job for life are wondering if they're going to get the pink slip. Many still-employed workers are taking steps to position themselves for self-sufficiency should the paycheck suddenly cease, and a growing number of ex-corporate employees are now working for their former employers as independent, homebased consultants. Although job loss may continue to be an important factor in one's decision to start a business at home, various surveys through the years have revealed that many people start businesses of their own simply because they want to be boss. Others have indicated they:

● think they can make more money working for themselves;

● are tired of their job;

● want a new challenge;

● desire a change of lifestyle;

● want to spend more time with their families.*

---

*In one New York Times poll on women's issues, 83 percent of working mothers said they felt torn between the demands of their job and wanting to spend more time with their family. Statistics indicate that more than half of all mothers now work full time, not always because they are seeking fulfillment. In these hard economic times, the extra income is likely to be needed.

Homemade Money

Today's homebased entrepreneurs are coming from a diverse group of individuals, including:

- people from all walks of life who have lost their jobs;

- dissatisfied job holders who lack advancement opportunities;

- satisfied job holders who simply need more money;

- men and women who must work at home because of children or adults in their care;

- disabled people who cannot find employment in the traditional workplace;

- senior citizens who need supplemental income;

- hobbyists interested in profiting from leisure-time interests.

As you embark on your road to extra income or self-sufficiency, remember this: Almost anyone can make extra money at home, but it takes a certain degree of skill, experience, and knowledge to actually turn a homebased money-making venture into a *profitable business*. Be realistic about the amount of profit to be derived in the early years of a business because so much will depend on the amount of time and money you invest in it. Small business owners often tell me that making lots of money is not nearly as important to them as making *enough* money for their particular needs. I agree. To me, the most important thing is that I am doing exactly what I want to be doing, secure in the knowledge that I'm spending my life in the most satisfying and profitable way possible. Too few people today are able to make such a statement. Like most others in the 1950s, I grew up with an employee mentality. I fell into self-employment quite by accident, and I'd be lying if I said that being my own boss for more than three decades has been easy. It hasn't. But if I could do it all over again, I'd start ten years sooner. I hope the information in this book will enable you to share the same enjoyment, satisfaction, and sense of pride I feel each morning as I get up to go to work . . . in the comfort and privacy of my home.

Overview of the Work-at-Home Industry

Smart Tip

There's only one way to read this book: with marking pen in hand. Try a yellow highlighter pen and underline or otherwise mark all the information that's important to you. When you have finished the book, go back to the beginning and follow up on every mark you've made. The more marks, the more opportunities.

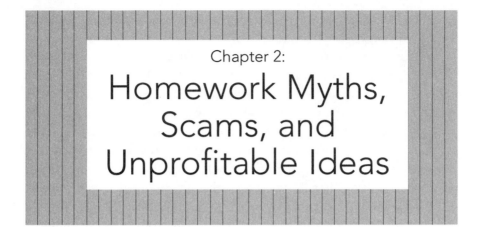

Chapter 2:
Homework Myths, Scams, and Unprofitable Ideas

You have to be a much smarter consumer than twenty years ago. You have to be careful about where you go on the Internet, who you give information to, who you believe.

—Frank Abagnale, author of *The Art of the Steal: How to Protect Yourself and Your Business from Fraud* (Broadway), from an article in *USA Weekend.*

When people ask if you want the good news or the bad news first, what do you say? As a positive-thinking person, I like to get the bad news out of the way first so I can concentrate on the good.

Although millions of people now work at home, "homework" is not that easy for the average individual to get. This chapter addresses some misconceptions people have about making money at home, mail order schemes or business ideas that violate postal laws or are simply unprofitable, scams aimed specifically at business owners, and work-at-home/home-business "opportunities" on and off the Internet. It concludes with information about a number of things you cannot do as a business because they are in direct violation of copyright or licensing laws.

You may be too smart to fall for most of the slick advertisements and Web sites that promise easy money for little work and no skill or experience, but you may not be aware of all the work-at-home schemes and mail order ripoffs described in this chapter. In addition to these specific examples, there are hundreds of variations of each scheme. People are getting conned every day and authorities can't begin to keep up with all the fraudulent schemes con men are devising. The Internet has only made the situation worse. No matter how they are described or what riches are promised, always remember the old adage, "If it sounds too good to be true, it probably is."

While this chapter is admittedly a burst-your-bubbles collection of information that could be thought of as bad news by some, the good news is that all this "bad news" is likely to save you a great deal of time, money, and frustration, not to mention a possible run-in with legal authorities. I know you'll thank me later for bringing all this information to your attention at the beginning.

Work-at-Home Misconceptions

Myth: *All you need to make money at home is a typewriter or computer.*

Many people with typing or secretarial skills believe that all they need to start making money at home is a list of companies who hire people like them. Alas, there is no magic list, and although you may find work-at-home directories in print and scores of "opportunities" on "homework Web sites," a careful reading of listings will reveal that what companies are really looking for are capable *self-employed individuals or freelance business professionals* who are interested in working as independent contractors. I was astonished when a prison inmate wrote to ask how he could find gainful employment by mail doing typing. He had the equipment and skills, so figured he could do the work. Maybe so; but who do you suppose would send a typing job to a prison inmate? Some common sense is called for here. If you have word processing or secretarial skills, your best bet for getting "homework" is to call on businesses in your area to let them know you are an experienced professional who's interested in working on a part-time basis as an independent contractor.

Homework Myths

Myth: *If you have great computer skills, you can work at home for some corporation.*

In truth, telecommuting (also called "telework") opportunities are available only to a small segment of the population. To do computer-related work at home, you usually begin by first being an employee of the company in question. Then you hope the company will be receptive to the idea of your doing work at home that for years has been done in the office. While some companies today do use telecommuters, others have been reluctant to try such a program. Once believed to be the wave of the future, this work-at-home option is out of favor with many employers, and those who do favor it prefer to work with existing employees who may be allowed to work at home only one day a week or for no more than six months out of a year. Thus, telecommuting opportunities do not exist for the average individual looking for computer-related work to do at home. Self-employed individuals with computer expertise, however, may find many opportunities to work with corporate clients as an independent contractor.

Myth: *There are many opportunities to work at home doing knitting, sewing, or assembling products for manufacturing companies.*

Certain manufacturing plants—not many—may have a limited amount of contract work available to individuals who live near enough to pick up and deliver finished materials on a daily basis. Training may be offered or required. If you don't have such a manufacturer in your backyard, don't waste your money on a directory that promises to lead you to such companies, and don't send any money to anyone on the Web who says they can find this kind of work for you. When you can find local manufacturers in need of help, typical product assembly work may include packaging material in plastic bags, adding tags, inserting pins into promotional badges, adding buckles to belts, or hand-wrapping fishing rods. Sewing and craft work may include mending sweaters, stitching shoe parts, making ski masks, neckties, tote bags, or T-shirts, trimming threads on commercially woven placemats, or putting in coat linings. Good work for a few, perhaps, but awfully boring to most. There may also be limited opportunities for craftworkers who can do machine knitting, sewing, or figurine painting, but if you have such skills, you would be better off starting a small business of your own.

Homemade Money

Myth: *You can make money selling handmade products made from kits.*

Beware of ads that begin, "$341.04 weekly possible making baby bibs at home!" or, "Make our kitchen aprons for fun and profit—$344.08 weekly!" Such advertisers say all you have to do is buy their supplies and materials, make products to their specifications, and they'll buy everything you make. Don't believe it! There is *no market* for products that come in "supply kits" offered in opportunity ads. Since this is a scam thousands fall for every year, it deserves extra attention here. These people—mostly mothers who want to stay home with the kids and make money, too—are quick to believe the magazine ads that say it's easy to make money selling craft items such as baby bibs, potholders, aprons, jewelry, Christmas ornaments, pillows, and the like. The promoters of such schemes will guarantee your complete satisfaction and a full refund of your money, but they simply won't do this. They may offer to buy all the products you make, but they won't, and their reason will be that your work does not meet their standards. And it never will because they have no intention of ever buying anything from anyone. These advertisers are simply out to sell you cheap product kits. But you don't have to take my word for it. Just listen to what some of my readers (all women) have reported:

- "I figured because you see handmade items advertised in virtually every catalogue there must be an abundance of work-at-home opportunities," writes Dorothy in Illinois.
- "I pored through craft magazines and began writing for free information. After receiving a number of responses, I narrowed these down by type and pay and then called the Better Business Bureau in each respective area. A couple of them said they had no information on companies in question, but the Better Business Bureau in San Francisco did say that one company on my list was a member of the BBB (although this was not to be taken as an endorsement). I congratulated myself on being smart enough to check them out before sending a money order for $47.90 for the cost of their kit, directions, and rush handling.

  "Two weeks later my anxiously awaited package arrived. What a disappointment! I had settled on an ornaments kit because I don't sew very well. What I received was a couple of bags of beads, some fishing wire, and some complicated instructions for an ugly little thing that looked sort of like a wreath with about 8 dangling columns hanging from it. I returned the kit immediately, asking for a refund minus the $10.45 I had agreed to in the initial mailing to cover 'shipping, handling and inspection.' I decided this was their gimmick: they send out an ugly little complicated kit. Their customer is disappointed and sends it back, which still gives the company $7.50 off each respondent and an extra $2.95 if they are excited enough to request rush handling, as I did."

- Virginia, in Missouri, reported that she kept the jewelry kit she ordered and sent the completed products for payment, only to be told they were unacceptable. "I spent three months trying to get it right and finally gave up," she said.

- Cathy, in Florida, had made pillows for gifts for years, so she bit on the ad that promised her money from pillows. After receiving her $50 kit and sending the finished pillows back to the company, she was astonished to learn that her work was considered borderline. "My friends told me I'd been taken, that these companies do this just to get the kit money," she wrote. "I still defended my work by saying I had only a couple of pillows that did not meet their standards, and when I got them back I would just fix those and send them all back. Since I have worked in quality control myself, I was very surprised to see that not one of my 'mistakes' was marked in any way—which made rework impossible. That was when I knew my friends were right."

- Nancy, in Michigan, went so far as to file a complaint with her local BBB only to find that many others were in the same boat. "We were asked to complete all types of legal papers against the company," she said, adding that the State Attorney General's office was investigating the matter.

As Dorothy pointed out, an unfortunate side effect to such scams is that once you respond to one ad, your name is automatically added to every "sucker list" in the country. "Not a day goes by," says Dorothy, "that I don't receive work-at-home opportunity ads or 'you-have-won' garbage in the mail. I've turned many of the chain letters and other offers over to the postmaster, but the sheer volume of such mail finally wears you down to the point that you just throw it away."

Myth: *You can get paid for reading books.*

Legitimate book publishers either have their own in-house proofreaders or easy access to professionals in this field. They don't need inexperienced people off the street. If you are well educated and want to seriously pursue this kind of work, check the annual *Writer's Market* for legitimate publisher listings and needs, and read *Make Money Reading Books* by Bruce Fife, which explains how to set up a successful freelance reading service in your home. (A college education will help but isn't necessary.)

Some unethical directory publishers may include the names and addresses of publishers in their useless work-at-home directories, but book publishers do not authorize such listings. Another variation of this scam is when you are asked to buy a book that gives all the inside secrets of this "plan" for "only $29.95." Still another variation is that you will be offered the opportunity to "be trained as a proofreader" at home for some imaginary editorial or publishing service. After paying a nonrefundable fee for this worthless "education," you'll be told that you haven't passed the aptitude test. That's because there was never any real work in the first place.

Myth: *You can make a million in MLM (multilevel marketing).*

The MLM industry has always been plagued by scam operators who promise quick riches for little or no work. "Thousands of people have bought the MLM promise and have nothing but full garages and empty wallets to show for it," says one writer in this field. Avoid any plan that offers commissions to recruit new distributors, and beware of plans that ask you to spend money on start-up kits of inventory and sales literature, training programs, or sales leads. "Many multilevel distributorship schemes are nothing more than sophisticated chain letters," says the U.S. Postal Inspection Service. "They operate on the pyramid method of selling and claiming participants can earn lots of money by selling products using many levels of distributors below them."

MLM attorney and author, Jeffrey A. Babener (MLMlegal.com), has lectured and published extensively on multilevel marketing law. He urges MLM entrepreneurs to study a company carefully before joining a new program. "Because of the abuses of the 'rotten apples' of the industry, multilevel marketing has become a closely scrutinized and regulated industry," he explains. "Over the years, it has come perilously close to extinction as a result of prosecution by regulators who claimed the industry promoted pyramid schemes under the guise of legitimate marketing. Regulations regarding multilevel marketing companies in the United States are a constantly changing patchwork of overlapping laws that lack uniformity and vary from state to state. The basic thrust of these statutes is that marketing plans that require an investment or purchase by sales representatives for the right to recruit others for economic gain are prohibited. Under these statutes, multilevel marketing companies must be bona fide retail organizations that market bona fide products to the ultimate consumer."

(See Chapter Four for a discussion of your true financial opportunities in the MLM/Network Marketing industry.)

Mail Order "Get Rich" Schemes

Myth: *You can get rich quick with no effort at all.*

In a free country, people can place magazine ads for anything they wish, provided it does not violate postal laws. But con artists pay no attention to such laws, and magazine publishers generally accept all the ads they can get. Publication of an ad, however, does not mean a publisher has endorsed the advertiser in any way. It remains the reader's responsibility to use common sense in deciding whether to send money to an advertiser.

"Opportunity classifieds" appear in many magazines, and it's not unusual to find the same ad in several publications at once. Readers may be asked to send from twenty-five cents to a dollar to receive information. So far, you're not out much. But what most people receive next are instructions to send larger sums of money for start-up kits, "secret information," or books of questionable value. This is where you must become especially cautious. Don't be too eager to believe snappy advertising copy implying you can get rich without a considerable investment of time or money. If it were this simple, we'd all be on Easy Street.

The full-page ads are even more convincing to the uninitiated. Bold headlines proclaim you can get rich sooner than you think, or "Secret money-making system revealed!" or "Just mail two letters . . . and make $15,000 in one month." The convincing copy in such ads often tells the sad tale of a man or woman who, on the verge of bankruptcy, suddenly discovers the secret to wealth, and now, out of the goodness of their heart, they are going to share it with *you.* (How lucky can you get!) To prove just how profitable their ideas are, the ads often include a list of their bank deposits for the past twelve months, along with a statement from their accountant swearing it's true. I don't doubt it. Thousands of suckers are sending such advertisers ten or twenty dollars for an information product that probably costs less than a buck. These promoters have discovered the secret to wealth all right—they've learned how to pick the pockets of gullible opportunity seekers.

I fell for one of these ads once. The picture of a lovely woman and the promise of "two volumes—a complete set of my ideas and systems" made me part with twenty dollars. What I got were two skimpy little books on how to get rich in mail order—information I found completely worthless. Like many others, I justified this expenditure by charging it to "research" (or perhaps we should call it "live and learn"). Whenever you read an ad that speaks in vague terms about what you're going to get for your money (besides the promoter's "secrets"), and never quite explains exactly what you'll have to do to earn the promised income, don't bite. An order is likely to bring you only a worthless book on mail order or some other "plan" of little interest to you. Remember that *no one* ever shares their secrets of success in a full-page ad "out of the goodness of their heart." They're in it strictly for the money. *Your* money.

Myth: *Some chain letters are legal, and will put a lot of money in your pocket.*

All chain letters (like pyramid schemes) are illegal, but we continue to receive them in both our regular mail and e-mail because postal authorities simply can't keep up with all the con artists out there. Some people think they are getting around the illegality of chain letters by saying they are offering a "mass merchandising mail order program," or simply a hobby or recipe exchange. But since some states have laws against pyramid schemes of any kind—even when no money is changing hands—a no-money recipe or hobby chain letter may be as illegal in your state as one that asks you to send money. Often, you are asked to order a report for $4 to $10 that will not only prove to be worthless, but is likely to put your name on a mailing list being investigated by the U.S. Postal Inspection Service.

"Chain letters are illegal," postal inspectors confirm, "and they don't work." If you participate in a chain letter promotion, you may be in violation of federal and state laws, so the smartest thing you can do is give the chain letters you receive to your local postmaster. (You can also register a complaint online at the Federal Trade Commission's Web site at FTC.gov.)

But what about chain letters that say, "This letter is entirely legal"? Just remember, con artists are used to lying and they're difficult to stop. As fast as postal inspectors put one out of business, a new one sets up shop somewhere else. Once when I called the Postal Inspector's Office about a particular scam that was making the rounds, I was informed that each letter mailed was considered one count, and the penalty for mail order fraud is up to five years in prison *for each count*. Ouch! It doesn't pay to mess with the U.S. Postal Service.

In early 2002, the FTC began to publicize on television and the Web that they were cracking down on spammers who were sending deceptive e-mail chain letters. According to an FTC news release, seven defendants caught in an FTC sting operation agreed to settle charges that they were spamming consumers with deceptive chain letters. The letters were slightly changed variations on the same message. They promised "$46,000 or more in the next 90 days," or similar extravagant amounts to recipients who were to send $5 in cash to each of four or five participants at the top of the list. The letters instructed new recruits to place their own name and address at the top of the list and remove the name on the bottom. In return for the $5 payment, recruits received "reports" providing instructions about how to start their own chain letter schemes and recruit tens of thousands of others via spam.

"This chain letter deceptively claims the program is legal and urges recruits who question its legitimacy to contact the FTC's Associate Director for Marketing Practices. Well, I am the Associate Director for Marketing Practices," said Eileen Harrington, "and these chain letters are illegal."

In addition to the settlements, the FTC announced that it had mailed warning letters to more than 2,000 individuals who were still running this chain letter scheme. The addresses were culled from the FTC's unsolicited commercial e-mail (UCE) database. With consumers forwarding spam to the agency at a rate of approximately 15,000 e-mails a day, the FTC has collected more than 8 million spam messages since 1998.

In summary, if you start a chain e-mail or letter or send one on, you are breaking the law. If you've been a target of a chain e-mail scam, contact your ISP and forward the e-mail to the FTC at uce@ftc.gov.

Myth: *You can make good money stuffing envelopes or mailing circulars.*

According to the U.S. Postal Inspection Service, the most common work-at-home frauds involve stuffing envelopes at home and/or mailing circulars. In one of its consumer booklets the Service says: "The Postal Inspection Service knows of *no* work-at-home promotion that ever produces income as alleged. A homework scheme promoter will . . . take your money and give you little or nothing in return except heartbreak and grief."

Ads for such offers may speak of a "revolutionary home-mailing program" that will pay up to $300 a day. A typical statement in such ads is "we could never possibly reach the millions of people who need this information, so we're willing to let you help us." Of course the copy sounds believable—it's written by pros. If you fall for this type of scam, you'll probably end up paying from $10 to $40 for a package of literature that includes the same sales letter you got originally, along with instructions on how to put an ad in the paper. Then when people write to you, you try to sell them the same thing you just fell for. Not a good way to build a reputation for yourself, is it? As the Council of Better Business Bureaus, Inc., confirms in one of its consumer pamphlets, "Most of the ads are simply lures by the advertisers to sell information on how to set up your own business or conduct the same scheme as the advertiser's."

Myth: *You can build a profitable mail order business using a promoter's ads, catalogs, and products.*

I've always been quick to encourage individuals to market their own products and services by mail, but mail order novices should avoid promoters who want them to build a mail order business using their ads, catalogs, and products. How-to booklets and reports of questionable value—some of which have been circulating for over twenty years—are commonly promoted in this way. Although these business promotions are not illegal, they are bound to be unprofitable. What promoters neglect to tell interested prospects is that, although they supply the ad copy to sell such products, the dealer must place and pay for all the ads. The promoter may supply the mail-order catalogs, but dealers must pay for them, as well as the postage to mail them, plus buy their own mailing lists as well. What mail order beginners do not realize is that catalog mailings may yield only .5–1 percent order response—which is only 5 to 10 orders for every 1,000 pieces mailed. And that's if the list is good; if it's bad, it's entirely possible to get only one or two orders, or none.

Similar ads offer people the chance to sell a line of inexpensive imports or novelty items. Promoters say the beauty of this kind of business is that you need not buy products outright or stock inventory—simply send all orders to them for fulfillment. While such companies may indeed be legitimate, it is my belief that most of them are making their money first on the sale of catalogs (sold at highly-inflated prices), and second, from the sale of mailing lists unlikely to result in orders. (Often these are nothing more than names of other opportunity seekers.) The only time such a mail order endeavor might be profitable, in my opinion, is if the entrepreneur already has an established prospect or customer list likely to be interested in such items. As the Council of Better Business Bureaus cautions, and which I can affirm, "Building a solid, profitable mail-order business is a demanding, full-time task. Few inexperienced individuals can learn enough about the business before their capital or patience runs out."

Myth: *You can make money compiling mailing lists.*

The ad may read, "We'll pay you 50 cents for each name and address you compile. If you have a pen and can write down a name and address, you can do this to make money." Or maybe the headline says, "Don't throw away your order envelopes—trade them for cash!" In checking out one of these schemes, here's what I learned.

You are told to compile names by placing certain classified ads the company will provide (but which you must pay for). When (if) you get responses to the ads, you forward the names to the company, and will actually be paid fifty cents for generating this valuable sales lead for them. Meanwhile, the company will send "your" prospects a brochure or catalog that describes one of several money-making plans they offer (all legal, but useless). For example, you might place an ad telling people how to make money mailing letters, and what they would receive from the company would be information on how to order a manual that will tell them how to make up to $1,000 a day just for mailing letters. It may be described as "the opportunity of a lifetime" but is probably nothing more than a common mail order guide. So your participation in such a program only helps to push the snowball downhill, setting up other suckers for yet another get-rich scheme. Legal, yes, but what do you suppose the chances are for financial success?

Remember this: *Your* name will be on those classified ads, and if people are upset with the material they receive as a result of contact with you, who do you think is going to get the flak? Even if you really don't care about using your name to promote someone else's products, do you really believe you'd make money here? A classified ad might cost $25 to $50 or more. At $50, you'd have to bring in 100 prospects just to break even. So the company is spending a mere 50 cents each for their prospect names while you foot its advertising bill and get absolutely nothing in the bargain. While you're wasting your time and money on its ads, the company is keeping a tight rein on its cash flow and profiting from the sale of its expensive manuals.

Here's another variation of this scheme: A mailer from a promoter stated I would be paid six cents for every new name I could generate for them. On closer investigation, I learned that they buy only the names of people who have responded to opportunity or money-making ads. The promoter compiles such names into new opportunity-seeker mail lists that he will sell back to the very people who responded to such ads in the first place. (Examples: Those who do circular mailings, push MLM programs, or peddle useless information.) Now do you begin to see why your mailbox suddenly fills up with junk mail as soon as you bite on that first opportunity ad or chain letter invitation?

Work-at-Home/Home-Business "Opportunities"

You may find cyberspace exciting, but it's also an industry running amok, with billions of Web sites and too few rules and regulations being enforced. In addition to being wary of greedy, though not necessarily dishonest, entrepreneurs whose prices for Web services are out of line, you must also be wary of shady opportunists. You can be sure that the same con artists who have previously used the mail and telephone to prey on unsuspecting consumers were among the first to get on the Internet and World Wide Web. With their glitzy Web sites and deceptive e-mail message, they can make even the worst "opportunity" seem irresistible.

According to a TV news story in mid-2002, work-at-home scams cost consumers $29 million dollars in 2001. "We all want to believe that scams only happen to others, but virtually everyone is a potential prospect for a scam," says a fellow who lost $30,000 on a bad business investment. "Scams are like wildfire," he says, "totally out of control with no rain in sight. Many times the prime candidates to be ripped off are those who have been involved in a previous scam. Hoping to recoup their losses, people take unnecessary risks. Since legal aid can cost more in time, money and emotional strain than is worthwhile for small losses, few people report them. And losing larger sums of money can be so embarrassing to people that their embarrassment and shame far outweighs their desire to do anything about the loss."

It wasn't until 1996 that the U.S. Postal Inspection Service joined other federal law enforcement agencies to begin monitoring computer online services for fraud and direct marketing scams. By 2000, the Federal Trade Commission, the Department of Justice, and law enforcement officials from twenty-nine states had launched an attack (called "Project Biz-illion$") on traditional business opportunity scams that were then bilking hundreds of thousands of consumers out of tens of millions of dollars a year.

Charlatans on the Web

Although some operators have been closed down, many charlatans continue to separate people from their money with a fancy-looking Web page and unsubstantiated claims about the profitability of their "hot" money-making or investment opportunity. If you have an e-mail address, the spammers will find you, and as soon as you get online, you'll start getting messages that promise financial freedom with earnings of $10,000 a month or more working from home—no special skills or experience required. When you call the 800-number to get "free details," even greater riches may be promised to those who are "serious about making money." After you've heard the high-powered pitch, you'll be asked to leave your name and phone number to get the details from a real person in the "association" who is really very, very busy, but will take the time to speak to you if you're really, really serious about this opportunity.

At this point, it's hard for the average person not to be convinced by the kind of motivational pep talks these messengers deliver, because their copy has been written by an expert copywriter and is delivered by an expert speaker who will probably make you feel stupid for not wanting to "invest" in such an amazing income opportunity. Bypassing such offers, however, will always be the smart thing to do. If you do call the 800-number or visit a related Web site, you'll find it will cost you money to find out whether you want to do this kind of work or not and, until you pay, you won't have a clue as to what kind of "work" they're talking about. You'll be told that if you're not willing to take this small financial risk, then you're not the kind of person they're interested in working with. If you give your credit card number to this kind of con artist, all you're really doing is throwing money away and possibly opening yourself up to identity theft (see sidebar on this topic).

So many so-called opportunities on the Web are beautifully presented with a considerable amount of information, but nothing specific on what you have to do to actually make the fortune being promised. Always, at the bottom of the last page, you'll be told you have to send a certain amount of money for "complete details," and that it is fully refundable if you decide this opportunity isn't for you. But don't hold your breath waiting for that refund check.

Even legitimate business opportunities are tainted by con artists on the Web who make them sound much easier than they are. Take medical billing for example. Although some people actually do this for a living, it's usually because the individual had a medical background to begin with or had previously worked in a doctor's office and then arranged to do this work at home. The FTC has found that few consumers who purchase one of the medical billing business opportunities are able to find clients and earn enough income to recover their investment in software, training, and technical support. (Those promised "doctor lists" are worthless because doctors never request this kind of listing.) The FTC has brought charges against several companies for misrepresenting the earnings potential of medical billing centers, and you'll find more information on this topic on the FTC's Web site.

I shudder when I think how many people are going to be suckered into get-rich-quick schemes now that they're so easy to sell on the Internet. It was bad enough when they were limited to magazines, but Web sites and e-mail have given con artists a lot of power. "The biggest thing folks need to watch out for is contact information for the various 'biz opps' that are available," says Tammy Harrison, a representative for Home-Based Working Moms (HBWM.com). "If you are researching something, be sure to find a *real person* to converse with, and get their full name and address. When talking to the company, get references and check those references out as well. Anyone who is truly legitimate will give you anything you ask for to research them as business people as well as their company. Then take whatever information you can find on the company to the Better Business Bureau (BBB.org) and other sites that are watching out for the consumer. Also check to see if the FTC, State Attorney General's office or some other governing body has made rulings or statements on various schemes or business opportunities, and be sure you know what you're getting into before you spend any money on a business opportunity of any kind."

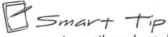

Go to www.BBB.org. There you will find a search area where you can type in the name of a company or other information you may have about it, and turn up any bad reports people may have filed on this site. You are also encouraged to file your own scam reports here.

Work-at-Home Seminars

Even when you find a "real person" offering information, you must be cautious. For example, many people have been ripped off by seminar presenters hawking various business opportunities. After spending a few thousand dollars in advertising, an "organization" blows into town to host a week's free Work-at-Home Seminar, and they may walk away with a few million dollars from sales of their worthless 900-number businesses, network marketing plans, and "business-in-a-box" opportunities priced from $495 to $2,500. People are pushed to order by fast-talking seminar presenters who say the offer is limited, that the price will be a few hundred dollars higher the next day, and only so many of each business package can be sold (a lie), so people grab their credit cards and buy something before they've had a chance to even understand what they're buying. Later, they find refunds are impossible to get.

Smart Tip

"Don't invest in any opportunity until you hunt down—independently!—at least half a dozen people who have actually succeeded in the business," says Lesley Fountain, FriendsinBusiness.com. "If it's legit, they won't be hard to find. I guarantee it."

Electronic Payments

Fortunately, the Internet is now making it easier for people to broadcast news about disreputable companies. Many sites allow visitors to post their own reports, and this kind of news also circulates in discussion lists. After Angela in Hudson, New York, told me she had been ripped off by National Home Employment Services (NHES), I checked the BadBusinessBureau.com site and found thirteen other reports by people who had been scammed by this company.

Angela told me how this particular scam works: "From their Web site and on other sites and job boards on the Internet, they advertise employment opportunities, targeting people who want to work at home doing 'administrative work.' They claim they have a client base looking for people to do this kind of work from their homes, and they guarantee their one-time application fee of $29.99 is completely refundable if you do not receive at least ten offers of home employment within seven to ten business days after your application has been processed." Of course, the only e-mail Angela ever received was from the company's "Position Fulfillment Department," confirming her application had been received. There were no offers of work, and she could not get a refund of her application fee.

Before you authorize an electronic payment for any kind of "business opportunity," make sure you know who you're dealing with. Con artists on the Internet always ask for payment by money order or some kind of electronic payment because this makes it difficult or impossible for you to get your money back. "When you authorize payment in the form of an e-check, you are giving someone your bank routing number and account number," says Angela. "Since no signature is needed to place a draft against your account, they can now draw from your account whenever they want, and some people have reported this has happened. Although you can close a bank account, this is easier said than done. First you must contact everyone to tell them you must change your billing method, then you must keep your account open until all these merchants have switched over to your new method of payment." (As an extra precaution while Angela was waiting for all this to happen, she placed a stop payment on her account for any $29.99 drafts that might come through from the company that defrauded her.)

"Plants" on Discussion Lists

Finally, a word about discussion lists. Beware of bulletin boards, chat rooms, and mailing lists where one individual is loudly proclaiming the value of a particular business opportunity in direct response to someone's question. In reality, both people may be "plants" and part of the scam. Before believing one person's claims about a particular opportunity, do your own research, as explained in this chapter.

Identity Theft: The #1 Scam

Half a million people are victims of identify theft each year, according to the Privacy Rights Clearinghouse, and the FTC says this is the #1 scam today. The FTC advises *never* to give your credit card number to anyone on the phone unless you initiate the call, and never put your Social Security number anywhere on the Web or even in an e-mail message. (If someone actually needs this information for tax purposes, mail the information or call it in.)

Be especially careful of what information you put on application or information-gathering forms on the Web—or anywhere else for that matter—because many con artists run ads designed simply to get people's confidential financial information so they can use it for fraudulent purposes. Many Web sites ask for this kind of information so they can sell your name to advertisers who will bombard you with junk e-mail. For more information on this topic, check the U.S. government's central Web site for identity theft info at www.consumer.gov/idtheft/index.html or the FTC.gov Web site.

Identity theft cons aren't limited to the Internet, of course. On the news one evening was a story about how someone in Chicago placed an ad offering work, then interviewed dozens of people in a fancy office that turned out to be only a front rented for the day. All those people filled out application forms asking for a lot of confidential information, including their social security numbers—just what a con artist needs for identity theft.

Scams Against Business Owners

Among the top ten Internet scams of 2001—in addition to chain letters—were e-mails offering info on how to investigate people or spy on them, credit repair services, and virus e-mails with deceptive subject lines and hidden code that causes one to spread them to friends.

Scams against businesses are endless. To give you an idea, here is a list of the categories of scams I found on various sites on the Internet, including The National Fraud Center, the Federal Trade Commission, and the U.S. Postal Service:

- **Advertising Materials.** You are asked to advertise on printed materials that will never be printed or distributed. (Get proof of other promotions completed and contact selected advertisers for a reference.)
- **Cramming.** A crook with access to your phone number and address can "authorize" your telephone company to add charges to your phone bill for services (Internet access, paging, voice mail, etc.) never ordered.
- **Bogus Invoices.** Crooks send invoices to companies for Yellow Pages renewals or office supplies never ordered, hoping the invoices won't be checked. (Always keep a follow-up record of things you've ordered.)
- **Paper Pirates and Toner Phoner.** You are notified, supposedly by someone from your regular office supply company, about a "last chance" to buy paper supplies or toner cartridges at a "special" price. Either you won't get the supplies at all, or they will be inferior. To double-check the validity of such offers, always call the company back to verify the "special deal," but don't use the number given to you by the caller.
- **Calling Card Charges.** Thieves pick up your PIN number (peering over your shoulder or using binoculars) when you make a telephone call in the airport and then use your card number to make calls.
- **Pay-Per-Call Scams.** You have called a number believing it to be toll-free, only to find very high charges for that call on your phone bill. Some of these numbers are specially routed so as to incur extremely high charges of hundreds of dollars.
- **Slamming.** Your phone bill is suddenly higher because another company has stolen your long distance service. (Avoid this by asking your phone company to put a "pick freeze" on your long distance service provider so only you can change this service in the future.)

Homework Myths

- **Internet Services.** Con artists offer various Internet services (Web site, banner ads, directory listings, etc.) and take your money but never perform the services. (Before buying such services, get a written contract with complete contact information that can be verified. Also get references from others who have used the service.)

- **ISP Account Updates.** If you receive an e-mail request that appears to be from your Internet Service Provider (ISP) stating that your account information needs to be updated or that the credit card you signed up with is invalid or expired and the information needs to be reentered to keep your account active, do not respond without first calling your ISP. According to the FTC, this could be an attempt to steal your identity. (See "Identity Theft" sidebar.)

- **Domain Name Registration Scam.** If you get an e-mail notice saying you must renew your domain name or lose it, make sure it's the company you originally signed with because many companies are sending such e-mails in an attempt to steal accounts from other companies (much like the companies that try to steal your long-distance service). Any notice from an unknown company should be discarded. Never click on an imbedded URL that will supposedly take you to a site for more information as this will automatically transfer your name to the e-mail sender, who will then claim you have requested this transfer.

- **IRS Audit Scam.** If you ever receive an e-mail saying you're under audit, and you must return a questionnaire within 48 hours to avoid penalties and interest, *do not respond*. The IRS does *not* notify taxpayers about pending audits via e-mail. This is merely a ploy to get your social security number and other confidential information that could lead directly to the theft of your identity. (See sidebar on this topic.)

Other scams, such as Nigerian money orders, PBX phone scams, fax fraud, prize promotions, and charitable solicitations are discussed on the National Fraud Center site at Fraud.org. Several other sites on the Web are devoted to educating consumers about scams, and you'll find them listed in Section II under "Scams and Frauds." With just a little research, you can learn how to cut down the number of spam e-mails you receive and learn whether certain business opportunities are for real or just another scam.

Smart Tip

Spammers often send their mail from fake addresses, saying you can get your name removed from the list by clicking reply and typing "remove" in the subject line. *Don't do this.* This will only confirm that your e-mail address is good, and your name will be forever planted on that spammer's mail list.

Ten Money-Making Ideas That Violate Copyright Law

The average person does not understand the copyright law and thus often breaks it unknowingly, sometimes only to his or her embarrassment, other times at some cost on the wrong end of a lawsuit. As a business person, however, you cannot afford to be ignorant of this federal law. The following information is vital to this book's readers because some may consider starting a business based on the intellectual property of others—property that is protected by copyright law.

Below you will find information that will help you avoid violating the legal rights of others. (See Section II of this book for additional information about copyright laws and their applicability to your homebased business.) The following information does not constitute legal advice but it has been checked for accuracy by Mary Helen Sears, an attorney in Washington, D.C., whose practice is mainly devoted to patents, copyrights, trademarks, and related matters.

First, a few words about copyright infringement and the penalties for same. This is a complex area I will only touch on here, but here's a good rule of thumb: A copyright is infringed whenever one violates the exclusive rights covered by copyright. It requires only "substantial similarity" to establish infringement, and the penalties may be especially harsh when such infringement affects the profits of the original author or creator while resulting in profit to the user. In addition to legal fees, copyright damages may be $100,000 or more. By heeding the warnings below, and double-checking questionable situations with an attorney who is knowledgeable about copyright law, you should be able to avoid this legal problem.

1   Do not copy, for purposes of resale either as a design or a finished product, the designs on handcrafted products or commercial gift

items. All commercial manufacturers and most professional craft designers/sellers protect their work by copyrights or design patents.

It is all too common today for a person to copy commercial designs or buy a pattern to make products for sale. Sometimes such buyers will modify the design or pattern a little bit, thinking this will suddenly make it their own. In spite of what you may have heard, it is not all right merely to "change one thing," or use a different color or material. Merely changing the way a design is used does not alter the fact that it is a copy. A work does not have to be identical to the original to be a copy, but has only to repeat a "substantial part" of it, according to the Copyright Office. Unless you can legally define the words "substantial part," you should avoid altering commercial patterns and designs for sale as your own "original designs." (See sidebar, "A Little Copyright Story.")

A Little Copyright Story

A woman decided to modify a pattern she had purchased and offer it for sale in a crafts magazine. She called the advertising department of that magazine and told them she wanted to advertise a pattern that was based on someone else's design. "It's okay as long as you've made a few changes," she was advised.

So the woman took her savings to pay for the ad, and upon publication, a friend of the original designer saw the ad and sent her a copy. Whereupon the original designer contacted her lawyer, who in turn informed the advertiser that she had infringed on a copyrighted pattern and must stop selling it immediately. Furthermore, all proceeds from the ad had to be directed to the original designer.

Moral of story: Never take advice on important matters unless the person giving the advice is an authority on the topic.

Homemade Money

In the crafts industry, the illegal use by consumers of copyrighted patterns and designs is known as "pattern piracy," and it has long been a matter of concern to professional designers, writers, and pattern publishers, many of whom who have either instigated lawsuits or are considering them. How can you stay out of trouble here? Generally speaking, you may not encounter problems if you sell your "borrowed designs" only to individuals at a church bazaar, home party, or through your local consignment shop, *but you must never "go commercial" (enter the wholesale marketplace) with products that use someone else's patterns or designs.* Some designers sell all rights to a publisher while others sell only "first rights" (which means they have retained the exclusive right to sell finished products or kits made from their own patterns and designs). When you see a design you like in a book or magazine, you have no way of knowing whether the designer or the publisher owns the copyright, but if you see something you'd really like to produce in quantity, you have nothing to lose by writing to the designer (in care of the publisher) to see if you might get permission to make multiples of the item for sale. Sometimes this permission will be granted without charge; other times, a fee or royalty may be part of the deal.

2   Do not make for sale any reproductions of such copyrighted characters as Snoopy, Raggedy Ann and Andy, the Sesame Street Gang, or the Walt Disney characters unless you have written permission from the copyright holders to do so. Anyone who uses such designs without permission, and without paying mightily for the privilege with a licensing agreement, is asking for legal trouble.

Yes, we have all seen handmade products bearing such designs, but with few exceptions, these crafters are in violation of the copyright law and just begging for a lawsuit. For example, the sale of licensed Disney merchandise is a multimillion dollar industry, and the corporation is aggressive in its efforts to protect its rights. They have sued many retailers for selling items with copyrighted Disney characters on them (and the craftspeople who make such items are just one step behind the retailers).

Commercial patterns or kits of such characters—which have been offered to buyers by licensed manufacturers—are designed for personal use only. Unless a magazine, book, or pattern specifically warns against reproduction for profit, however, the innocent person who makes handmade items for sale in the local craft shop or church bazaar is not likely to be held liable in a court of law.

3 Do not make reproductions of any kind of any picture, photograph, painting or other piece of artwork you may have purchased.

Many people think their purchase of a particular object gives them the right to reuse the design or image on that object. This is not true. The creator of that object owns the copyright, and that copyright can be conveyed to another person *only in writing, or by other transfers that occur by operation of law.* If you buy a painting from an artist, all you own is the physical piece of art. The artist still owns the *image* of that artwork, and only he or she has the right to copy it as prints, postcards, greeting cards, calendars, and the like, or to grant the right to copy to someone else in the form of a license.

4 Do not photocopy—for sale or trade—any pattern, article, or other printed material from any book, magazine, newsletter, etc. because such use denies the creator the profit from a copy that might have been sold. (Even when there is no copyright notice, you must assume such work is copyrighted.)

5 Do not photocopy any part of any copyrighted publication—particularly books and manuals—for use as a teaching aid unless you plan to use it only once, or are teaching a charity group without charge. And the amount of material copied must be "reasonable." Never, for example, make several copies of an entire book (as some teachers have done) for use in a classroom setting.

6 Do not reprint and offer for sale any previously published material still protected by the copyright law (not in public domain—see sidebar), even though such material may no longer be available from the original publisher. That publisher, or the creator, still owns the copyright to that material, whether he or she wants to do anything with it or not.

7 Do not duplicate records, cassettes or tape recordings, videotaped television shows, or computer software for sale, or trade. Sound recordings, audiovisual works, and software are fully protected by copyright laws.

8 Do not copy and republish recipes from books or magazines exactly as they have appeared. A group of previously published recipes can be

republished in new form, however, provided you make changes such as: (1) the recipe's title, (2) the order in which ingredients are used or the amounts of ingredients used, and (3) the way the instructions are written on how to put the recipe together.

9 Do not use poems or poetry written by other people without their written permission. Novice self-publishers often use the work of well-known poets in their newsletters, magazines, booklets, or on greeting cards or calendars, etc. But the use of an entire poem is a flagrant violation of the copyright law because it represents the use of a whole work of an individual creator who is receiving no financial benefit from such usage. *Giving credit to the creator is not enough.* The use of one or two lines of a poem, or a paragraph or two from a book or other publication, may be considered "fair use," according to the copyright law, but some publishers are now asking that even such limited usage be cleared with them beforehand. The same rules apply to all words in general. Never "lift" material from books, magazines, newsletters, etc. for inclusion in your own articles, books, or speeches without giving full credit to the creator. Even then, you must be concerned with the amount of material that is quoted and whether it falls into the "fair use" area of copyright law mentioned above. When in doubt, always request permission from the writer or publisher in question.

10 Finally, a special note for computer users who work with scanners or graphic art software to create illustrations or Web graphics: *Do not alter original line artwork or commercial art illustrations for your own use.* Thanks to affordable computer technology, high-tech copyright infringement has reached epidemic proportions. Many people, ill-informed about the copyright law, believe they can simply scan in someone else's images, change this or that, then claim the illustration as their own because it's now in their computer. *This is not true.* While some "borrowing" with credit to the artist may fall under the "fair use" doctrine of the copyright law, it would be dangerous for the average person to do this. (Remember what I said about the definition of "substantial" in point 1 above.) Fortunately, there are now many sources on the Web where you can find free clip art and graphics. Just type those words in your browser's search engine to turn them up.

As you have seen, the Copyright Law is complex, and nothing to mess with. Your library will have books on this topic, should you wish to pursue it, and the Copyright Office itself offers a wide selection of explanatory circulars, free on request. (see "Copyrights" in Section II). In the end, my best advice to you is . . . *to be safe, be original.*

The Celebrity Rights Act

I'm closing this "bad news chapter" with a few words about a little-known law that business beginners should pay serious attention to. Your state may or may not have a Celebrity Rights Act, but that will not protect you from a lawsuit if you are caught selling unlicensed products and services that fall under the provisions of this law.

It specifically prohibits any person or company—without permission—from producing or advertising a product or providing a service that in any way utilizes the name, voice, signature, photograph, or likeness of a deceased person during a period lasting 50 years after his or her death.

Material in the Public Domain

You can use material in the public domain, which means material on which the copyright has expired or has not been claimed. Some people believe that anything published before 1910 is automatically in the public domain. Not true. Copyright duration before the 1978 Act varied greatly and many copyrights were renewable. It can be risky to use any material that appears to be in the public domain, simply because someone else may have obtained rights by putting it into new form, and claimed a copyright on that new form. Dover Publications, for instance, has reorganized and reformulated many books that were once in the public domain and obtained copyrights for their own new forms. Thus, in all cases, if you plan to use previously published and copyrighted material for your own profit, you would be wise to obtain a legal opinion from an attorney who specializes in copyright law.

Homemade Money

How does this law affect product makers and service providers? I recall a crocheter who designed a Marilyn Monroe doll for sale to her mail order customers. If she's still selling this particular doll or its pattern, she's inviting legal trouble; and if you're an entertainer who plans to dress up as Mae West or Charlie Chaplin and do imitations for profit . . . don't.

My husband has a handpainted plaster bust of W. C. Fields hanging in his office. The company that made it, and the retailer who sold it, may have violated the above law without knowing it. Such replicas cannot be made without special permission from the estate of W. C. Fields. Note that the Celebrity Rights Act affects not only the manufacturer or creator of an unlicensed product or service, but distributors and retailers as well. All can be sued, according to the owner of Roger Richman Productions, Inc., the Beverly Hills agency that represents the heirs and estates of such personalities as Marilyn Monroe, W. C. Fields, the Marx Brothers, Abbott and Costello, Mae West, and others.

Not all states need a special law about this because there simply aren't enough celebrities in some states to warrant it. Regardless of whether there is a state law or not, you may be sure that somewhere there is an attorney or agency looking out for the rights of deceased personalities. Here's an alphabetical A-to-Z list of commercial uses affected by this Act: advertising, animation, apparel, barware, calendars, ceramics, collectibles, dolls, domestics, figurines, games, gifts, handcrafts, jewelry, lithographs, look-alike services, mirrors, mugs, office supplies, party goods, photographs, premiums, prints, promotions, publishing, records, reproductions, sound-alikes, souvenirs, stationery, syndication, textiles, timepieces, toys, T-shirts, video cassettes, wall decor, wax museums, and all other general uses mentioned above.

Uses *excepted* are: plays, books, magazines, newspapers, musical compositions, films, radio or television programs, political and newsworthy material, single and original works of fine arts, and certain advertisements. In the event you want to obtain a license to use a particular personality's characterization in some way, Richman suggests you contact the Screen Actor's Guild (SAG.org) or the Academy of Motion Picture Arts and Sciences in Los Angeles (Oscar.org).

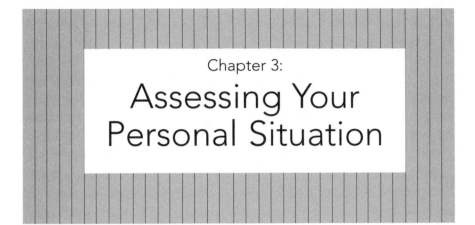

Chapter 3:

Assessing Your Personal Situation

People are always blaming their circumstances. I don't believe in circumstances. The people who get on in this world are the people who get up and look for the circumstances they want, and, if they can't find them, make them.
—George Bernard Shaw

Whether you're a homemaker about to launch a part-time business on a shoestring, or a corporate executive who's thinking about investing your life savings into a full-blown entrepreneurial venture, you need to assess your personal situation before you begin to work at home. The first part of this chapter is for nervous beginners who wonder whether they've got what it takes for success, and what they are letting themselves in for when they start a business at home. Readers who are comfortable with the idea of being their own boss and confident of their business abilities may want to skip to midchapter to the section, "Home Business Pros and Cons."

Are You a Good Home-Business Candidate?

Before you launch a business at home, you need a clear understanding of yourself, your capabilities, *and* your limitations. You must know your strengths so you can build on them, your weaknesses so you can shore them up.

Find out if you're a good home-business candidate by taking the following "test." There are no right or wrong answers, of course; I just want you to do a little thinking about your strengths and weaknesses. After you have answered the questions, ask a family member or close friend to answer them with you in mind. If there is disagreement, it could be that you're trying to fool yourself, or you haven't let other people see the real you.

YES   NO

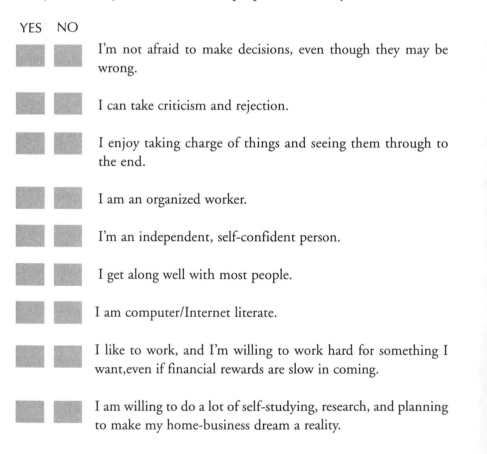

I'm not afraid to make decisions, even though they may be wrong.

I can take criticism and rejection.

I enjoy taking charge of things and seeing them through to the end.

I am an organized worker.

I'm an independent, self-confident person.

I get along well with most people.

I am computer/Internet literate.

I like to work, and I'm willing to work hard for something I want, even if financial rewards are slow in coming.

I am willing to do a lot of self-studying, research, and planning to make my home-business dream a reality.

Assessing Your Personal Situation

As you may have guessed by now, the more "yes" answers you have, the more likely a home-business candidate you are. Having a couple of "no" answers doesn't mean you have to give up your business dream, but it could be a sign of trouble to come.

For instance, the person who is afraid to make decisions will certainly encounter difficulty the first time a major business decision has to be made. The person who cannot take criticism and rejection may crumble the first time a customer says "no" to a sales pitch. People who are reluctant to take charge, or unwilling to accept responsibility, should not subject themselves to the stress of managing a home business. On the other hand, all of these problems might be overcome if you were to join forces with a partner who did have these desired business qualities.

If you answered "no" to the questions about being organized, having confidence, or getting along well with others, this is an indication that you would benefit from some self-help books on these topics. With time and effort, anyone can learn the secrets of organization, develop a greater degree of self-confidence, and improve working relationships with other people.

If you are not yet computer literate, I urge you to acquire computer/Internet skills as soon as possible, for they will not only enrich your life, but make operating any kind of business so much easier and more efficient. If you are already using a computer to access the Internet, and know how to do online research, you'll be miles ahead of others who are still trying to avoid the Internet as they begin their homebased business.

I do hope you answered "yes" to the last two questions, because a home business definitely requires concentrated effort, time, and energy, to say nothing of the three Ps: Patience, Perseverance, and Planning. From experience, I can assure you that your home business, whatever its kind or nature, will take twice the amount of time and energy of any salaried job you may have held in the past; and, unless you are extremely lucky, it will also take longer than you think to make a profit from your endeavor. Be patient in your financial success expectations. Allow at least two years, and as many as five, depending on your type of business, the time, energy, and money you give it, and the skills and experience you bring to it.

Your Opportunities for Learning

Today's home-business beginners have a greater chance for success because so many others have gone before them and are now sharing their experience and knowledge on the Internet, in books, magazines, newsletters, and success tapes and videos. Today's small business owners also have the added advantage of computer technology, which makes it possible for them to operate much like Fortune 500 companies. In addition, there is a wealth of help available from government sources, community colleges, and other learning centers, plus individual teachers and authors like me.

If you do not possess business management and marketing skills and feel you cannot acquire them through self-study, one option is to work with someone who does have a head for business, such as a spouse, partner, other family member or friend who can be your business partner. "Do what you do best and hire out the rest," is excellent business advice, but it's expensive to hire outside business services, which is why I've put so much detail into this book. You may be surprised by how much you can do on your own with a little time and effort. When you do need outside help, I hope you will support the home-business industry by hiring another homebased business to help you. In addition to finding them all over the Internet, many communities also have helpful directories of homebased professionals or organized networking groups where such contacts can be made. You can also connect with such professionals (check your local chamber of commerce) by joining a home-business organization or reading entrepreneurial magazines on your newsstand. (See "Other Resources" in Section II to connect with many of the product and service providers who have contributed information to this book.)

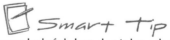

Good advice is always helpful, but don't let other people tell you how to run your business. There is much to be said for following the dictates of your heart, trusting your intuition and gut instincts, and marching to the beat of a different drummer. As you develop your own business ideas, read, study, and carefully weigh the advice and experience of others while also remembering that your way might be as good or better than anyone else's.

Identifying Special Skills and Talents

Many people who think they do not possess the necessary talent and skill to start and operate a successful business are often surprised to discover their true abilities and potential for success once they get going. Thus, what you may be doing best a year or two from now compared to the things you now do best, will no doubt amaze you. Once you have started your business, I wager you'll soon be saying, "I can't believe I'm actually doing this. I had no idea I was capable of such things." Here's a little assignment to help you identify your many talents and skills. Title three sheets of paper:

1 Special Skills and Talents

2 Work Experience

3 Practical Know-How

Include education, hobbies, abilities, volunteer activities, job experience, favorite home activities, extracurricular or social activities, etc. For example: Do you have good communication skills? Do you enjoy using the telephone . . . meeting people . . . speaking in public? Do you have a flair for design or decorating . . . skill as a cook . . . a fundraiser . . . a tour guide? Are you a speed typist? Do you have writing ability . . . good word processing skills. . . graphic art or design skills? Special technology or Web skills? Do you have a "green thumb?" Are you good with children . . . animals. . . older adults? Do you sew . . . do stitchery . . . make handcrafts? Do you have teaching experience . . . accounting or bookkeeping skills . . . legal training . . . nursing skills. . . managerial ability? Any experience in sales? Are you an organizational wizard. . . a "take charge" person . . . a creative thinker . . . a problem solver? Are you especially knowledgeable about one thing in particular? Is your background unique? Are you a Jack or Jill of all trades? What do you do that others might like to do? You've got the idea, I'm sure. And you probably have more skills and talents than you realized.

Homemade Money

Donna M. Snow, who has trained women in successful entrepreneurship at HerSmallBusiness.com, suggests you brainstorm for business ideas on paper by listing all your skills in sets. "Then give all of them a score from one to five," she advises, "with one being most enjoyable and five being the least enjoyable (for you). Don't erase or scratch out anything. Just keep writing until you can't think of anything else. Then take a look at all the things you placed in the number one position. Can they be combined to create a livelihood for you? Is there one skill or hobby that stands out? Ask friends and family what they feel you are really good at, what makes you stand out from the crowd. Don't make the mistake of limiting yourself to your new business choice by whatever industry you happen to be working in at the time. Although your skill sets can be utilized and should be included, don't limit yourself to skills acquired in your career. This is not your only option. You will be surprised at how many ideas you come up with just by putting all the aspects of your life down on paper."

In addition to giving you an ego boost, this little exercise will automatically suggest new business ideas. Keep your worksheets handy as you continue to read this book. Add to your list each time you are reminded of something else you know or do well. By the time you have finished, I guarantee you'll be impressed, particularly if you're a homemaker who has thought of herself for years primarily as a wife and mother. This book is not for women only, of course, but my thirty years in this industry have convinced me that more women than men own businesses at home or want to start them. (Women have always outnumbered men at all the home-business conferences I've attended, and the SBA's research also shows that, in the past decade, women have been starting businesses at twice the rate of men.)

Mothers still represent one of the largest categories of new and would-be home-business owners, and a growing number of sites on the Web now cater to their special needs and interests. Liz Folger is the author of *The Stay-at-Home Mom's Guide To Making Money From Home*, an eBook she has published on her BizyMoms.com Web site along with many other home-business eBooks by moms and dads in her network. In one of her e-mail newsletters, she said: "I'm one of the lucky women who have decided that working at home is the best discovery since the invention of the peanut butter and jelly sandwich. No, I don't have the newest car and I haven't gone on an exotic vacation lately. But I do know who is spending lots of time with my kids and teaching them values and beliefs I hold dear. Me! Plus I've found work that I enjoy. Now how many people can say that?"

Since the very job of homemaking tends to release a woman's creative abilities, it is not surprising that so many home businesses are closely allied to such homemaking arts as cooking, sewing, child care, needlecrafts, handcrafts, music, art, gardening, interior decorating, and pet care. Often out of need, boredom, or accidental discovery, the idea for a home business just sneaks up on a woman and before she knows it, she's making money.

A Special Message for Women

Observers have noted that the ability to focus on a task in both its large and small dimensions, despite distractions and limited resources, is characteristic of women's role in the home and is also needed for entrepreneurial success. The displaced homemaker, who is frequently turning to entrepreneurship, is finding that experience gained nurturing a family is useful in nurturing a business. In addition, many observers comment that women entrepreneurs show a greater willingness than male entrepreneurs to admit ignorance, to seek help, and to do their homework. Many entrepreneurial women need only business training and equal opportunity to be successful.

—From an Annual Report to the President's Interagency Committee on Women's Business Enterprise

Why People Avoid "Business"

My communication with women has shown me this fact: The homemaker who suddenly starts to make extra money at home seldom feels like a businesswoman, and she may never feel as though she's "in business," even though she may continue to make money at home for several years.

This reluctance to look upon a money-making activity as a business is common among women in general and particularly prevalent among the thousands of men and women who sell art, crafts, and other handmade items. Yes, money is being made from such homebased enterprises, but little *profit* is being realized by the majority of these people. That's because so many of them are part-time hobby sellers who lack business expertise and an understanding of the crafts or giftware marketplace. Unfortunately, their failure to look upon their endeavor as a business makes profit almost impossible to attain.

Success in a home business begins with the right attitude: a money-oriented mindset for success. *You have to want money to make it, and you must desire success to attain it.* Without a professional, businesslike attitude about what you're doing, you are destined to remain small-time forever. If that's what you want, okay. But I'm betting that what you really want is more than pin money or even part-time income—and you can get it *if you're willing to work for it.*

Why are so many people so hesitant to approach their homebased, moneymaking activity as a business? The simple answer is . . . *fear.* The very word "business" seems to scare some people half to death, particularly women who have never held outside jobs. And a certain number of men and women alike are apt to shun the idea of a business by saying, "Who, me? Nah, I just want to make a little extra money." In reality, some of these people are not ambitious enough to build a real business. Others are afraid they would fail if they tried, and still others are afraid of success. "Fear is the darkroom where our negatives are developed," says motivational speaker and author Zig Zigler. Your goal must be to turn those negatives into positives.

Why People Fear Success

Why do people fear success, of all things? *Because it signals change.* If a home business were suddenly to take off, it might require a greater investment of time and money, a restructuring of one's home to accommodate growth, out-of-town business trips to find buyers or participate in trade shows, and perhaps the hiring of employees or sales representatives. At this point, the whole family lifestyle would have to change. Since many families are reluctant to accept change in any form, this is not a concern to regard lightly.

Speaking of family, I'm sure you're aware that the definition of "family" has changed in recent years to include a growing number of single moms and dads with children. According to the 2000 census, the number of American single-person households amounted to 26 percent of all households, while households with married couples and children under 18 dropped to 23.5 percent, from 45 percent four decades ago. Today there are also nearly 5 million people who are living together without benefit of marriage. I do not believe in living this way, but I cannot ignore the fact that many couples who aren't married do operate businesses together. (If you decide to go this route, take care to protect your legal interests in the business as discussed under "Legal Forms of Business/Partnerships" in Section II of this book.)

Meanwhile, back to married couples and the problems that sometimes arise when a business is begun at home. Many women have told me it would have been impossible for them to build a business without the full cooperation and support of their husbands. If a man is unsupportive and is going to use the home business as an excuse to criticize the way his wife does housework, she's going to experience stress with a capital *S* and not every woman can handle it. In a case like this, I would suggest that the home business idea be dropped unless the woman feels compelled to follow her dream, is confident of her abilities, and is reasonably sure she can handle whatever comes. Some women need to ask themselves this disturbing question: "If my business succeeds, will my marriage survive?"

Sometimes a husband may see his wife's emerging successful business as a threat to his own place in her life. More than anything, I think, a woman's desire to give to her family is the one thing that ultimately holds her back from great financial success. Many women have told me that their family simply must come first, and they must be careful to keep their business small for that reason, even though greater profits would come with growth.

But sometimes sudden growth comes anyway. If you're a married woman, and your new business takes off like a shot, could your husband accept the fact that you might end up making more money than he ever did? Divorce, of course, is not unknown in home-business land. Reminds me of what one woman told me at a conference. . . about how her overwhelming passion for crafts had changed her life, led her to a soft-sculpture shop of her own and, ultimately, a divorce. She said things got so bad that at one point her husband picked up a piece of lint from the carpet and sarcastically asked, "Can I throw this out, or *do you plan to make something with it?*"

Fortunately, far more marriages seem to thrive on the entrepreneurial lifestyle than dissolve in divorce. Many of my readers have reported that working together as a couple has enriched both marital and personal lives. As home businesses of all kinds continue to be recognized as a vital economic force, we'll continue to see more and more couples (both married and unmarried) striving for a full-time, self-supporting business of their own. If such couples are wise, they will work together from the very beginning, each assuming a certain responsibility for the business as well as for the home and family.

"The main ingredient in a couples' working relationship is love and cooperation," says Connie and Tim Long, partners in North Star Toys since 1980. "These values must never be neglected. You can discuss something and argue a point and be bull-headed and generally go through all kinds of emotions that seem to get deeper and deeper into the hypnosis of conflict, *but* if you keep the goal that you will not sacrifice your love for each other, and that you are dedicated to resolving any issue or conflict, you can always work it out. Nothing could or should be allowed to go unfiltered by these two values."

Is Something Holding You Back?

People have many reasons for not doing something about their dreams and ambitions. Here are some of the more common excuses, and my rebuttal to them. Check the ones you have been using lately. (If none apply to you—my congratulations!)

☐ **I'm scared because I don't know anything about business.**
The education you give yourself will dispel many of your fears. This book is a good beginning. Think of it as a crash course in home-business basics. The more you learn, the less frightened you will be.

☐ **I don't have a good education.**
In a home business, a formal education is not nearly as important as the

education you can give yourself. If you can read and are willing to study, you can learn what you need to know. Increase your education by taking special courses, attending workshops and seminars related to your interests, and by surfing the Internet. (Many courses are now available online—see "Other Resources" in Section II.) Also join appropriate organizations and network with others who share your dreams.

☐ I have no money to start or expand a business.

Many home businesses can be started with a small amount of cash, and there are ways to generate capital even when one has no collateral for a bank loan. (See "Business Loans and Other Money Sources" in Section II of this book.)

As I see it, there is no "right amount" of money required for a home business except that you *do need enough for your particular needs*. (Those needs can be determined by preparing a written business plan, which you will learn how to do in Chapter Eight.) A major benefit of starting with only a small amount of money is that you automatically limit your financial risks. Small expenditures mean small mistakes, and the lack of money can actually be a benefit because it will force you to think more creatively.

☐ There's no room in my home to set up an office or workroom.

I know people who run home businesses in house trailers, apartments, and RVs. You just have to let your home know who's boss! Don't let it dictate the way you live in it. Make room for what you want to do by changing the way you live. Many people lacking a desk or office literally start a business on the kitchen or dining room table. (My first office was a tiny pantry off the kitchen. I laid a shelf across the back of the wall, resting it on the shelves on either side of the panty, and set up my typewriter.) Claim any drawers you can find, and rearrange closets so you can have one just for the business. Consider the use of a room divider to turn one large room into two, and take a serious look at the back porch, the garage, or the basement. You have space somewhere—the trick is in learning to use it efficiently. Books and magazines will give you ideas.

☐ My family won't support my efforts.

You may be surprised by the support you'll receive once you have started and shown your family how serious you are about what you are doing. (See Chapter Twelve, "Maintaining Control.")

I'm always being interrupted in anything I do at home.

And you'll continue to be interrupted until you lay down the law by telling family and friends that you must work and that you cannot be disturbed at certain times of the day. Establish a work schedule for yourself—even if it's only two hours a day—and stick to it.

I'm too old to start a business.

You're only as old as you feel, and no one is too old to make money at home (as this book proves). It takes only a good moneymaking idea and the ambition to see it through. Talk to older people you know who are working. Some of their ambition is bound to rub off on you.

I'm handicapped!

If you have a physical handicap, gain the courage you need by reading books and magazines written especially for handicapped people. (Ask your library for a list of them.) Also discuss your ideas and dreams with friends and professionals who might be able to help you. A home business may allow you to carve out an exciting life for yourself.

My job leaves me with no time for my home business idea.

The lack-of-time excuse is often a cover-up for one's fear of the unknown. First you need to change your attitude about time. Everyone has the same number of hours to spend each day. As someone once said, "Some people count time; others make time count." Many people automatically find time by not doing certain things they used to do— things that no longer seem important after the business is begun. Regardless of your situation, I urge you never to let lack of time stop you from trying to achieve the things that are important to you. My own experience leads me to believe that we only find time for special things by simply beginning. Then, mysteriously, the needed time materializes in direct reversal of Parkinson's Law (i.e., that work expands to fill the time available). In this case, it is time that expands to make room for all the things we want to do.

The Cowards Never Started

In many ways, home business entrepreneurs are like the pilgrims who came to America on the Mayflower. Some have the courage of their convictions, others don't:

"It was alright to talk about it. They made plans. They had a moment's vision, a fleeting dream. But in the end, some lack in their moral fiber, some gnawing, nibbling fear held them back. They never started. . . they stayed where they were. They dropped back. They failed somehow to release within themselves that power which lies in every individual, and is released only when he starts forward in a straight line for the object about which he has dreamed. The man who never starts, never feels that sense of power."

—From *The Cowards Never Started*, by Ray Dickinson (Franklin Publishing Co., Inc., 1933)

Home Business Pros and Cons

There are many special advantages to having a business at home:

- If you are a caregiver, you can continue in that role, whether you're caring for kids, a sick or disabled spouse or partner, or aging parents.

- If you're handicapped, a home business may be a perfect solution to your special employment problems.

- If you're older and without employment but not yet eligible for social security, a homebased business can be a wonderful bridge, giving you not only personal satisfaction but income that otherwise might not be possible. (Of course, many people already on social security are finding that a homebased business not only provides extra income, but a way of staying active and involved in life.)

- Whether young or old, male or female, as a self-employed individual, you are in control of your own time and working hours. (Of course it goes without saying that you'll push yourself relentlessly, but at least you'll be the one doing the pushing, and where stress is concerned, that makes all the difference.)

- In your own office at home, you can enjoy the companionship of pets; have the luxury of a smoke-free environment if you don't smoke, or smoking when you feel like it if you do. You can also choose your own kind of background music or work in silence, as preferred.

- The high overhead costs that kill so many new businesses are low, sometimes nonexistent, when your home becomes your place of business. Also, when you're at home all day, you dramatically cut the chances of being burglarized.

- By working at home, you automatically save money on clothes, lunches out, transportation expenses, and day care costs.

- You don't have to earn as much when you work at home, because a home-based business enables you to shelter a sizable chunk of your gross income from taxes through a variety of tax deductions outlined in "Business Expenses and Tax Deductions" in Section II of this book.

A homebased business offers intangible benefits as well, especially where children are concerned. Working at home means being there for your family in ways that were never possible before. Single moms and dads and couples alike may find their relationships with their children greatly strengthened, particularly if they are old enough to have a small part in the family business.

A business that does reasonably well can also increase one's self-confidence and make one aware of special talents and abilities previously undiscovered. Women, in particular, have often told me how their businesses have increased their self-esteem and feeling of worth.

And all of us who work at home share a smug satisfaction about being able to stay at home when others have to face gridlock on the expressway or risk their lives driving in blizzards, heavy rain or fog. We're grateful we no longer have to face other commuters on trains or buses, or fight for a seat in the restaurant at lunchtime. We're happy to be able to work in the most comfortable clothes and know that the office is just a few steps away. If this isn't a terrific way to live, I don't know what is.

Yes, it's true that homebased business owners put in awfully long workweeks, especially in the first few years of their business. But in the end, we decide when to start and when to stop. No boss is telling us what to do, and this adds to the quality of life. Curiously, the same things that make a business at home most satisfactory are also the ones that cause problems. For example:

- You're in control of your own time and working hours, but you'll soon find you tend to be self-exploiting in that there is no one to tell you when to quit and go home. (Business owners in my network have reported they often work as many as 80 hours per week.)

- You may have total privacy from the world in your own home, but not from your family. Your children, spouse, or partner may intrude into your daily work schedule, and household responsibilities have a way of perpetually interrupting productivity. (It's difficult for the average homemaker to find large blocks of time for serious work. Most are lucky to find even twenty scattered hours a week for their business.) Even without children, interruptions are the norm. Houses naturally demand attention when things go wrong, and spouses don't like to be taken for granted. The "Honey, I know you're busy but . . . " line has always annoyed me, but it's something I had to adjust to. As my husband, Harry, put it many years ago, "When the day comes that your business comes before me, look out!" (Now that he's retired and I'm still working full time at home, having some of my time has become even more important to him.)

On the Lighter Side: As soon as you start a business at home, you will never again have enough time to do everything you want to do. As someone once said, "If it weren't for the last minute, nothing would ever get done." You'll stop polishing your copper-bottom pots, forgotten food will turn green in the refrigerator, and you'll soon adopt the attitude, "If I can't see it, I don't need to clean it." Gourmet cooking will quickly fall by the wayside, and if you're a woman who has been preparing fantastic meals for years prior to starting a business, the oven is not the only thing that's going to heat up when you start throwing quickie meals on the table. A homebased business will also curtail your social life. Either you'll be working in the evenings or on weekends, or you'll simply be too tired to think about entertaining guests, let alone cleaning house for them. Before long, you'll find yourself identifying with the Tupperware lady who shared this insight on housekeeping: "'When I can write my name in the dust on my coffee table, it proves one thing: that I'm literate."

"Self-Employed Individuals" vs. "Entrepreneurs"

Have you ever taken one of those entrepreneurial quizzes to see if you've got what it takes for success? If you have, and you got high marks, congratulations. But if your score was disappointing, don't take it to heart. Some of these tests are not all they're cracked up to be, and while they're meant to be helpful, in some cases they tend to discourage good people with a lot of potential.

Although I've been profitably self-employed for most of my life, I've never felt comfortable with the "entrepreneur" label. Once, when a highly-rated entrepreneurial quiz was making the rounds, I took the test just for the fun of it. As a successful self-employed individual at the time, I figured I'd score high. Imagine my surprise when the test revealed I was "unlikely to succeed."

This information was both amusing to me and useful because it gave me interesting perspective on the difference between classic entrepreneurs and self-employed individuals like myself. There are two entrepreneurial traits I lack, which set my score back. First, I tend to be inflexible; second, I care too much about the feelings of others. The classic entrepreneur, you see, operates in a flexible and spontaneous style, but like so many others who have started businesses at home, I am more comfortable with a *planned, predetermined way of life*, both at home and in business. I set guidelines and timetables for my business and I don't like to leave things up in the air. I am less willing to change course in a venture after it is under way, and once I make up my mind on an issue, I'm not easily swayed from my opinion.

These things set me—and thousands of other successfully self-employed individuals—apart from the classic entrepreneur who typically has an *impersonal, logical approach to business*. Unlike typical entrepreneurs, home-based business owners tend to be caring individuals who are truly concerned about the needs of others, and their commitment to providing worthwhile services is important to their success.

The test I took did confirm that I'm a "go-getter" who understands the importance of finishing tasks thoroughly and on time, and that I'm disciplined and have learned the secrets of managing my time effectively. (Stated philosophically, this means that each day we are faced with many situations in which we must choose between self-discipline and self-gratification. The choice is not always easy.) A cautionary note on my test said, "Because of your nature, you may have to temper your desire to do everything yourself—make an effort to delegate responsibility." (Oh, if only it were that simple—as you may soon learn for yourself.)

My major entrepreneurial weakness has always been my difficulty with my "outer sphere adaptability." Like most people, I prefer to work in my own "comfort zone." Although I couldn't have attained my present position as a leader in my field without stepping outside my sphere on many occasions, this is not to say I've ever felt comfortable doing it. As your business grows, you, too, will find many opportunities outside your immediate comfort zone of friends, contacts, and resources, and you'll have to explore new territory, too, whether you call yourself an entrepreneur, freelancer, self-employed individual, or plain vanilla "home business owner." So get used to feeling uncomfortable. It's a natural part of being in business for yourself.

Or as the well-known quilt designer and author Jean Ray Laury says: "If you are being pulled out of your comfort zone, out of your area of competence, you are being challenged. Anything that challenges tends to push us to the extremes of our abilities . . . and that's when we discover things about ourselves." (See sidebar, "Creativity and Your Comfort Zone.")

Taking a Chance on Yourself

If you're out of work and without interesting job prospects, you have little to lose by launching a homebased business now. If you have a strong desire to be self-employed, but are being held back because of a full-time job, you may have considered quitting and "going for it." While I would not recommend this to everyone, sometimes it is the best solution. Sometimes a person really does have a profitable idea, the necessary skills, the right experience, the right market, and enough money to take the risk, plus the necessary confidence and determination to succeed in business. In that case, it may be now or never. In my case, it was also, "put your money where your mouth is."

After the publication of my first book in 1979, I began to receive a lot of mail from readers who had interesting questions and useful information to share. A couple of years later when I started a newsletter to communicate with these people, I began with the simple notion that this would be a little sideline business in addition to my full-time job. At that time, I was general manager of a small book publishing company, and it wasn't long before I realized I could not do justice to both tasks at once. Something else began to bother me, too. Here I was, sitting high and dry with the security of a good-paying job, telling other people they ought to start a business at home. It occurred to me that I wouldn't have much credibility if I didn't practice what I preached. So, in June of 1982, I took courage in hand and quit my job. It was a simple quote in *Reader's Digest* by Frederick B. Wilcox that finally moved me to action:

> "Progress always involves risks. You can't steal second and keep your foot on first."

It is sometimes necessary to take personal and financial risks to get what you want. I took the risk and it paid off. It might for you, too. *But don't quit your full-time job to start a full-time home business unless you're absolutely sure you understand the risk involved.* Stealing second is only part of the game. The question is whether you can make it to home plate before your money runs out.

This book presents a clear picture of today's changing home-business industry, your opportunities in it, and what you must do to achieve success as a self-employed individual. Understand from the start that doubt comes with the territory. With my husband between jobs at the time I started my business, and expressing concern that I was foolish to give up a good job to go out on my own, I had to overcome my feelings of doubt about whether I was doing the right thing. I worried about whether I was going to lose the money I'd borrowed from personal savings, which had been earmarked for a down payment on a house. Although confident on one hand, I was scared to death on the other. The memories of my own start-up thus prompt me to caution you to never risk more than you can afford to lose, be it time, money, confidence, or ego.

Creativity and Your Comfort Zone
by Dennis Gaskill, BoogieJack.com

Aside from talent being God-given, you must be willing to do your part in the creative process, even if it means looking like a fool. Creativity isn't found in the center of our comfort zone. It lives beyond the edge, so you must be willing to step out of your protective shell to embrace your creative side. That's where the magic is.

We are naturally unwilling to leave our protective shell to become truly creative. To go into the wilderness of our own unknown is risk taking. It is contrary to our nature because we are intentionally doing things we aren't quite sure of, and our nature tells us to stay in our protected area where it's safe, where we won't be ridiculed or laughed at. But guess what? Stepping out of your comfort zone opens whole new worlds!

Step out of your protective shell and what you'll discover will be exciting and enlightening. What you'll discover will be yourself. Not the you others taught you to be, or that you evolved into. Not the you that you or others think you should be. But just you—creative and wonderful you! You may not be a fool, but you must be willing. As Tennyson once wrote: "The shell must break before the bird can fly."

Why Businesses May Fail

I once heard a speaker at a business conference say that most people who start businesses aren't entrepreneurs, "but merely technicians suffering from an entrepreneurial seizure." Unfortunately, a lot of people with good ideas don't make it in business because they fail to become technically adept in the areas of business management and marketing. Through the years, I've communicated with thousands of people who were engaged in a variety of part-time homebased, moneymaking activities. Many of these people did not consider themselves to be "in business," and those who did often lacked business expertise and marketing know-how.

Furthermore, many of these moneymaking activities were underground operations as far as the Internal Revenue Service was concerned. (While some people may think they are pulling a fast one on tax collectors, they are more likely cheating only themselves. That's because there are numerous personal and financial advantages in bringing a home business to the surface, as discussed under "Business Expenses and Tax Deductions" in Section II.)

Since no one knows exactly how many homebased businesses there are, we have no way of knowing how many of these businesses will eventually fail. Studies by the Small Business Administration indicate, however, that the failure rate of home-grown companies is 45–48 percent after five years.

Are You an "Intrapreneur" or "Ideapreneur"?
by Russ Schultz, WriteandReap.com

Not everyone is suited for self-employment. From the onset, you have to be willing to admit and accept it if you are not entrepreneurial enough or if you are not properly trained to attempt this type of lifestyle. With proper introspection, you may just discover instead that you function better as an "intrapreneur," someone who demonstrates personal entrepreneurial characteristics but prefers to remain as an employee in the comfort of a corporate or bureaucratic setting. Or maybe you qualify as an "ideapreneur," someone who has a lot of promising ideas or inventions, but not much initiative, opportunity, energy, or money to transform these ideas into a revenue-producing and profit-oriented enterprise at home. As you assess your situation, here are four additional questions you need to ask yourself:

1. Do you have a secondary source of income that will continue as the new venture is begun?
2. Have you done a budget and set aside six to twelve months of operating expenses?
3. Have you conducted a survey of the market and identified your target audience?
4. Are you willing to face the possibility of failure and return to your previous job and/or start over?

Assessing Your Personal Situation

Looked at in a more positive light, however, this means that more than half of all homebased businesses *survive five years or more*. In following the home-business lives of hundreds of individuals over a period of twenty years, I've seen tremendous coming and going here. Many newcomers, at first excited by the idea of working at home, soon become disenchanted when they realize a homebased business means commitment and hard work. Since such activities were never really businesses in the first place, it's hard to think of them as business failures when they cease. As I stated years before we had statistics to back up my beliefs, at least half of all wannabes won't last long enough to become a real business. Yet this is no reason for you not to try! You may be the exception, but even if you're not, I guarantee that your entrepreneurial experiment will teach you wonderful things about yourself you will never learn otherwise.

Some homebased businesses fail or close not because they are unprofitable or unsuccessful, but simply because of some uncontrollable event in the owner's life that makes cessation of the activity necessary. A marriage, a divorce, a death, a birth, loss of one's home to a fire, hurricane, flood, a sudden illness—all these things and more have a great impact on one's business plans and the overall business-failure or closure rate of homebased businesses. Here's a good example. As I was writing this chapter, I received an e-mail from Darlene Graczyk whose Errands and More business had been featured in the last edition of *Homemade Money.*

"I closed my business in 1995 after seven wonderful years of being self-employed," she said. "I fell in December and broke my right leg in multiple places that required two surgeries to repair. I was in non-walking casts for three months, walking casts for another two months and then tons of therapy in order to get back on my feet. As you can imagine, my business required me to be able to walk (some days run), stand long periods of time with the baskets, and generally be able to go nonstop from morning to night. It quickly became apparent that my career needed to change into a desk job and, with having nearly twenty years of seniority at State Farm, it didn't make sense to go elsewhere."

Darlene now has a dream job and says she is happier than she ever would have thought possible, because her job allows her to use her creativity and all the organizational, people and customer service skills she acquired during the operation of her homebased business. This is just one example of how a home business can be a springboard to something even more satisfying and profitable down the road. Rest assured that the time, money, and effort put into a new homebased venture will always bring some kind of reward, even if it isn't the one you envisioned in the beginning.

Overcoming Your Fear of the Unknown

Whether you will succeed or fail in business will have much to do with your attitude and whether you really need money or are just playing around with business for the fun of it. The more you need income to supplement your family income or provide a full-time living, the more likely you are to succeed in business.

In fact, your very need for money can literally empower you to do what is necessary for financial success. I speak from experience here because some of my most profitable ideas have come to me when I was in a state of financial panic, trying to figure out how I was going to pay the next month's bills.

I often remember what Linda Ellerbee once said in a revealing interview. "I got into journalism when my husband left me to raise two children," she said. "I'll tell you this: Ambition to get ahead can't hold a candle to fear. You can run twice as fast with something chasing you."

Since fear is one of the biggest hurdles business owners face—not only in the beginning, but throughout the life of their business—this topic needs some special attention here. In my surveys of hundreds of people who attended my day-long seminars through the years, I often asked people to write on a slip of paper the one big thing about business that scared them the most. In analyzing hundreds of responses, I found the same fears named over and over again. Read the following list of "Hot Fear Buttons" and see how many you have:

I'M AFRAID OF . . .

Being in debt

Poverty in my old age

Losing money

Assessing Your Personal Situation

Losing face

Making expensive mistakes

Getting in over my head

Getting in trouble with the law

Getting in trouble with the IRS

Getting in trouble with my spouse/partner

Getting ill or dropping dead with no one left to fill the orders.

I'M AFRAID I'LL HAVE . . .

Too many interruptions

Too many expenses to handle

Too little time for it all

Too little business to keep going

Too much business to handle.

I'M AFRAID I WILL . . .

Get bored working only for myself

Let my work ruin my family either financially or emotionally

Fail in business and lose the investment

*Be so successful that it challenges
my relationship with my spouse/partner*

*Get swallowed by the business so I end up
as stressed as I was in my full-time job.*

I'M AFRAID I WON'T BE ABLE TO

Discipline myself and stay motivated to work

Make ends meet financially

Find and keep customers

Sell myself

Meet the expectations I have set for myself

Convince others that what I'm doing is right

Avoid burnout

Cope with rejection

Handle success

*Deal with failure (and the discovery that
I may not be competent or just can't hack it).*

In the above list, do you recognize the common denominator? Although fear can be verbalized in many different ways, what it all boils down to is *fear of the unknown*. And that's good news, because *knowledge* is the antidote to fear. I once heard someone on the radio say that *knowledge equals information times experience*, which made me realize I was not sharing my knowledge with others, but merely sharing *information* with them. Thus, you can use all the information in this book to increase your own knowledge, and once you have that, you will also have an understanding about what you can or cannot/should or should not do.

When you set out on a new road of discovery—which is exactly what a home business is for most people—it's natural to be frightened, even scared silly. But that may be good for you, according to Rod Steiger. "Terror is a great foundation for creativity," he said when recalling his early days as an actor cast against Marlon Brando. If fear is the main thing holding you back from starting a business, ask yourself what's the worst thing that could happen if you tried? Failure? Of course. But failure can be a beneficial experience because it teaches you what *not* to do the next time around.

I certainly have had my own share of failures. In fact, my first home business was profitable only in terms of experience, knowledge, and friendships gained (not a bad bargain at that). There was very little financial profit, so when the business ended, I felt like a failure. But only for a short while. Then I began to realize the important lessons failure had taught me. In looking back, I saw that failure in one area is often a necessary step to success in another.

Smart Tip

"Failure does not take something out of you; failure builds a lot of necessary character and personality qualities into you," says a success expert. "You are not weaker because you fail, you are tougher, stronger, more determined—and much wiser."

Since the very act of beginning involves the unknown, most of us have a tendency to shy away from it. Yet we cannot make gains either as individuals or business owners if we do not constantly explore unknown territory and test our new ideas and theories. If you have a business idea in mind at this time, but are being held back for one reason or another, use this time to sharpen old skills, acquire new ones, and gain an education in business basics. As Ben Franklin put it, "An investment in knowledge pays the best dividends."

Starting a business right now may not be nearly as important in the long run as being able to do it well when the time is right. Each new thing learned will broaden your economic base; each new skill acquired and sharpened will increase your income potential. Everything you do to develop your skills and business expertise will be like depositing money in a special savings account. Invest in yourself! You'll never find a more worthy investment.

"Don't be afraid to try something you really want to do," says writer and self-publisher John Cali. "I hesitated for years to get into something I really loved because I was afraid I'd fail. Then a good friend told me that the only way to know if you can fly is to jump off a cliff. So I jumped off the highest cliff I could find. Much to my surprise, I found I could fly."

Press On!

Your biggest hurdle will be giving yourself permission to fly. If you fail to press on while the light is green, you will spend so much of your life in the amber zone waiting for "just the right moment," or "a time when most people will understand" that you will find yourself on your death bed surrounded by regrets.

—Charles R. Swindoll, *The Finishing Touch* (Word Publishing)

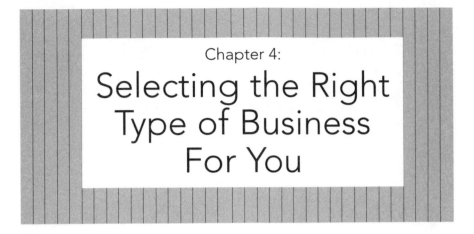

Chapter 4:

Selecting the Right Type of Business For You

If entrepreneurs suffer from a common malady, it's impetuosity. They rush off in a burst of enthusiasm to start businesses and are dumbstruck twelve months later when they fall flat on their faces. They mistakenly think a great idea is all it takes to launch a business. On the contrary; a good idea is only the spark that ignites the entrepreneurial fire.

—Donald Frey, retired CEO of Bell & Howell Corp, as quoted in *Entrepreneur* magazine

Once you've assessed your personal situation and identified skills, talents, and experience that might be used in a homebased business, you should think about the type of business you want: a *product* business, a *service* business, or a combination of both. The reference charts in this chapter provide an overview of the many different kinds of product and service businesses and how sales are made. In addition to stimulating the idea-generating process for a new business (see also next chapter), these charts will come in handy later on when you're ready to start thinking about business expansion or diversification. As you study them, try to relate what you see there to the self-profile you recorded on your skills/talents/experience worksheets in the previous chapter. (If you haven't completed this little exercise yet, do it soon because these worksheets will be helpful to you in brainstorming for moneymaking ideas.)

To help you better understand your product-business options, this chapter also includes a discussion of things you should consider if you're planning to start an arts and crafts business, sell products by mail, or get involved with a direct sales or network marketing program of any kind. You'll also find a brief discussion of home business franchises at the end of the chapter.

 Smart Tip

There is no new thing under the sun, according to the Bible, but every product or service in the world can be changed, improved, presented, or sold in a new way or simply offered to a different audience. That's what makes business so exciting and your moneymaking opportunities so many and varied.

Two Basic Kinds of Business

In spite of the hundreds of individual things you might think of that could bring in extra income, there are just two kinds of businesses after all: *product-oriented* and *service-oriented*. Let's analyze them, two by two.

1. **Product-Oriented Business.** Your selection of a product business will have much to do with the way you plan to make sales and deliver products. (See sidebar, "Direct and Indirect Selling Methods.") Product businesses fall into two main categories, as indicated on the "Product-Oriented Businesses" chart in this chapter: (1) Products that are self-created (or manufactured) and made for sale at retail, wholesale, or on consignment; and (2) products made by others and either purchased for resale or sold to others on a direct-sales or drop-ship basis. (In drop-shipping, you do not have to handle inventory. You merely solicit orders, then forward them, with appropriate payment and a shipping label, to a publisher or manufacturer who ships the order directly to your customer.) If you put your business on the World Wide Web, you will also have the option of selling both products and services through affiliate programs, a diversification strategy discussed in this book's companion marketing guide.

2. Service-Oriented Business. Service businesses also fall into two main categories: (1) Services performed at home (work generally performed *at* home after sale of service), and (2) services performed from home (some or all work performed away *from* home after sale of service). From-home businesses are now called "mobile businesses," and there are literally thousands of them operating today. An important consideration in starting a service business is whether you will perform the service offered or hire others to perform it. If so, you must consider what you will have to pay others to perform the service and whether your profit will be sufficient.

Both at-home and from-home services are sold to two primary markets, as indicated on the two service-oriented business charts in this chapter: (1) Individuals at home, and (2) people in the business community (including business professionals, companies, shops, stores, organizations, and institutions).

Because many services can be adapted for sale to both business and consumer markets, there is some overlapping here. I believe, however, that the true profit potential of any service business can best be analyzed by viewing it from this marketing standpoint: *Simply ask yourself which market you are most qualified to serve and best able to reach.* The same logic can be applied to product businesses, too.

Direct and Indirect Selling Methods

There are only two ways to get a product to the ultimate consumer: directly or indirectly.

- **Direct selling to consumers.** Examples of direct (face-to-face) selling methods include fairs, shows, bazaars, flea markets, home parties, network marketing, in-home demonstrations, and other person-to-person sales.

- **Indirect selling to consumers.** Here, sales may be made to individual buyers through a Web site; through retail shops and stores, mail order dealers, or distributors; or through other wholesalers by means of sales calls, trade shows, sales representatives, special distribution programs, and trade advertising.

Arts and Crafts Businesses

Many people view arts and crafts businesses as nickel-and-dime ventures, and rightly so, given the millions of hobby sellers out there today. But today's arts and crafts industry also includes thousands of highly successful men and women who earn a living doing what they love to do most: working with their creative hands and minds. While a hobby business may be lucky to net a thousand dollars a year, many art and craft professionals are generating gross incomes of between $30,000 and $250,000. In fact, arts and crafts are now a multibillion-dollar industry that offers many opportunities to creative individuals who are willing to approach the sale of handcrafts and related products and services as a business. (See sidebar, "Arts and Crafts Industry Statistics.")

Because there is now so much competition in this industry, success here demands a serious commitment to the idea of business and marketing. The interesting routes creative people can take in this industry, and the many different ways products and services can be sold, are simply fascinating and virtually unlimited. (I've written four books on these topics alone. For hundreds of examples, see *Handmade for Profit* and *Make It Profitable* (M. Evans), and *Creative Cash* (Prima), available in bookstores everywhere and on my Web site, BarbaraBrabec.com.)

Most crafters get their start by selling in local arts and crafts shows, consignment shops, craft malls, or holiday boutiques. This helps them understand the marketplace, learn what consumers are currently buying, and how much they are willing to pay for certain products. Serious craft producers who don't mind making the same products over and over ultimately perfect their production techniques and move into wholesaling. Many who will eventually tire of selling at retail often discover new talents and skills in the process that enable them to move into successful careers as craft designers, writers, teachers, speakers, or consultants.

Cindy Groom-Harry is but one example of what can happen when one's creative skills are taken seriously. After years of designing her own crafts, Cindy went on to sell many original projects to craft magazines. In 1989, she resigned her teaching job to pursue designing and consulting for manufacturers full time. Cindy was one of the first designers in the industry to see the importance of working with manufacturers on a consulting basis, and it was her membership in the Society of Craft Designers that helped her build a network of designers and sparked the idea for her homebased designing and consulting business. As this business grew, Cindy and her husband, Lee

Selecting the Right Type of Business

R. Harry, incorporated as Craft Marketing Connections, Inc., and moved the business outside the home. Today, with a staff of eight, Cindy and Lee provide their clients with such services as conducting research, creating new products, developing and handling comprehensive marketing programs, advertising, and public relations activities. Or, as Cindy puts it, "We help manufacturers introduce their products into the craft industry. We create designs, write instruction sheets for making those designs, and then help companies with their marketing and sales plans."

Smart Tip

To succeed in a crafts business, first zero in on your special talents and abilities to develop products or services currently in demand. Then read available crafts marketing books to learn how to perfect the methods used to promote and sell them to the right market.

Exploring Your Marketing Options

If you're planning to sell products you will make yourself (art, handcrafts, stitchery, fiberarts, etc.), you must give thought to where you're going to do the actual production, where you're going to store supplies and finished inventory, and how you're going to sell the products themselves—directly to consumers, through retail outlets, trade shows, by mail, on the Web, etc. These are important considerations since you may not have the kind of space that's necessary to make and store a large volume of goods or the physical stamina to haul merchandise to one show after another. In addition, you may or may not enjoy interacting personally with buyers or have the ability to travel to make sales calls or deliveries. Thus your personal preferences or situation will largely determine the way you must try to sell your products. Here is a list of the many outlets creative people sell to/through today to reach both individuals and wholesale buyers:

- Arts and crafts fairs and shows
- Art and fine craft galleries
- Craft consignment shops
- Home shops, studios, and open houses
- Home parties

- Holiday boutiques
- Craft malls and rent-a-space shops
- Gift shops and other retail shops and stores
- Corporate clients
- Beauty shops
- Realtors and local builders
- Pushcarts in shopping malls
- Schools, hospitals, clinics, retirement centers, and nursing homes
- Marketing cooperatives and co-op shops
- World Wide Web

In the past few years, there has been an explosion of craft sites on the Web, opened by individual artists, crafters, needleworkers, designers, teachers, authors, and publishers in the crafts industry. Although being on the Web is not a fast way to riches, many of the individuals in my network who have launched Web sites are reporting good sales. Once you get your crafts business rolling, you may well want to consider some visibility on the Web, either through a site of your own, or one of the sites that now help artists and craftspeople sell their work.

Smart Tip

Two organizations on the Web offer inexpensive Web site design and hosting services. To save money, check out the National Craft Association (NCA) at CraftAssoc.com, 1-800-715-9594, and CraftMark at www.CraftMark.com, 1-800-335-2544.

The secret to success here is to think of your Web site as just another marketing outlet. You can't rely on it to bring in sales unless you aggressively promote the existence of your site to your customer and prospect base and make it easy for people to buy with a credit card. (Putting your business on the Web is one of the many marketing topics discussed in this book's companion marketing guide, *HOMEMADE MONEY: Bringing in the Bucks.*)

Product-Oriented Businesses

Self-Created (or Manufactured) Products

Made for sale at retail, wholesale, or on consignment. Involves inventory. Product examples:

Arts and crafts*

Books/directories

Fine art and prints

Food products

Furniture

Garments

Greeting cards/notes

Herbs, plants

Household items

Kits (craft, hobby)

Patterns and designs

Periodicals

Special reports and booklets

Rubber stamps

Tools, equipment

*The crafts category is so broad as to be almost indescribable. Basically, it includes anything made of wood, metal, clay, glass, fiber, fabric, and all materials in between, and covers such specific items as gifts, decorative accessories, miniatures, toys, dolls, novelties, jewelry, clothing, sewing, weaving, needlework, and so on.

Products Made by Others (Manufacturers or Publishers)

Products purchased wholesale and resold (at retail or wholesale). Involves inventory. Product examples:

Advertising specialties

Antiques and collectibles

Books and booklets

Calendars and posters

Craft supplies and materials/kits

Crafts and needlework (finished products)

Flea market goods

Food products

Housewares

Imported gifts and novelties

Jewelry

Nutritional products

Office supplies

Perfume

Stationery/note cards

Products generally purchased for resale in direct-sales situations or on a drop-ship basis. May or may not involve inventory. Product examples:

Cleaning supplies

Cookware

Cosmetics

Craft and hobby kits

Diet/health products

Giftware

Greeting cards

Housewares

How-to books

Jewelry

Lingerie

Perfume

Toys

Service-Oriented "At Home" Business Ideas

Generally sold locally, in person; some also sold and performed by mail or e-mail/Internet. (The listings below are merely examples--no attempt has been made to list every possible service one might sell.

Services Sold to Individuals

Auditing services (utility, tax bills)
Beautician
Calligrapher
Child care
Class instructor (cooking, sewing, crafts, writing, etc.)
Consultation (career, weddings, fashion, business, art, beauty, diet)
Custom design (crafts, gifts, clothing)
Dressmaker or tailor
Food specialist (party food preparation, special diets, menu planning, party cakes)
Hairdresser (cutting, shampoos)
Mechanic or small engine repair (where zoning laws permit)
Pet care (kennel, grooming, training, dog walking)
Repairs/restoration specialist (art, antiques, furniture)
Tax preparer
Taxidermist
Teacher or coach (piano, voice, special education, drama, speech, art, sewing, etc.)
Telephone salesperson
Therapist
Writer (family memoirs, resumes)

Services Sold to Business Community

Accountant
Ad consultant or agency
Agent (literary, sales, booking entertainment, insurance)
Artist/crafts designer (architectural commissions, interior design)
Artist/designer (brochures, catalogs, books, printed materials, signs)
Bookkeeper
Calligrapher (diplomas, scrolls, certificates, etc.)
Clipping service (publicity mentions)
Computer programmer or other services
Consulting (by phone, mail, Internet)
Copyediting service
Copywriting services
Counselor (investments, social services)
Financial adviser/planner
Marketing or PR services
Medical services (billing, transcriptions)
Printing consultant or broker
Publicist
Research services
Secretary/word processing (legal, academic, business)
Tax preparer
Web services (site design and hosting, management, marketing, etc.)
Writer (copywriting, press releases, resumes, newsletters, ghost writer)

Service-Oriented "From Home" Businesses

Services Sold to Individuals

Appraisal services (real estate, antiques, jewelry)

Auctioneer

Baby-sitter

Caterer

Chauffeur

Chimney sweep

Computer training

Construction services/building repair

Escort (children, the elderly)

Hairdresser or barber (house calls, shut-ins, hospital patients)

Insurance agent

Interior decorator/designer

Landscape/gardener

Maid or butler

Medical insurance claims processing

Mover (furniture, equipment)

Party entertainer (singer, instrumentalist, magician, puppeteer, clown)

Party planner/coordinator

Personal shopper or delivery service (gifts, groceries, meals, medicine)

Photographer or videotape services (people, events, possessions for insurance records)

Private teacher/tutor (math, music, horseback riding, swimming)

Repair services (large appliances, electronic equipment, home repair)

Sitter (house, pets, people)

Snow removal service

Studio instructor (dance, exercise, music, etc.)

Tradesman (plumber, carpenter, painter, etc.)

Services Sold to Business Community

Computer services (technical)

Consulting

Coordinator (special events, projects)

Courier/messenger (bonded)

Craft demonstrator (trade shows)

Efficiency/organizational expert

Entertainer (supper clubs, organizations, private groups)

General contractor

Human resource development consultant

Instructor (sports, drama, dance)

Janitor (offices)

Model

Photographer (specialized—medical, horticultural, etc.)

Plant or floral service (flowers/plants delivered and maintained)

Producer (cultural events, shows, plays)

Sales representative/agent

Speaker (seminars, workshops, keynote addresses)

Stenographer/secretary (have pen, will travel)

Tour guide (museums, parks, sightseeing buses)

Translator

Arts and Crafts Industry Statistics

It has long been known that America's handcraft industry was making a significant contribution to the economy, but there were no statistics to prove it until early 2001, when the Craft Organization Directors Association (CODA) released the results of its landmark study. It confirmed what many industry leaders instinctively knew all along: Craft businesses are contributing nearly $14 billion a year to this country's economy. Here are some surprising facts and figures from the CODA study:

- There are 106,000 to 126,000 craftspeople working in the United States today.
- These business owners (79 percent of whom are homebased) are generating sales of between $12.3 to $13.8 billion per year.
- The average gross sales/revenue per craftsperson is $76,025.
- Income from craft activities comprises 47 percent of household income on average, and 22 percent of craft households derive all of their income from craft.
- Retail sales account for 52.9 percent of annual sales, with just over one-half of these sales being made at craft fairs.
- The average craftsperson derives 27 percent of annual sales from wholesale, and 11.2 percent from consignment to galleries.

In summary, the CODA study findings have validated the crafts industry as a vibrant and growing network of small American businesses while drawing added attention to small and homebased businesses in general. These statistics are expected to prove to business and government leaders that craft is a viable and sustainable industry worthy of investment and support.

Mail Order Businesses

Not everyone understands that mail order is not a type of business, but simply an effective way to market a wide variety of products and services. But since so many people think in terms of starting "a little mail order business," the topic needs discussion here.

Today's $1.7 trillion mail order industry is also referred to as the direct mail or direct response industry. Most people learn this business the hard way—through trial and error—but beginners could save themselves a lot of money and heartache if they would only study some of the classic how-to mail order books on this topic before placing ads, renting mail lists, or creating printed materials. With determination and a willingness to learn the rules of the game, the average person can master the principles of marketing by mail. But remember this: For every astonishing mail order success story, there are thousands of stories of failure. Unless you have a lot of money to invest up front, it will take time to achieve financial success in a traditional mail order business that involves the purchase of goods for resale through a catalog.

On the other hand . . . I would be the first to encourage you to get involved in mail order marketing if you

1   Have one terrific product to begin with;

2   Have ideas for related items you can add to your line; and

3   Can reach your targeted market through inexpensive classified ads or publicity (both print and online).

Although I no longer sell anything by mail, I made a good living for twenty-five years by selling this way. I began in 1980 with just one product, soon following with a newsletter and special reports, self-published books, and workshops. In spite of rising postage and delivery costs, mail order is still the preferred way to sell thousands of products. Today's busy shoppers don't seem to mind paying higher shipping costs to get a needed product, because this kind of shopping saves them a considerable amount of time and shopping frustration. Thanks to the Internet, more and more consumers are shopping on the Web, so if you're serious about selling your own products by mail, make plans now for your own Web site. Color brochures and catalogs are costly to print and mail, but with a Web site, you can showcase hundreds of products and give customers access to your catalog 24 hours a day.

The beauty of a mail order business is that you can control its size and dollar volume by increasing or decreasing the number of ads, direct mailings, or online promotions to bring in business. The curse of a mail order business is that, if you don't have employees, you can never get away for more than ten days at a time because the orders just keep coming, and someone has to quickly process and fill them. (See also "Mail Order Laws" in Section II.)

Ten Characteristics of a Good Mail Order Product

As with any endeavor, a mail order business will grow in direct proportion to the amount of time, money, and effort invested in it. Good products and prompt service are important keys to success. Following are the characteristics of a good mail order product:

1 It is a product not readily available elsewhere, either in retail stores or from other mail order firms. The more exclusive the product, the better.

2 It will appeal not to a wide universe of buyers, but to some special-interest group of individuals—often a relatively narrow market that large companies are not interested in because profits aren't great enough. (Sales that would be "peanuts" to them might represent a substantial amount of money to you.)

3 It is an item in which people will not quickly lose interest.

4 It is an item people can use, appreciate, and understand; one that offers a benefit of one kind or another. (Products should be unusual in that they are not readily available elsewhere, but not so unfamiliar that people would hesitate to buy them. People won't buy something if they don't understand what it is or why they should have it.)

5 It is easy to describe in writing.

6 It photographs well and looks good when pictured in a print catalog or on a Web page.

7   It is easy and inexpensive to pack and ship for arrival in customers' hands in undamaged condition. (The more fragile the item, the higher your shipping costs will be since you will need special packing materials for it. Also, anything that can be easily damaged in shipment will probably result in your having to replace merchandise from time to time.)

8   It is small, so many items can be stored in a minimal amount of space.

9   It retails for less than $25 and has a profit margin of 65–70 percent. (To compensate for increased overhead costs, the price of a mail order item should be at least five times what it cost in materials and labor to produce.)

10   It is a product of high quality. (While you may be able to sell a bad product, the customer who bought it won't buy from you again. This is vitally important, since the real profits in mail order come from repeat sales to satisfied customers.)

Thinking About Importing? Unless you have found a source of supply on your own by visiting a foreign country, you will need to connect with agencies that can provide the names of firms that export products. Each country has a consulate office in the United States, many of which are located in New York City, Chicago, or Washington, D.C.

If you are importing raw materials, you may be able to deal with individual firms in other countries. But if you are interested in importing handmade goods, you probably will have to work through special marketing organizations for each country. For example, all goods from Poland must be channeled through Cepelia in New York, handmade items from Greece are marketed through the National Organization of Hellenic Handicrafts, and so on. Each country's consulate office will put you in touch with the specific marketing contacts you'll need.

When merchandise from a foreign country arrives in this country, it must go through customs, so consult a customs broker in advance of ordering any goods. You can clear only a certain dollar value of shipments through customs yourself, and this may affect the quantity of merchandise you order at one time. In addition to customs regulations, there are state and local requirements about licensing and the payment of sales tax. Check with your state treasury department about this.

Direct Sales Businesses

Over 4 million people are now involved in direct selling as a full-fledged career or a profitable second job, and over 80 percent of them are women who have learned that direct selling fits nicely into their family lifestyle. Like the network marketing companies discussed below, direct sales companies also encourage their distributors to recruit party hostesses, bringing them into the dealer network and generating income on another level. Many companies, such as Mary Kay Cosmetics, Lady Remington, Shaklee, Watkins, Avon, Tupperware, and Discovery Toys are eager to work with sales-oriented people who want to build profitable part- or full-time businesses, and the profit potential here is excellent. You'll find their ads in many consumer and business magazines on the newsstand as well as on the Web. In deciding which products to sell, be sure to compare the offers of several companies, noting:

1 Startup costs;

2 Cost of promotional catalogs, brochures, delivery bags, etc.;

3 Whether you have to pay for merchandise in advance of receiving payment from your party customers;

4 Local competition (ask companies for the names of dealers in your area).

Products available from direct sales companies can be sold in a number of ways, including sales to one person at a time, through meetings, home parties (see sidebar), by mail, or on the Web. Some product sellers have their own Web sites, while others simply sell on online auctions, a topic discussed in this book's companion marketing guide.

A Mary Kay Success Story Twyla Menzies is a good example of the profit potential possible when one becomes involved in the sale of good products offered by reputable companies such as Mary Kay Cosmetics, the number one seller of skin care and color cosmetics. When Twyla joined Mary Kay as a beauty consultant in 1981, she had no idea of the financial possibilities here.

"Initially, I was only interested in making the same $200/week I was then earning at my 40-hour-a-week job," she says. "I soon discovered I could earn that much with only 6–8 hours a week in Mary Kay. It was important to me when I joined twenty years ago to be able to schedule my work around my children's schedules. Now it is important to me for the same reason, only as a grandmother."

After attending her first annual Mary Kay seminar, Twyla learned there was no limit to her sales possibilities if she would consistently hold three beauty shows a week and spend some time on the phone. By doing this, she obtained Directorship nine months later. "My income is not limited to what I, alone, can produce because my income is extendable through others," she explains. "As a Mary Kay Director, I receive a 13 percent Director's check on every member of my unit in addition to a 13 percent commission check on those people I have personally recruited. And, as a Senior Director, I also receive a 4 percent commission check from my spin-off unit in California."

A "beauty show," by the way, is nothing more than an event where three or more women gather together to have a facial, says Twyla. "Products are tried before purchase, and the products are made available on the spot, so that while the method of application is fresh in their memory, they take it home with them to reapply the next day. The consultant collects the money (check, cash, or credit card). When ordering from the company, we pay tax on retail at time of purchase, and then we collect the tax back from our customers."

Although large profits are certainly possible in direct sales companies such as Mary Kay, few sellers get rich quick. Like all other businesses, the amount a person can earn is directly tied to the amount of time and effort expended. The majority of Mary Kay consultants work part time and earn less than $30,000 annually in commissions or prizes, but Twyla is one of the exceptions. "Mary Kay has more women making over $100,000 a year than any other direct sales company," she says. In singing the praises of this company, Twyla added that it was one of the first direct sales organizations to offer a family retirement program. Now into her second decade with Mary Kay, Twyla has qualified for ten vehicles, although twice she took the cash option plan instead of a car. For the past ten years, because of the flexibility of her work, she has had time to be involved in a prison ministry. "I believe The Mary Kay company has thrived because it was founded by the late Mary Kay Ash on the principles of God first, family second, and career third," she says. "In that order everything works; out of that order, nothing works."

Selling Through Home Parties

Home parties, or "party plan selling," is one of the most successful types of product marketing ever invented. Where not specifically prohibited by zoning laws (see Chapter Seven), this type of marketing works anywhere, even in the smallest rural community, and anyone can learn to do it. Any commercial product line, including jewelry, cosmetics, cleaning products, kitchenware, lingerie, toys, and gifts, will sell this way, and many individual craft producers have also found home parties to be a terrific way to sell handcrafted merchandise, craft and needlework kits, and patterns.

The party plan concept is simple. You arrange for parties to be held by friends or relatives, who in turn suggest the names of other friends and relatives who might like to hold a party. A host or hostess at each party supplies refreshments and earns points according to the sales volume of the party and the number of additional parties booked. The salesperson plans the presentation, supplies any necessary game or door prizes, and displays wares for sale. Orders are taken, but merchandise is not delivered until later. This job falls to the host/hostess, who also must collect payment for the seller. (A deposit, especially on custom-designed or personalized items, is recommended to discourage later cancellations.)

Detailed information on this type of marketing will be found in Barbara's book, *Handmade for Profit* (M. Evans).

Working with Web-Based Product Companies

Many good companies on the Web now offer business opportunities for individuals who want to build Web sites to sell their line of products. One example is AtHome America (formerly known as Country Peddlers), a network of online stores that provide a comfortable shopping experience. Michelle Winterhalter, who has been associated with this company for eight years, agrees it offers a good income opportunity for anyone who likes to sell.

"It has been very lucrative for me," she says. "In fact, when my husband got laid off, we decided he did not have to return as we could now live on this income alone. Not only that, this company offers a very positive, supportive environment where the recognition and applause is in abundance, the creativity flows, and we're all treated like family." Over the past seven years, Michelle has built her business around four small children, and she currently coaches and manages 125 other homebased sellers from her site, AtHome.com/Shelle.

AtHome.com specialists have their own Web sites, which they set up themselves using a template provided by the company. Each specialist maintains his/her own site and pays a small monthly fee for it. Each site is independent, but all orders go back to the home office's main site, carrying a link that identifies the source of the order. Income is limited only by the amount of work the seller is willing to do to promote sales.

MLM/Network Marketing

You'll recall my earlier mention of MLM (multilevel marketing) companies and scam operators in Chapter Two. (See also sidebar, "A Typical MLM Pyramid Scheme.") In promoting their products, new MLM programs often point to the success of such established direct sales companies as Tupperware, Amway, Shaklee, and Mary Kay Cosmetics to prove how well the MLM concept works. But the big corporations in this industry no longer want to be thought of as MLM companies because MLM has had more than its share of bad apples through the years, and is still fighting a bad reputation. That's why so many now refer to themselves as *direct sales companies* that offer *network marketing opportunities.*

Actually, MLM selling is similar to mail order selling in that it is not really a business at all, but merely a way of marketing products. New companies in this industry do not market through regular retail outlets, but through individual distributors, and the kind of products most often sold this way tend to serve niche markets larger companies are not interested in. The most successful MLM products seem to be household products, personal care items, and herbal and vitamin products, some of them imported from other countries. Often, these new products will benefit from a demonstration or explanation on how to use them for best results. Although people involved in network marketing are running businesses based at home, most do not think of themselves as "home-business owners" because they are simply selling the products of other companies. Instead, many simply think of themselves as "homebased professional network marketers."

Although selling is a big part of what they do, few MLM distributors are salespeople, which isn't necessarily a problem. "People who are strictly sales-oriented will fail in network marketing," says one network marketer. "You can't be successful in a program unless you use and believe in a product, and you must also be willing to teach and train others how to build their own business—in other words, duplicate your efforts. A solid MLM program must be based not on how far *you* can go, but how many people you can bring with you when you climb the ladder of success. Thus, if you are not willing to teach and train, you cannot be a successful network marketer."

MLM guru and author Charles Possick, believes as many as 10 million families in the United States may be involved in MLM selling. "For 98 percent of them, one of the best bonuses of an MLM distributorship is the fact that they can buy products at wholesale prices," he says. For example, a large family that wants to add vitamin supplements to its diet could save a small fortune by joining an MLM program that offers the products it needs.

Smart Tip

The only way to succeed in this business is to find a good product you're excited about, and make it available to other people who will also get excited about it. If they also want to sell it to friends, you will profit by bringing them into the program as a "downliner."

Building a Successful Downline

Many people believe that MLM selling is about getting other people to sign up under a distributor and do all the work. But anyone entering MLM with this idea in mind is going to fail. Like all businesses, MLM companies come and go; 90 percent of them are likely to fail within ten years. This automatically affects the distributors who were handling their products. So when a company goes under, the MLM sellers who were promoting its products naturally start looking for new products they can get excited about, and they may sell them indefinitely, or only until they find something they like better. Thus there is a lot of coming and going in this industry, and many, many companies promoting to all known MLM sellers, trying to convince them to stop selling what they're presently selling, and to start selling their product. "But this is okay," says Charles Possick. "Being able to pick and choose is what freedom is all about."

In an article for *Home Business* magazine (February 2001), MLM attorney Jeffrey A. Babener said, "Network marketing is only a second job for most people, so huge earnings for the average participant should not be expected." He then indicated that the 90 percent of distributors who do network marketing on a part-time basis might expect initial earnings of $300 to $400 a month in sales, but those who do network marketing on a full-time basis may eventually generate up to $40,000 a month in sales. "There is no cap on possible income," he adds, "because those incomes are the result of hard work, talent and good fortune. But they are not the everyday case."

Veteran Shares Success Secrets. Jackie Ulmer works about 35 hours a week on her Web-based business, StreetSmartWealth.com. She won't say how much money she's earning because she believes that when people see how much some people are actually making in MLM, they immediately begin to think they can't do it, and they don't even start. "So many people have this preconceived notion of network marketing being all flash and hype and I personally can't stand that," she says. "It's not my style at all. It's a lot of hard work, and the payoff is great, but I never want people to think it's a breeze. I have a very lucrative business that is centered around network marketing. I have built it exclusively online, meaning I don't go to meetings, have home parties, or do mailings. Everything I need is available online or through a conference call. I find and work all my prospects online, and teach others to do the same."

Jackie has developed multiple streams of income by working with two different though complementary MLM companies (health and wellness products and personal care items), by adding selected affiliate programs to her Web site, and by writing eBooks related to network marketing. Her first book, *Building a Successful Network Marketing Business*, was published by BizyMoms.com, and she was working on other eBooks as this book was being written. The reason so many people fail in network marketing, she says, comes down to a few simple things:

● People are not clear or realistic about what it's going to take to succeed in their business. They don't understand the importance of investing time, money, and energy into something that won't necessarily pay well at the beginning. Usually they are told by an overenthusiastic sponsor how easy it is and how you "just do a little and the money rolls in."

- They don't choose a business or a sponsor from a business standpoint. They get excited because a friend calls and promises them they are going to make big money. The product looks okay, and so does the company and pay plan, so they get started. But true success revolves around having the right product or service, a good pay plan, a solid company, and a good sponsor and system with which to work the business. Above all, one must believe in each aspect of this. The best way to start is with one good company. Find one that fits, learn it, master it, and then consider what direction you want to take your business.

- They fail to understand exactly what is expected in terms of marketing. Will they be doing party plans? Calling cold lists? Working leads lists? Advertising? Having in-home business meetings with a "warm" market of friends?

- Without a boss pushing them, some people find it hard to stay motivated. Many people who start a business do not believe in themselves or their ability to really succeed at it. Two or three people may tell them no and they think that means no one is interested. Because they aren't clear on why someone has said no, it's easy to slip back into the same old rut and forget about the business and those silly dreams of living a great lifestyle.

In summary, you're as unlikely to make a million in MLM as you are in any other business, but through hard work and attention to business and marketing details, you might find this kind of homebased business extremely profitable, and just perfect for you.

A Typical MLM Pyramid Scheme

The author's legal rights were violated in 1992 when an MLM entrepreneur in Minnesota began to use "Homemade Money" as the name of his business and MLM opportunity magazine. Barbara coined these words in 1984 and, over the years, they automatically acquired trademark status because of their long-time use in connection with her name. The use of her book's title by an MLM company was detrimental to her business because she had a reputation as a provider of high-quality business information. Using legal means at her disposal, she was finally able to resolve this problem.

The brochure advertising the "Homemade Money" MLM opportunity emphasized the five-get-five-get-five concept that so many MLM promoters use, and which is so misleading. It read:

"If everyone in your downline sold 5 monthly subscriptions, your organization could look like this:

1..............5
2..............25
3..............125
4..............625
5..............3,125
6..............15,625

"When you multiply 15,625 subscribers, times a $50 commission, times twice a year, you get, $1,562,500."

To understand why this illustration doesn't hold water, consider these remarks by Leonard W. Clements, publisher of *Market Wave* (MarketWaveInc.com), a business analysis newsletter focusing on the MLM industry: "First, there is a high attrition rate in MLM, so we must assume that 90 percent of your people will drop out. But the above numbers assume that all 15,625 people will get into the program before even one gets out, then all 90 percent will drop out at once. If you are going to assume a 90 percent drop out rate, you must assume it from the beginning. In other words, four or perhaps all five of your original first level people are going to drop out! In truth, you may have to sponsor twenty people to find five that will go out and sponsor five others. And they will have to do the same."

Home-Business Franchises

Without question, franchising is a dominant way of bringing a new product to market, but the primary aim of this book is to help people with limited funds start low-investment, "from scratch" businesses that utilize existing skills, knowledge, and experience. Nevertheless, for the benefit of those who may be wondering about buying one of the many home-business franchises now available, some introductory information on the topic is included here.

This industry experienced aggressive growth in the past decade, and there are now a growing number of franchises suitable for operation from home base. Start-up costs generally range between $10,000 and $40,000. In one of its informational booklets, the U.S. Department of Labor states:

> Starting fresh with a new business certainly permits you the most freedom, since you are not restricted by what has gone before and are not regulated by someone else's rules. On the other hand, there are distinct advantages to buying an established franchise. Here, the purchaser or franchisee receives the right to operate a business under the leadership of a well-known distributor or manufacturer. In return for a fee and royalty payments, the franchisee has immediate access to a proven product, a consumer image, publicity, and goodwill. In many instances, the franchisor provides the goods as well as the training and techniques for conducting the operation. If the franchise is a sound one, the likelihood of success in one's own business is increased.

The disadvantages of a franchise are that you, the franchisee, must conform to someone else's standards; sell only their product at their price; share in their distributor problems, even though they are not of your doing; possibly end up with management that is unresponsive to your needs; and, of course, share the profits.

Before buying a franchise, consider whether you might be able to start a business similar to some of the franchise packages. A couple of women who attended one of my workshops told me they had long debated about buying a $17,000 housecleaning franchise. They finally decided they knew as much about housecleaning as anyone, and could learn the rest on their own. They launched their own cleaning business and did very well with it. Sure, they had to do a lot of business research; acquire their own industrial cleaning equipment; find their own wholesale sources for cleaning supplies; and

Selecting the Right Type of Business

develop their own special work methods, marketing techniques, advertising materials, and so on—things that are usually provided in a franchisor's package—but they saved $17,000 and got to keep all the profits they generated.

Not everyone has entrepreneurial abilities, which is why franchise packages were originally developed. On the other hand, a lot of people have abilities they don't realize until they begin a business of their own. As I see it, when you buy a franchise you are paying someone else to do your homework. If you have the money and can afford it, great. But if you have more time than money, consider trying it yourself. Remember, an investment in a franchise does not automatically guarantee a market for the product or service being offered. The job of finding and selling all those customers is still going to be your responsibility. Further, with a franchise business, somewhere along the line you might want to move your business in a new direction, expand to a new area, or simply change the image you're projecting to the public, but you won't be able to do this because such things are controlled by the franchisor.

Unfortunately, there are scam operators in the franchise field, too. Under the FTC's Franchise Rule, franchise sellers and many business opportunity sellers as well must provide potential purchasers with a complete and accurate "basic disclosure document" containing twenty categories of information, including the identity of current and former franchisees. The Rule also requires that sellers who make claims about actual or potential earnings must also provide written substantiation for those claims.

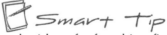 Smart Tip

If you're still sold on the idea of a franchise, first visit other franchises and investigate a company's reputation and track record by contacting the Better Business Bureau and consumer affairs department of your State Attorney General's office.

Be wary of come-ons that emphasize promises of unrealistic profits or guaranteed earnings in a protected market area. Money-back guarantees may be worthless, too, since a promoter may say you haven't "operated according to instructions" even when you believe you have. Never sign a contract until an attorney has checked out all clauses related to exclusivity, inventory, royalty rates, purchase requirements, and investment obligations.

Summary

"You can stop looking for the perfect business plan—it doesn't exist," says Georganne Fiumara, founder of Mothers Home Business Network, on the Web at HomeWorkingMom.com. "Businesses, like babies, are born with unlimited possibilities but must evolve through trial and error."

As you now realize, no one can tell you what type of business you ought to start because there simply are too many variables in the picture. This is a decision you must make yourself. In selecting a business to run with, you may be concerned that, even after all your deliberation, you've made the wrong decision. That's a definite possibility; but you're not going to know for sure until you begin, and since nothing new and exiting is going to happen until you do begin, don't dillydally too long in the dreaming stage. Or, as Georganne puts it, "Don't wait for all the pieces to fall into place before you begin to work. Ideas evolve and tend to take on a life of their own once you set them free."

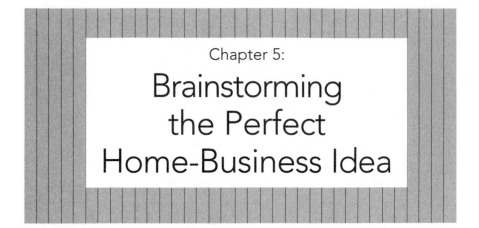

Chapter 5

Brainstorming the Perfect Home-Business Idea

Getting an idea should be like sitting down on a pin; it should make you jump up and do something!
—E. L. Simpson

Now that you know the *type* of business you want to start (product or service, or a combination of both), you need to focus on picking a particular business that's right for you—something that will not only fit into your personal lifestyle, but will actually be profitable. The many real-people examples in this chapter will help you relate your own interests, dreams, experience, and personal situation to a particular business activity. (Read this chapter with your skills/talents/experience worksheets in hand.)

"I wish I could discover or devise a magic formula for combining all my talents and interests into one tremendously successful package," someone once said to me. That's the trick, all right, and I believe that each of us can create some magic in our lives through a combination of concentrated self-study, patience, determination, and perseverance.

"Perseverance," said Longfellow, "is a key element of success. If you only knock long enough at the gate, you are sure to wake up somebody." Right now, I'm the one who's knocking on your gate, trying to wake you up to the many home-business possibilities awaiting you.

☑ Smart Tip

Ideas don't keep. If they aren't captured the minute we get them, they may be lost forever, like dreams briefly recalled in the morning. Or, as someone once said, "To err is human; to forget, routine." To store your good ideas until you have time to do something with them, set up a series of "Good Idea!" file folders into which you can drop notes and clippings for later referral.

Read, Listen, and Observe

Reading is absolutely essential to business success, and many people have been spurred to action after reading a good home-business guide. A few months after launching CalliDesign.com, Richard Tuttle e-mailed me to say my *Creative Cash* book had given him a tingling feeling in his stomach, but he just couldn't force himself to make a career change at that time. "I have worked in the information technology industry since its infancy, but over a period of time, I became burnt out and wanted something different," he said. "Then I came across *Homemade Money*. After digesting it in one night, I waited a week and then sat down to read it more slowly, marking as I went. By the time I finished it the second time, I knew I had to go out on my own. I have been doing freelance work since then, teaching others how to do things on the Web, from Web design to making Web applications, and I love it!"

Home-business ideas also abound in daily newspapers and on radio and television. Still others will come as you begin to circulate in the business community, join organizations, attend workshops, seminars, and trade shows, or network with other business owners. Many people have gotten their best ideas just by watching what others do, then figuring out a way to do the same thing better. As you begin the idea generation process, your main goal should be to get your brain vibrating with ideas, on both a conscious and subconscious level. Your mind is like a giant computer—the more input you give it, the more you'll get back. Throughout your entire life, your subconscious mind has been gathering all kinds of information, impressions, and ideas, storing them for possible future use. You know a lot more than

Laughable Home-Business Ideas

Some of the "profitable" ideas in moneymaking books are good only for laughs. In the days when Harry used to open all the mail for Barbara's mail order book business, he often wrote funny notes to her in the margins of letters or advertising material. A flyer promoting a book of home-business ideas stated:

"Selling dust from your vacuum cleaner is just ONE of the unusual money-making ideas in this book!"

As a not-so-subtle reminder that the house needed cleaning, Harry wrote in the margin, in red ink and with lots of exclamation points: "BUY THIS!!! We have a fortune under our feet and don't know it!!!"

you think you know, and now is the time to retrieve some of this data for your financial profit. By constantly stimulating your mind with new information and ideas, you will automatically release some of what's already hiding in there on a subconscious level.

As you read and think, pay attention to what's happening with the economy. Due to the downsizing of so many companies in recent years, there are now fewer employees to do the work, and this has opened the door of opportunity to many business service providers. If you're a corporate worker who has recently lost your job, the examples in this chapter will give you perspective on how to package your existing skills and know-how into a successful business.

As more and more workers have less and less time, the demand for personal services is also growing. Regardless of the economy, there will always be people who have money to buy the products and services of small businesses. What they may lack most of all is time, so they willingly pay others to do for them what their own time won't allow. The fact that small enterprises can give the kind of customer service larger businesses can't afford to provide is often the key to success. In the end, the amount of money you'll earn from any business activity will be directly proportional to the number of people who are benefiting from your effort. "Before you start a business,

The Source of Ideas

Some of my best business ideas came out of sheer desperation when my back was against the wall. Remember: the most impressive plants can grow out of manure piles.
    —Investment Adviser, Howard Ruff, in an interview for *Business Age*

• • •

Big ideas come from the unconscious. But your unconscious has to be well informed, or your idea will be irrelevant. Stuff your conscious mind with information. Then unhook your rational thought process. If the telephone line from your unconscious is open, a big idea wells up within you.
    —David Ogilvy, founder, Ogilvy and Mather

• • •

To get a sound, profitable idea, we have to learn to look past the end of our nose. We have to obliterate our preconceptions and prejudices. Look around. Observe what is successful. Then, start brainstorming. Ask yourself a thousand questions and try to answer them. Ideas do not hide from us. They are everywhere we go, in everything we do. They are not beyond reach. But some of us are mentally blind.
    —John Sheehan, writer

decide what type of people you most like to help and what you most like to do," advises freelance writer and marketing consultant Martha Oskvig. "My business keeps growing as I keep serving the needs of others."

If you happen to be a mom who's looking for home business ideas or a way to get your business on the Internet, one of the best places to begin is at Liz Folger's BizyMoms.com site. "Ever since BizyMoms first debuted, the Ideas section has been our most popular area of the site," says Liz. "Each idea is a story written by a person with that type of business—real stories from real people. We have so many now that our ideas have been split into two alphabetical sections. Now there is also a department devoted to helping moms make money with a Web site."

As emphasized earlier, your home-business idea doesn't have to be new and different to succeed. Every product or service can be changed, improved, presented or sold in a new way, or simply offered to a different audience, giving you unlimited opportunities for profit.

Smart Tip

By reading more, listening closer, and paying keen attention to what's going on around you, you will methodically pack your brain with the kind of stimulis that could lead to a "brilliant brainstorm" when you least expect it.

Keeping Technology in Mind

Computers and recent technological advances continue to affect not only the way millions of people live and work, but the types of new businesses being started and the methods being used to manage and market them. That's why it's so important for you to plan any new business with an eye to what's happening where technology and the Internet are concerned.

Although you will ultimately need a computer to efficiently manage your growing business, this does not mean you have to offer a computer-related service or product to make money at home. In spite of all the computers, robots, lasers, and digital technology in our lives, there will always be a demand for business and creative skills only human beings can perform. In fact, John Naisbitt, author of *Megatrends*, believes that the more high tech our lives become, the more we will need to balance this situation with what he calls a "high touch" counterpart. This suggests a continuing demand for personal services of all kinds in areas that call for increased human contact. I also interpret this to mean there will be a continuing demand for high-quality handcrafts and other finely made goods that will satisfy people's nostalgic longings for "the good old days."

Creative people may well have an edge in our high-tech future, according to Ric Tombari, a professor of management at California State University. In an article for *Entrepreneur*, he said creative individuals would make up the majority of future entrepreneurs, adding: "Because creative people are less structured and better able to consider and accept new ideas, they will have an easier time charting a course through the constantly changing business world."

See Chapter Eleven for tips on how to learn the latest computer technology and put it to work in your homebased business.

Find a Need and Fill It

How many times have you or a friend said, "If only I had someone to do (such-and-so) for me"? Maybe you're the person who ought to be doing this job, or maybe you can develop a salable solution to the problem that will enable others to get the job done easier, better, faster, or cheaper. Often, in solving problems for yourself, you accidentally stumble onto a good idea for a business.

Before you actually launch or expand a business, spend time checking out the market for your new product or service (see Chapter Eight, "Planning Your Moves"). When in doubt, follow the "find-a-need-and-fill-it" rule. Since it is easier to sell a product or service for which a need already exists, look for problems that are being created because the right product or service doesn't exist, then challenge yourself to provide it. "Great opportunity has often come dressed as something missing, and great rewards are given to those who find a way to provide what's missing to others," says motivational speaker and author Barbara J. Winter.

Loses Weight, Gains a Business. After shedding 125 pounds by using low-fat, low-sugar recipes she developed herself, JoAnna Lund realized a lot of other people had the same problem she had just solved. Encouraged by a friend, she gathered her recipes into a book called *Healthy Exchanges*, borrowed money to print a thousand copies, and sold them in a few weeks. In her first eighteen months, from marketing efforts only in the state of Iowa, JoAnna sold over 42,000 books through radio publicity and local workshops. Clearly on to something hot, she quickly launched a companion newsletter to keep her fans loaded with new recipes, and within fifteen months had captured 11,000 subscribers from her book-buyers database. It was at this point that she began to promote beyond her own state and publish a second book.

Brainstorming for the Perfect Home Business

JoAnna has always said that her success is due to the fact that she is "just a common person with a common problem solved with common sense," but she adds that her business would not exist if she had not first achieved a major goal: to lose weight. After grossing $300,000 in her first year of business, JoAnna encouraged her husband, Clifford, to quit his truck-driving job and join her in the business. Before he knew it, he was co-host of her *Healthy Exchanges* radio show, was handling all the mechanics of getting JoAnna's booklets printed, and was no doubt shaking his head in wonder at what a woman can do when she sets her mind to it. Since I first interviewed JoAnna in 1993, her business has expanded far beyond the boundaries of the home-based business she once envisioned.

Typesetting/Editorial Services Answer Local Need. A common need by many in both small and large communities is typesetting and editorial services. "Who needs a freshened up resume? In these economic times, plenty of people do," says Susan Young, who lives in a small community in Alabama. In addition to other endeavors, including the opening of a retail gift shop in 2000 (PeachKittyStudio.com), Susan has offered a local clientele her typesetting and editorial services since 1989. "Someone is always needing a new or revised resume or brochure, or news release," she says, "and I can earn up to a hundred dollars an hour for such jobs." Susan has learned there is also a market out there for anyone who can take a handwritten manuscript and put it into a publishing format (spacing, grammar, editing), because not everyone has a computer or can even type, for that matter. If you can offer editing or ghostwriting services or design original computer graphics, your opportunity for income automatically increases. "If there's a need, fill it," says Susan. "It's money in your pocket."

 Smart Tip

As you brainstorm for new ideas for a business or products or services you might sell—and after you have filled your mind with ideas and impressions gathered from many sources—ask: "How can I combine these ideas in a way that is different from what everyone else is doing?" *That* is creativity!

Do What You Love

I always admired actress Katharine Hepburn and her work philosophy: "If you have to support yourself, you had bloody well better find some way that is going to be interesting," she once said in an interview. Actress Greer Garson had it right, too, when she said, "Starting out to make money is the greatest mistake in life. Do what you feel you have a flair for doing, and if you are good enough at it, the money will come."

I can't overemphasize the importance of loving what you do. It's one thing to be stuck in a job that makes you miserable, but when you start your own business, you have many options, and your primary goal, besides picking a business that will actually make money, should be to pick an activity that gives you genuine pleasure, even on the worst days. If you start a business you don't love, you'll be tempted to throw in the towel the minute things get rough—and sooner or later, they will.

Smart Tip

Don't agonize over the specific business you should start, but focus instead on just getting started in an activity that gives you pleasure. Few people end up doing what they originally started anyway because the very act of being in business leads them in new directions, and opportunities often come out of the blue when least expected.

Crafts Column Leads to Production of Cable TV Show. Jeanne Baratta originally started selling wearable art at craft fairs in 1990 but put the business on hold while her children were young. As they entered school, she picked up on her crafts business again. Later, when art classes at her children's school were scrapped due to budget restraints, she developed a Cooperative Art Program for the school that won the prestigious Parent Partnership award from the National Catholic Education Association. This experience helped position her for a new opportunity a few years later.

"You never know where something can lead," says Jeanne. "I set out with the idea of getting some of my designs published in a magazine, and ended up producing a television program for my local cable station. It all started because I needed some writing experience to get my designs published, so I submitted an article to my town's Web site to gain this experience. It was a hit, and I was asked to write a regular column that soon gave me quite a following. After being invited to an open house at our local cable station, I was asked to put together and host a television program showcasing crafts, cooking, gardening, etc. I was dumbfounded and, of course, quite excited. Martha Stewart, look out, here comes Elf!" (Jeanne's latest enterprise, KitchenElf.com, has grown from its beginnings in 1999 to include a line of custom gift baskets and an offering of craft classes for adults and children.)

Juggling Leads to a Book Publishing Business. Pleasure from a home-based business is often greatest when one is able to turn a passionate hobby or leisure time interest into a business. Bruce Fife once worked as a clown and juggler on the side, but found he loved it so much he wanted to do it full time. That desire led him to something he enjoyed even more: writing and publishing books. Under the name of Piccadilly Books, Bruce has now written or co-authored and published some four dozen titles related to his personal interests, including clowning and juggling, ventriloquism, magic, health, and entertainment. Using the experience gained as a book publisher, he has also written books on how to make money reading books, how to become a literary agent, and how to get published. (See a complete list of titles at PiccadillyBooks.com)

Lost Job, Found a Business. When Tim Long lost his teaching job, he turned his woodworking skills into a new career as a cabinetmaker and trim carpenter. He made his first toy when a friend needed a birthday gift for a child and later began to make toys for his own children. Before long, both Tim and his wife, Connie, were working together to create products for sale. "We've been creating quality wooden toys and puzzles since 1980," says Tim, who emphasizes that the main ingredients in a couples-working relationship are love and cooperation. The Longs, who are now on the Web at NorthStarToys.com, are not formally trained in their business activities, but say they have good common sense. "We find out what we need to know by reading about it or asking someone for help."

Once, when Tim was being interviewed for an article and was asked if a hobby still can be fun after it becomes a job, he replied, "It's a blast. As soon as it stops being fun we're going to stop doing it and look for something else."

Writing Hobby Blossoms on the Web. In choosing a business, don't pick a business idea merely because it's working for others or because it offers more money than something else you'd prefer to do. Cindy Thomas turned her love of writing into a full-time activity on the Web in 2001, first by launching several free sites in a writer's network, and then building a permanent site at JCTPublishing.com that will house all her current and future writing interests. "I explored various options for about ten years," she says, "but nothing ever worked out. I could never figure out why, until this past year. *What I was trying to do wasn't for me, but what had worked for someone else.* Writing is what I do best, what I love to do, so I've come to the conclusion that one's best home business is what a person does best, and what they love to do, perhaps a hobby turned into a business."

Someone once said, "A conclusion is the place where you got tired of thinking." I can certainly relate to Cindy's comments about writing. When I was still struggling for survival in my publishing and book-selling business, I interviewed Twyla Menzies, an enthusiastic Mary Kay salesperson who was making five times the money I was then generating. "Why don't you get involved in this program? You could make a fortune!" she insisted. Why not? Because I've never been interested in cosmetics, I wouldn't enjoy giving facials, I don't like direct selling, and I certainly wouldn't want to spend my evenings throwing home parties—not for any amount of money. It took me awhile to achieve my major goals and reach the level of income I was striving for, but even when the money wasn't there, I loved my work, and I've long been content in the knowledge that I'm doing the kind of work best suited to my lifestyle, personality, experience, and skills. That kind of contentment is what I wish for all of you who are striving for a more satisfactory way to earn a living. *If we must spend a third of our lives working, then let it be at something we truly enjoy doing!* Or as entrepreneur and author Harvey Mackay puts it, "Find something you love to do and you'll never have to work a day in your life."

Of course, self-employed individuals have an entirely different view of work than their 9-to-5 counterparts. You've surely heard the old joke about how entrepreneurs are happy to work sixteen hours a day for themselves just to avoid working eight hours for someone else. Entrepreneurs may sleep only six hours and work most of the remaining eighteen, rarely having time to squeeze in anything that remotely resembles relaxation, but when I talk to such people, I often hear, "But I don't mind because I really love what I'm doing." One couple put it this way: "Although we work longer hours than we ever did in our lives, it doesn't feel like work because we enjoy it and because it's something we've chosen to do. It's a lifestyle more than work. It's hard to define as work. We just don't think of it that way."

Build on What You Know and Do Best

In trying to find the home-business idea that's right for you, look for marketable products or services that are compatible with your work background or business contacts, or those that tie in to your professional or personal fields of interest. If you already have a good understanding of the field you'd like to enter as a business owner, it will be much easier to market your business.

Nursing Leads to Successful Consultancy Business. My research shows a close connection between previous work experience and successful home-business start-up. Susan Kilpatrick has a Bachelor of Science degree in nursing and is board certified in Case Management. In 1992, she turned this experience into M. Susan Kilpatrick & Associates, Inc. "I consult with insurance carriers, attorneys, governmental entities and even other legal nurses on issues of healthcare," she says. "For instance, with insurance carriers, I work more frequently with carriers of Workers' Compensation. When a worker is injured, they call upon me to ensure the care is appropriate, timely, and cost-effective. I coordinate medical appointments, hospitalizations, etc. and make sure the patient is progressing as he should. Many of my patients are those injured in catastrophic injuries and their needs are huge. I also write Life Care Plans that project the medical needs for the remainder of the injured person's life. Insurance carriers need these figures for settlement purposes. For attorneys, I review medical records to determine issues such as malpractice or negligence on the part of physicians, nurses, etc. I also assist attorneys in their depositions, do medical research of odd diagnoses, and assist with demonstrative evidence for jurors. In addition to the malpractice work, I also work with attorneys who defend physicians and hospitals. Government work is everything rolled into one! I love the work, although it does get a bit intense at times. Until flying hither and yon became tiring, I was also an expert witness. Now I just enjoy being able to work in my jammies in my home office."

When One Thing Fizzles, Try Another. Building on what you know and do best could be a financial life saver if you happen to lose your job. Philip White started an electrical contracting firm in 1993 and operated it for several years. Like many other self-employed individuals, he found it difficult to build a good retirement program, and this prompted him to close the company and take a job. "I found a great job with a large corporation that offered 401k, insurance, vacation, overtime, and all the other niceties normal working folks have become accustomed to," he said. "Unfortunately, I was laid off a year later and forced back into either working for myself or looking for another company in need of my services on a full-time basis."

At that point, Philip fell back on his lifetime of experience and know-how. This time around, however, he is focusing on offering engineering services instead of electrical contracting because the last economic downturn was particularly hard on this industry. He is now on the Web at RigelEngineering.com. "I have learned a lot about operating a home business," he says. "There are some excellent benefits but there are many negative aspects as well. Home businesses are not for the faint of heart."

Special Research Leads Mother to Write Books. As we go through life, we often acquire special knowledge about a particular topic or field that suggests an idea for a business. Julie Yarbrough began to write and publish her own books when her research on health issues led her to some surprising discoveries. "I spent most of my life with various health ailments that could not be explained and was often led to believe it was all in my head," she says. "After an allergist tried to put me on a drug I did not want to take, I began to search for answers on my own. Then, when my son was diagnosed as autistic, my research became more intense and I finally began to find all of my symptoms in allergy and diet-related articles. I was shocked because no doctor had ever mentioned diet as a possible cause, but I soon discovered that every health complaint had a dietary connection. It's not just a matter of eating vegetables and taking supplements. They are vital, of course, but it's also necessary to remove the foods, chemicals and medications that are actually causing the health problems. I am now writing books to help others, while my health, and that of my son, continues to improve."

Chance Remark Prompts New Business. Often, the idea for a business comes from something someone has said to us somewhere along the line, something that may actually have been buried in our subconscious mind for many years. Yvonne Conway has been a licensed professional cosmetologist for fifty-two years and owner of My Line, a mobile beauty service, for the past nineteen years. But this business wouldn't have been born at all if not for circumstances and a chance remark by Yvonne's mother twenty years earlier. Yvonne, who recently turned seventy, has been self-employed for most of her life.

"My husband and I had an amusement game business for twenty-five years that we thought would provide our retirement," she says, "but in time the business died due to people losing interest in this form of entertainment. We started another business, but it, too, was killed by circumstances beyond our control, and suddenly we found ourselves close to bankruptcy, our retirement dreams shattered. At this fork in the road, we decided my husband would stay with the sinking ship and I, then fifty, would look for work elsewhere. After examining the prospects of college and vocational classes and small local business opportunities, I decided to explore an idea my mother had planted in my head twenty years earlier. I recalled the time she told me about a friend in a nursing home who yearned to get her hair and nails done, and my saying it was too bad you couldn't carry a beauty salon with you. Twenty years later, I thought, *why not?*"

Yvonne offers haircuts, permanents, shampoo sets, hair coloring, manicures, and pedicures. Her motto, "This hairdresser will come to your home, office, or jail," got her quite a bit of publicity, and the demand for such services in her area (Olympia, Washington) was so great that her son, Craig, launched a similar service called Haircuts on Wheels, Inc., a year later. Yvonne's clients are mostly elderly or confined, while Craig serves young families and professionals. "Convenience is the key word," says Yvonne. "Tight schedules, poor health, or just plain snob appeal makes mobile services viable in any and all realms of society."

After seven years in business, Yvonne wrote and self-published *Mobile Hair and Beauty Services—Your Guide to Profits on Wheels*, a comprehensive how-to manual that helped many others follow in her footsteps. She doesn't plan to reprint this book, but many copies were distributed to libraries over the years so your librarian may be able to obtain a copy for you.

Making Money in the Country

Some people have the mistaken idea that if you live in a small town or "way out in the country" your chances for building a profitable homebased business are not as good as they might be if you lived in a metropolitan area. But that's not true at all. Take my book agent and her husband (my tax accountant) in rural Iowa, for example. As a literary agent, Barbara Doyen success-fully competes with literary agents in New York City because her publishing savvy and skill in negotiating a book contract has made her invaluable to authors and publishers alike. In addition to managing the Doyen farm, Bob is an Enrolled Agent with a successful tax accounting business. Although his specialty is working with farmers in his area, he can work with anyone by phone, fax, and mail.

There are literally hundreds of things you can do or sell to generate extra income or build a part- or full-time business in the country. (See "Country Businesses Idea Checklist.") The more ways you can communicate with clients or customers and deliver your products and services, the greater your options. For example, if you can travel, you won't be limited to starting an "at-home" service business, but can start a "from-home" service that involves travel to one place or another.

Sales Reps for Professional Crafters. Being able to travel has enabled Malcolm and Sandy Dell in Orofino, Idaho (population 3000) to make a good living as sales reps for professional crafters. After only a few months in business, the Dells were representing over thirty lines and selling to over 200 retail stores in five states—mostly in rural communities with a population of between 5,000 and 40,000.

"We represent mostly small manufacturers from rural towns in fourteen states, although a couple are larger distributors with a significant line of products," says Malcolm. "Examples of our products include handpaint-ed/woodcrafts, metal art, specialty foods, handmade soaps, candles, herbals, coin jewelry, coloring books, mugs, keychains, gold and silver jewelry, medallions, etc."

To sell even more products, the Dells launched a wholesale-only Web site in 2001 at LewisClarkGifts.com to bring buyers and sellers together. Here, product sellers will also find a helpful online course, "Taking Your Products to Market: A Primer on Wholesale Marketing Channels."

A Soapmaker's Selling Strategy. Many product sellers in rural areas complain because the market for their product is limited, or people won't pay the price needed to make a profit. In that case, you don't have to change your business, but you will have to look for new markets outside your own area if you hope to survive. (For a variety of ways to do this, see this book's companion marketing guide, *HOMEMADE MONEY: BRINGING IN THE BUCKS.*)

Brainstorming for the Perfect Home Business

Soapmaker and lady farmer Pat Fountain, Hearts-Delight.com, has the right idea. A separate building on the farm houses her soapmaking operation and shop where she sells to local customers occasionally through the year and especially during her annual Christmas boutique. To increase her income and local market, Pat also teaches "Homemade Beauty" and "Natural Home" classes to promote her soaps while also educating people about the benefits of using non-chemical products. The bulk of her sales, however, comes from wholesaling her goat-milk soap products to gift and craft shops across the country and retailing to individual buyers on the Internet. "Thanks to the Internet," she says, "I've also found new wholesale accounts, such as a group of spas in the Virgin Islands that now buy my products."

The Power of a Few Words

People are often prodded to start a business because of a quotation that strikes home. (Remember the you-can't-steal-second-base quote that moved Barbara to action?) For copywriter Bob Westenberg, it was a little-known Thoreau quote he had carried in his wallet for seventeen years. "I read it again when I was transferring stuff from my old wallet to a new one I'd gotten on my fortieth birthday," he recalls: *"As young men we gather the materials to build a bridge to the moon, but in middle life we use them to construct a woodshed.'* I decided right then that I would either go on my own that year or throw away that dirty, dog-eared little scrap of paper. Today it's framed on my office wall."

Country Businesses Idea Checklist

Certain businesses do better in rural areas than others. The following types of businesses appear to be most popular with farm families and other individuals living in rural communities.

Food Businesses

Baked foods (breads, pies, cookies, cakes; for local restaurants, stores, individual customers)

Cake baking (birthdays, weddings, anniversaries)

Catering (using local commercial kitchen facilities)

Candy making

Chemical-free beef

Cider and vinegars

Deer farming

Gourmet foods (sauces, seasonings, soup mixes, flavored popcorn)

Honey and honey products

Jams, jellies, juices, wines

Maple syrup and related products

Meats (frozen, freeze-dried, smoked, game)

Soy nut snacks

Yogurt and specialty cheeses

Special Farm Crops

Birdseed

Christmas trees

Commercial food production (raspberries, strawberries, blueberries, seedless grapes, miniature vegetables, mushrooms, nuts, fruit trees, sweet corn, other fresh market vegetables)

Culinary herbs (fresh or dried)

Fish (catfish, salmon, trout)

Flowers (fresh or seeds) and ornamentals

Sod/turf

Special grains

Sprouting seeds (Mung beans)

Services for Farmers

Auctioneering

Bookkeeping/taxes

Consulting (crops, animals, equipment)

Dairy service (for vacationing families)

Excavating

Grain bin insulation

Repair services (home appliances; farm machinery, implements)

Restoration services (antique furniture; old farm equipment)

Rose arbors and yard accessories

Brainstorming for the Perfect Home Business

Small Business Services

Accounting
Burglary alarms/systems
Computer services
Consulting
Fertilizer service (lawns, golf courses)
Financial planner

Insurance
Marketing services (varied)
Secretarial/word processing
Virtual Assistant business (VA)
Web site design/management

Popular Arts and Crafts Businesses

Animal traps
Christmas boutiques
Corn shuck crafts
Custom artwork (portraits of children, pets, horses, farmhouses)
Custom leatherwork (chaps, saddle bags, bridles)
Deersksin and sheepskin products
Doll and toy making
Down comforters and pillows
Farm-themed handcrafts (cows, pigs, horses, chickens, geese, bunnies, duck decoys, nature items, dried miniature corn, hay bales, grapevine baskets and wreaths, corn shuck crafts)

Feather pillows
Fishing lures and tackles
Handcrafted products of wool, fur, or hide
Teaching arts and crafts
Quiltmaking, needlework, sewing
Woodcarving

Other Country Businesses

Bait shop/worm production
Bed-and-breakfast inns
Bees and beekeeper supplies
Campground areas
Cross-country skiing
Dog kennel (grooming, showing, obedience classes)
Farm tours
Garden products and accessories
Greenhouse
Gun dogs (boarding kennels; training)
Handyman service for elderly
Hunting guide
Intermediate care for elderly

Hunting lease operation (pheasant, quail, other game birds)
Home parties (party plan sales, all types of products)
Live and dried plants
Petting zoos
Poultry and eggs
Self-publishing (cookbooks, patterns, how-to booklets)
Sheep farming (selling sheep's milk, cheese, fleece, yarn, gift items)
Upholstery and furniture repair
Vegetable stand
Videotaping services

Starting a Business on the World Wide Web

Once begun, many businesses can enjoy increased success by moving onto the Web, a topic discussed in this book's companion guide, *HOMEMADE MONEY: Bringing in the Bucks.* But countless businesses now on the Web actually began there, inspired by the success of a previous business or an individual's desire to do something new and exciting. Everywhere on the Web today you will find successful businesspeople doing all the things discussed above, from finding a need and filling it, to doing what they love, to building on what they know and do best. They read, listen, and observe, and, more than anyone, Web entrepreneurs understand the importance of change and the impact technology is making on peoples' lives and businesses.

Sell What People Need and Will Buy. Many entrepreneurs who got on the Web in its infancy have made a fortune by offering products, services, or technical expertise designed to help others who want to make money on the Web. Dr. Jeffrey Lant is a good example. Already a millionaire by the time he hit the Web in 1994, Lant realized the Internet was the transforming technology of his lifetime. "I saw that it was going to change the way businesses worldwide did business and that in this situation literally trillions of dollars would be made," he says.

Worldprofit, Inc. was begun by Lant and two co-founders as a homebased business in Cambridge, Massachusetts, and Edmonton, Canada, in 1994, and the company has been immensely profitable. It offers ready-to-go e-Properties that provide everything one needs to do business online. They are very popular, and they sell as fast as Lant and his staff can set them up. "I wouldn't be on the Internet if it didn't work, if there wasn't money to be made, and if I wasn't getting my share of that money," he says. "I came to the Internet expecting to work hard, study the business, perfect products and services, and profit accordingly. I never expected a free lunch or to 'get rich quick.' I wanted a long-term means of producing wealth, and I was willing to do what was necessary to get it. I remain as enthusiastic today about the prospects for smart people using the Internet to make money—indeed more so—than I was back in 1994."

Lant and his colleagues at WorldProfit.com have created a system that does work, does produce online profits and can be worked 100 percent at home, full or part time. "This system is the result of years of effort, considerable expenditure of both treasure and intellectual capital, and endless testing," he says. "Our goal was and is to allow people to make a good return on their investment by following a simple, proven system. It is not for people who believe that wealth can be produced without effort and that you never have to lift a finger on your own behalf."

As a business veteran who has earned his money the old-fashioned way, Lant finds such ideas ridiculous. "If you want to make money online, you must sell things that people must have in their lives, things that generate a good commission," he emphasizes. "The amount of junk being sold online is staggering! Vast numbers of people seem to think you can create the semblance of a product, then inveigle enough people to sell it and all will live happily ever after. Nonsense. The expression, 'build a better mousetrap and the world will beat a path to your door' still pertains today, but there are precious few 'better mousetraps' on the Web. If you are trying to get in quick and get out fast with fortune in hand, you are doing things the wrong way. The only way to build a lifetime income is to sell things people really need and will continue to buy."

Sculptor "Falls Into" Programming. Many people have successful Web-based businesses today because being on the Web in the first place automatically leads one in new directions. Michael R. Harvey is both a sculptor and a Web entrepreneur who offers Internet business tools at Ibiz-Tools.com and sculpture, crafts, and jewelry at three other sites. Once he got on the Web, his life and business began to change. As a friend observed, Mike was a sculptor first who "fell into" programming because he needed to bridge a gap with his Web site. I asked him how he acquired his new skills and brainstormed the multifaceted business he owns today.

"I always enjoyed techie stuff," he says, "so when I finally bought a computer and learned how to use it, I decided I wanted to showcase my work on the Web. I got on the Web and found places to learn HTML (HyperText Markup Language) and build my site. Then I started offering to do this kind of work for friends and art groups I was associated with. After a few years, I started learning PHP (server side programming) and MySQL (a database system). At this point it was still just a hobby, but then I thought, why not make a buck at what I enjoy? I managed to get a couple of small contracts through friends' word of mouth advertising, and things just grew from there. In a nutshell, I simply found what I enjoy doing and searched for ways of doing it that people would want to pay for," he says.

Michael now has several programs and modules available on his site, along with several online business and computer courses developed in partnership with his brother, Brian, a teacher. I asked Mike what advice he would give to home-business wannabes, on or off the Web. "Find something you enjoy," he told me. "Pick a hobby or something you always wanted to learn to do and *do it*. Don't expect to get paid for it at first, at least not much. Do it for yourself, your friends, family, or charity. Do it because you enjoy it, but keep looking for ways to do it better, more efficiently, and better than the next guy. And while you're doing this, keep your eye and mind open to how you might make a buck at this. At first, focus on just making enough for your expenses, your materials, tools, or equipment, then work from there."

That's good advice because you can't get anywhere until you start moving. And once you do, you'll be amazed by how one idea always leads to another until, sooner or later, you land in a place you never expected to find yourself, surrounded by opportunities for earning an income at or from home base, and proud of yourself for having the gumption to stick it out until you achieved success.

Moms Helping Other Moms to Success. Lest you think that Web entrepreneurs are all men, let me assure you that the Web is now loaded with "mom businesses" of all kinds, and some moms have made it their business to help other moms succeed. Donna M. Snow says my *Homemade Money* book was the first book she picked up when she decided to start her own business, and it changed her life. A single mother of six children between the ages of four and seventeen, Donna designs Web sites, trains women in successful entrepreneurship, and writes business columns for newspapers and Web sites. With no child support, Donna had great motivation to succeed in her business endeavors, and she is now passionate about helping other women succeed, too.

"I know there are many women out there struggling to reach their goals while dealing with kids or husbands who don't support them," she says.

Like most others on the Internet, Donna learned Web design on her own, a little at a time. "In the fall of 2000, I signed up as a site manager for HerPlanet.com, and as part of my responsibilities I was to build and develop content for HerSmallBusiness.com," she explains. "With the support of other managers in our network, I learned how to design Web sites, then went on to train other site managers in Web development." Today, Donna coordinates online events with chat technology and holds regular training sessions and business mixers at HerSmallBusiness.com while also managing SnowWrite.com, a full-service Internet production company she launched in mid-2002. At that time, Donna was also attending college to learn advanced Web programming and design so she would have a solid background in this industry.

Working Electronically As a Virtual Assistant (VA). To some, a "virtual assistant" is just a new name for "secretarial service," but it seems to have a better reputation than secretarial, and usually involves more high tech skills. Donna L. Gunter, SohoBizSolutions.com, says virtual assistance is "the art of helping successful people organize the details of their business and personal lives without being physically present. It works well only when a small business owner decides that the only way to move ahead in business is by delegating business details that do not need his or her personal attention."

Donna adds that VAs generally charge by the hour or on a monthly retainer basis. Some things a VA might do for a SOHO (small office/home office) business owner include:

- Providing office support (e-mail, make/return calls, send/receive faxes, schedule appointments, etc.)
- Researching (traditional and Internet)
- Planning (travel, meetings, or other special events)
- Managing special projects
- Arranging speaking engagements
- Doing technical work (newsletters, desktop publishing, computer assistance)
- Working with vendors (setting up accounts, establishing relationships with them)
- Creating office systems

Interestingly, Donna has never been a secretary or office manager. In her former life, she was a higher education administrator and an executive director of a nonprofit corporation. "My real desire in opening this business was the ability to move back to my home town to be near my family," she says. "Unfortunately, it's a small, rural town in East Texas with a high unemployment rate and very few job opportunities in the field in which I have my Master's degree. Being a VA enabled me to move back here and make a decent living without being dependent upon the local economy in any way. All of my clients are on the East Coast." (Another good example of how to make money in the country!)

Notice how Donna's previous job experience, heavily oriented to administrative work, made being a VA a natural fit. Although she does perform some secretarial services, her speciality is administrative work, such as being the training director of a virtual university and working with the officers of a regional chapter of a national organization. "I'm pretty picky about my client base," she says. "My work centers heavily around writing and marketing tasks as well as lots of idea generation on my clients' behalf."

For more information on this type of business, visit Assist University at Assistu.com, the premier virtual training program for virtual assistants, and see "Other Resources" for other online organizations for VAs. Donna also offers information on this topic in her newsletter, available on her Web site, listed above.

Change Is Part of the Picture

As I see it, the most successful homebased businesses today are those built around a good idea backed by a lifetime of acquired skills, working experience, and common-sense knowledge—coupled, of course, with a commitment to the concepts of business and marketing. Whether you are already in business or still groping for a profitable idea, your feelings about your chances for success are going to run hot and cold as you read this book. That's because everything in life—including business—is connected to something else, and whenever one thing changes, a lot of other things change, too. Thus your "business picture" is going to shift each time you gain new knowledge or perspective, and it will continue to shift throughout the life of your business as you acquire new information and gain entrepreneurial experience and business contacts. The many real-life examples in this book will automatically trigger new ideas on how you might change, improve, or redirect your own home-business plans.

Remember, too, that your choice of a business and your chances for success in it will be strongly influenced by such changeable factors as your personal lifestyle, financial situation, age, amount of business experience or education, your level of ambition, your professional attitude, your health, and the amount of support you receive from family and friends. Both your choice of business and marketing methods also will be affected by where you live (urban or rural area) and by the economy in your particular area (affluent or economically depressed) or the nation's economy in general. At this very moment, things are changing in the economy that could affect the marketability of your present business or budding idea. A new technological advance could just as easily render it obsolete as increase its potential a hundred-fold. And, just as some businesses are made extinct by technology, the social and economic changes now occurring will prompt a need for many new kinds of businesses. Implant these thoughts in your mind as you launch a new enterprise or become more deeply involved in your present venture: *Nothing stays the same. Remain flexible. Go with the flow.*

You are not yet far enough along in this book to realize what a *powerful success tool* you are now holding. The original *Homemade Money* changed the lives of tens of thousands of its readers, and thousands more will benefit from this new, expanded two-book edition. If you will only *act* on your good ideas, and use my two *Homemade Money* Guides together as your "success bible," you, too, may soon be thanking me all the way to the bank.

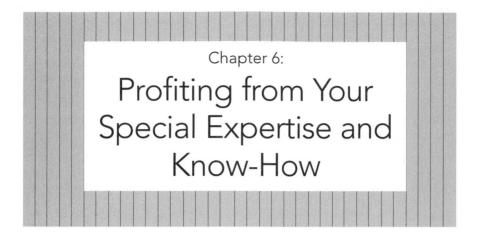

Chapter 6:

Profiting from Your Special Expertise and Know-How

An expert is someone who doesn't know more than most people, but has it better organized and runs a slide show.
—From the weekly journal of Denmark's civil engineers, as noted in the *Chicago Sun Times*

Your lifetime of experience and know-how may position you nicely to start a business based around one or more of these five activities: writing, publishing, speaking, teaching, or consulting. All of them fall neatly into one category called "The Advice Business," and any one of them can be either the basis for a new business or a way to diversify or expand an existing one. There are great opportunities for profit in this field and many good books and Web sites to help you realize your potential and find your niche as a professional adviser, teacher, information-provider, or consultant to individuals or the business community, or both. Let's take a closer look at each of these industries and see what you need to know to break into them.

Writing for Money and Recognition

Few writers today can earn their entire living by writing articles, but thousands of professionals write occasional articles for print and electronic magazines, earning both extra income and recognition in their field. The key to success here is the ability to deliver well-written material currently in demand by editors. To sell articles, you must have a good understanding of the writer's marketplace and, unless you're already a skilled writer, you may need to hone your writing skills to find acceptance for your work.

Successful writers are avid readers, of course. The first thing I did when I decided to become a professional writer in 1976 was subscribe to *Writer's Digest* magazine and buy five years' back issues. That reading and self-study, in combination with several books from the library—my "crash course in writing"—changed my life by giving me information that enabled me to earn a living for the rest of my life. I've never stopped studying my craft, but today I get most of my writer's tips and marketing information on the Internet from Web sites listed in "Other Resources."

Writers with skill in editing, copywriting, or ghostwriting may also find freelance opportunities with book publishers or corporations that need professional writers. This topic is beyond the scope of this book, but many books for writers explain how to break into this industry. Check "Other Resources" for books on this topic, and Web sites where you can get free how-to articles and market leads online.

Profits from Publishing

eBooks

Today when we speak of the book publishing industry, we're talking about not only the traditional trade book publishing industry, but the self-publishing industry as well, which includes both print and electronic books (eBooks). While the market for print books remains as strong as ever, it is sometimes difficult for beginning writers without an agent to attract the attention of a major trade book publisher, which is why so many authors continue to turn to self-publishing. (See sidebar "Self-Publishing vs. Trade Publishing.")

Profiting from Your Special Expertise

Thanks to the Internet, many authors can now be published electronically by one of the many eBook publishers on the Web. (See sidebar, "Tips for Beginning eBook Publishers.") If you are primarily interested in electronic publishing, you will find hundreds of resources on the Web simply by doing a search with your browser for such key words as "ebooks" or "electronic publishing." (A search for these words on Google.com turned up nearly 2 million Web pages for each of them, so you'll have your homework cut out for you.)

At this point, I'm still doing my own research on electronic publishing, but it appears that few beginning writers are making serious money from the sale of their eBooks. Exceptions are Web entrepreneurs who are selling technical information and know-how on computer-related topics currently in demand by would-be Web entrepreneurs, such as Web site design, eBook or newsletter publishing, electronic marketing strategies, and so on. Generally speaking, eBooks are more difficult to sell than "real books" because people don't like to (or have time to) read books on their computer screen, and today's hand-held eBook readers are still too expensive and unrefined for serious book readers to consider. This is not going to stop the electronic publishing industry, however, and the market for eBooks may change dramatically in the near future. Meanwhile, thousands of eBooks have already been published, and electronic publishing continues to attract the interest of many writers and Web entrepreneurs. Several publishers have begun to make many of their titles available electronically, and there is no question that this trend will continue. In fact, according to information found on eBookMall.com, consumers are already downloading thousands of eBooks every day, and an estimated 250 million people will be reading eBooks by 2005.

Some experts with their own Web sites and ezines are successfully selling their information-packed eBooks in the $30–$99 range while others are simply offering free eBooks designed to sell other electronic products or business services. The majority of eBooks, however, are priced much lower, with $9.99 quickly becoming the most popular price for an eBook. Many beginning writers are breaking into this field by working with established eBook publishers. Some charge an up-front fee to edit, publish, and promote an author's book while others do this work without charge, but take a higher percentage of each sale. When researching this topic on the Web, remember that eBook publishing is a new industry without set standards. Publishers make their own rules and set their own standards, so be sure to read all the fine print in any contract you sign.

When I decided to write my first eBook, *Money-Saving Tax Strategies for Homebased Entrepreneurs*, I chose to work with Liz Folger, a business friend. She and her husband, Ben, have developed a thriving business on the Web at Bizymoms.com. (You don't have to be a mom to be published there, however.) Through their site, Liz and Ben offer not only eBooks (home-business how-to guides written by mom-and-pop home-business owners), but electronic classes taught by BizyMom authors. The classes and Liz's weekly ezine encourage the sale of books, and additional sales are also made by other Web site owners who have joined the BizyMoms affiliate program. If you have specialized how-to home-business information you'd like to sell in electronic form, you would do well to start your eBook research here.

Smart Tip

To learn more about self-publishing your own book, visit Dan Poynter's Web site at paraPublishing.com or call 1-800-PARAPUB for information about his classic *Self-Publishing Manual—How to Write, Print and Sell Your Own Book*. Dan's Web site has hundreds of pages of information and free documents with links to many other self-publishing resources.

Special Reports and Booklets

Until the Internet changed everything, it was easy to sell information in printed form by mail, but the increasing costs of postage and paper, in addition to more people looking for free information on the Internet, have made printed reports and booklets more difficult to sell. In the years when I was selling my books by mail, I used to make several thousand dollars a year from the sale of inexpensive ($3–$10) special reports, booklets, and mini-directories that offered supplemental information not included in my books. I now believe the market for this kind of information is dying due to the proliferation of informative articles and free eBooks now available on the Web. The market for eBooklets and eReports, however, may increase as more people become accustomed to buying information this way. What must be remembered, however, is that we are all literally drowning in information today, so the only thing people are likely to spend money on will be highly specialized information that solves a problem or addresses a particular need.

Self-Publishing vs. Trade Publishing

Are you confused about the difference between self-publishing and being published by a trade publisher? If you write a book that is accepted for publication by a trade book publisher, your job will be almost finished by the time you have written the book and turned in the manuscript. Your next job will be to work with the content and copy editors, double-checking their suggested changes. You may or may not be involved in the preparation of the index. After that, you have no further responsibilities to the book, except to help publicize it whenever you can. You just sit back and wait for your royalty checks to arrive. It is the publisher's responsibility to pay the printer, send out press releases, place advertising, and handle distribution of the book. In all likelihood, you will have little or nothing to say about any of this, and if you're working with a large publishing house, your suggestions won't be welcomed. (The smaller the publishing company, the more likely you will be able to play a role in helping your book gain a market.) For a keen understanding of how to work with trade book publishers, read *How to Get Happily Published* by Judith Applebaum (HarperCollins), and check this author's Web site at Happily Published.com.

Conversely, when you publish your own book, you are in control from start to finish, and you assume all financial responsibility for it. You not only write it and see that it is typeset, proofread, and prepared for printing, but you also pay the printer, get out the publicity, place advertising, and figure out how to get the book distributed to the general public. This is not easy for even the most skilled person to do alone, but when it's done right, it's truly exciting, and often quite profitable. Fortunately, there are many excellent how-to guides for novices in this field, and you'll find my favorites listed in "Other Resources."

Note: There does seem to be a good market for booklets that can be printed in quantity and wholesaled to corporate buyers who may use them for promotional or advertising purposes. Consult with a booklets broker for more information on how to do this. (On the Web, begin your search for more information on this topic at TipsBooklets.com.)

Newsletter Publishing

Thinking about starting a subscription-based print newsletter? Think twice. In response to the Internet's impact on its industry, the Newsletter Publishers Association changed its name in 1999 to Newsletter and Electronic Publishers Association (NEPA), on the Web at Newsletters.org. They report the industry's sales are getting socked hard by online competition, and direct mail and renewal results have been in a continuous downward spiral since 1995. In other words, many people who used to pay for newsletter subscriptions have now turned to the Web's free information sources instead.

Prior to the Web's impact on newsletter publishing, even the most skilled publishers were lucky to get a 60–65 percent renewal rate, and second-year renewals rarely went higher than 70–78 percent. If you can't keep at least half of your first year's subscribers, something is definitely wrong with either the editorial content of your newsletter or your promotional or renewal efforts. Or maybe you're just trying to sell the right information to the wrong market. Either way, first-year profits from newsletter publishing are likely to be nonexistent, and if you're going to lose 35–50 percent of your subscribers every year, you can see that you'd have to hustle just to stay even. For that reason, a lot of novice newsletter publishes quit about the middle of their second year.

In the early 1990s when desktop publishing was all the rage, it seemed as though subscription-based print newsletters would inherit the earth. (There were about a hundred thousands newsletters in print at that time.) Lots of "big guys" were raking in money selling subscriptions to their high-priced business newsletters, and soon lots of "small guys" caught up in the home-business boom of those days figured this was a good way to make money, too. A decade earlier, I had launched one of the first newsletters ever published for home-business owners, so I was an old hand at this kind of publishing when this new wave of kitchen-table entrepreneurs, freelance writers, and other professionals jumped on the newsletter bandwagon. At one time, my PR list contained the names of at least two hundred newsletters aimed at home-business owners in all fields of endeavor. By 1996, however, most of those publishers were out of business, having learned that newsletter publishing wasn't all it was cracked up to be.

Unless you're a known personality with a large following—an author, teacher, seminar leader, consultant, etc.—you will find it difficult to get subscribers. Once you have them, the challenge is to keep them. As long-time newsletter publisher and author Barbara Winter puts it, "Publishing a newsletter is a lot like being an engineer on a train: at every stop people get on and others get off."

Barbara has been publishing her bimonthly newsletter, *Winning Ways*, since 1987. She has succeeded in this field because she is a good writer, an imaginative thinker, and a skilled speaker with a devoted following of fans. She brings in subscribers both through her Web site at BarbaraWinter.com and her regular speaking engagements and workshops. She has a 40–50 percent renewal rate with many longtime subscribers. "I do almost no promotion other than through my workshops, although I do get subscriptions from some online sources and from my book," she says. "But my newsletter is primarily intended to be a follow-up to people who have had a direct experience of working with me."

Print newsletters are a good choice only when they are in addition to something else you're doing to bring in the bucks, and only if you can figure out how to bring in subscribers without spending a fortune in magazine or direct mail advertising. After fifteen years of newsletter publishing, I was mighty tired of the relentless publishing deadlines and regular mailings I had to do to get new readers and keep old ones, so I ceased publication of my print newsletter in 1996 to focus on writing books full time. Although my newsletter had always turned a nice annual profit, its primary value to me was its power as an image and communications tool. Today, my Web site at BarbaraBrabec.com does this job for me at minuscule cost and with a lot less time and effort, and my promotional e-mail newsletter, *The Brabec Bulletin*, enables me to communicate at no cost with my steadily growing subscriber base.

Subscription-Based eNewsletters. If you're now thinking about offering a subscription based newsletter online, think again. Online e-mail newsletter publishing literally exploded in 2000 as list services such as eGroups (taken over by Yahoo.com in 2001) and other free ezine distribution services made it possible for everyone with a personal computer to become a newsletter publisher at no cost. Because there are so many free newsletters on the Internet now, it's almost impossible for the average amateur writer to sell paid subscriptions to a newsletter. (According to NEPA, conversions of 1–7 percent may be possible if you're selling hard-to-find, niche-content marketed to the right people at the right price, but this is not easy to do.) The best way to make money from an electronic newsletter is to build the list to a size large enough to attract advertisers. (For a discussion of electronic newsletter publishing for promotional purposes, see this book's companion marketing guide, *HOMEMADE MONEY: Bringing in the Bucks.*)

Directories

Directories, more than reports or booklets, often solve a particular business need and are thus more salable because this kind of information is not so easily gathered by the average individual or business owner. All kinds of information lends itself to publication in directory form, from collections of supplier names and addresses (specific industries) to listings of events, buyer markets (sales reps, shops, and stores of a particular nature), and media lists. The more up-to-date and detailed the listings, the more value it will have to the buyer.

Some print directories are distributed free of charge, with the publisher making a profit from advertising placed in the directory by listees. In this case, distribution must be sufficient to produce a satisfactory response for advertisers or they will not pay to be in future editions.

Smart Tip

It can be dangerous to pick up and print information "second-hand," not to mention it being a terrible disservice to one's readers to publish inaccurate listings. Never publish a directory of names and addresses without contacting everyone listed to make sure such publicity is desirable to them.

Tips for Beginning eBook Publishers

If you work with an eBook publisher, you'll have to meet their minimum page requirements, and they will determine the best price for the book. If you want to self-publish and market an eBook through your own Web site, however, I suggest you:

1. Focus on publishing highly specialized business or how-to information on topics that appeal to consumer or business niche markets you know how to reach and sell to.

2. Keep your books short enough (between 50 and 100 pages or so) that people will feel they can afford to print them out for reading or study at their leisure. (You might emphasize the practicality of this by reminding buyers that the cost to print a hundred-page book may be less [about five cents a page in paper and ink] than what they would normally pay to have a book delivered by mail or UPS.)

3. Keep your prices low enough that buyers will feel they're getting good value for their money.

4. Offer satisfaction or money back. (Few people will ask for their money back, but failure to give a refund to even one unhappy reader could harm book sales if that reader speaks badly about the book on discussion lists or bulletin boards.)

Money in Your Mouth

If you have the "gift of gab," you can promote your business, earn additional income as a speaker, or build a full-time speaking career talking on topics that relate to your business or personal interests. Although I no longer travel and do speaking engagements, between 1980 and 2000 I presented dozens of day-long home-business workshops across the country, working mostly with community colleges or small business development centers (SBDCs) that took care of all advertising and other arrangements. Like many other speakers in the home-business community, I fell into speaking as a natural result of my wide visibility as an author and industry leader. This, coupled with word-of-mouth advertising, generated all the speaking engagements I wanted to do. Over the years as I gradually raised my speaker's fee, I found $500/day plus expenses to be the most community colleges or SBDCs could afford to pay, so I moved into a different market (small business conferences) that paid more. Here, what most conference directors wanted was a forty-minute keynote speech and a short workshop related to the theme of the conference.

Opportunities for Professional Speakers. "Talk may not be cheap, but it certainly pays," says Dottie Walters, publisher of *Sharing Ideas* (the leading speaker's newsmagazine) and author of many books, including *Speak and Grow Rich*. "Each year, more than a million paid speeches on every possible subject are presented at conferences, conventions, workshops, seminars and meetings of all kinds," says Dottie. "Being a professional speaker will lead you in many different exciting directions. As the world of professional speaking expands at an ever-rapid rate, opportunities for all kinds of speaking, training, teaching, writing and related products are accelerating."

Dottie's agency, Walters International Speakers Bureau (Walters-Intl.com), books over 20,000 speakers who present every topic under the sun. Many of them earn $5,000 or more (plus expenses) for a keynote address. Says Dottie, "A grandmother may speak on 'Getting Liberated' while another teaches executives 'Good Etiquette for Business Meals.' Some speak on strategy, negotiation, or implementation; time management, communication, sales or humor. Many are authors of books on these subjects. We often book characters from history who appear in costume, including Ben Franklin, George and Martha Washington, and General George Patton. A galaxy of famous personalities are alive and well and appearing on the platforms of the world as professional speakers. Even Mahatma Gandhi can speak for your convention."

If you plan to educate yourself to all the possibilities on how to sell your intellectual know-how through speaking, you should also read *Money Talks* by Jeffrey Lant, a man who has made millions by practicing what he preaches. In this book, one of several Lant has self-published, he explains how to profit from the lucrative world of talk with workshops, seminars, lectures, institutes, conferences, and more.

Teaching Others What You Know

Organized people with enthusiasm, patience, and the ability to communicate their knowledge to others make the best teachers. A college degree or teacher's certificate seldom is required, but it may help command higher prices. (So will experience. The more you have, and the better a teacher you become, the more you can charge.) You may elect to teach a skill (art, lace making, woodcarving), present a special-interest class (astrology, gardening, writing), or share your business expertise (marketing, computers, taxes).

Opportunities in Adult Education Centers

"Non-credit learning is not one mass market, but an almost endless number of tightly focused niche markets," say Bart Brodsky and Janet Geis, authors of *The Teaching Marketplace* (now out of print). "Identify your prospective students by vocation, hobby, special interest, geographic area, and lifestyle," they advise. "You can turn almost any life experience into a rewarding career teaching free-lance or part-time. You can customize the length of a class, the price, location, and number of participants. You don't even need to be affiliated with a school."

Adult education centers provide opportunities for everyone. "Many colleges, universities and community colleges offer programs in adult and continuing education in addition to their regular credit courses," says a program coordinator for a state university. "We're constantly on the lookout for qualified teachers. At one time or another, the University has offered, or been interested in offering, courses in folk art, holiday package wrapping, calligraphy, cooking, sweatshirt painting, crochet rug making, color wardrobe, silk scarf painting, needlepunch, oil painting, wearable art, and horticulture."

While arts and crafts classes are very popular with program directors, a broad range of business-related topics are also in demand. When a self-publisher in my network decided there was a market for courses in starting a homebased business, he sent course proposals to ten Continuing Education departments in his area, and seven of them eventually booked workshops. He later expanded his client list to 20 by adding seminars on mail order, self-publishing, and computer businesses.

Fee Guidelines. An image consultant told me her first "pitch letters" netted a response from every school she had written to, but her delight turned to shock when she discovered how poorly some of those teaching jobs would pay. In time, however, the low-paying jobs she accepted turned out to be quite profitable because they brought her additional business and made her more of a recognized authority in her area.

A low-paying teaching opportunity can be made more profitable by having something to sell to students, such as a book or materials kit related to your class or workshop. The program coordinator may allow you to offer it separately or elect to build its cost into the course fee and pay you directly in addition to your teaching fee. For example, in the day-long home-business workshops I used to teach, sometimes one of my books was a required text; other times, all of my books were offered as optional purchases at day's end. In the latter case, I generally sold books to at least 85 percent of my audience, making these workshops quite profitable.

Some schools do not allow sales of any kind, so be clear on this point before you agree to teach. If product sales aren't possible, be content with the exposure you will get from school catalogs and the positive impression you will make on your students. Use your class roster sheet to add student names to your mailing list and send them a brochure or catalog later.

Whether you will be teaching at an institution or in your own home, set your per-student or per-day price according to what others are charging for similar classes. If no standards exist, set a price you feel is fair, based on what you might pay if someone else were giving the class. (So much depends on the area in which you live and the demand for your particular knowledge or skills.) Payment for adult education courses varies across the country. One teacher told me she received $500 for a 15-hour course taken for credit, but thought this rate might be higher than average. Another teacher reported receiving $20 per contract hour for "one-shot" classes of from one to four hours in length. While some teachers in my network have told me they receive similar payment for courses, others work on a split of total income derived from a course. This is especially beneficial to teachers who can enlarge a workshop audience through PR efforts or use of their own mailing list. A 60/40 split seems to be common, with the teacher getting 40 percent. Thus, if a day-long course is offered for $29 and attracts 40 students, the teacher would get $11.60 per student times 40, or $464, a tidy profit indeed. The more students, the more money.

If you are interested in teaching, but lack a reputation that will bring speaking engagements your way, start to build one now by offering to give a free talk at the library or to some local organization. If tutoring individual students is more to your liking, establish an hourly rate per student, keeping in mind that you are providing a special service that may be unavailable elsewhere. Charge accordingly.

Teaching in Craft Stores

Many skilled artists and craftspeople get started in teaching by offering to teach a class at a local craft supply store. This will be of particular interest if your class is designed to sell more of their supplies, and a teaching relationship with a shop is a good way to open up a new market for patterns or how-to books you may sell.

"Most shops are willing to consider new teachers if you take the time to ask," says pattern designer Terrie Kralik, who teaches at quilt and fabric shops in Coeur d'Alene and Sandpoint, Idaho, and sells on the Web at MooseCountryQuilts.com. "To compete with other professionals in the area, you may have to offer something different to be accepted, and some shops may be new to scheduling classes and need your help getting started. Sometimes you will have to decide if the distance you must travel is worth your payment, or if you're willing to teach at unusual hours or weekends to fit their schedule. As I meet more quilters from other areas, I've been asked to teach quite a distance from home. The rules are a little different for that kind of teaching, but it opens up a lot more doors and takes you to new levels of your craft."

Teaching Online

This topic needs a whole book of its own! Crafters were among the first to discover the profit potential of electronic teaching (which is considerable), but all kinds of information providers are now finding ways to conduct classes or coaching sessions on the Web.

At KarenBooy.com, crafts designer and publisher Karen Booy offers an online twelve-week course ($75) on how to start your own successful craft business. "Each weekly lesson includes both instructional materials and guide sheets to help students direct and organize thoughts and ideas into a workable plan," she explains. "Opportunities for one-on-one feedback with me and online class members are provided through a discussion list."

At QuiltUniversity.com, many quilting experts offer classes on a variety of quilt-related topics. They collect all fees and do all organizing of classes. Teachers get 80 percent of student fees. "To succeed in electronic teaching, your voice has to come through, the same as in a book," says Myrna Giesbrecht, one of the teachers on this site. "You have to know your topic and be very organized. The images are your examples. The text must be very clear. You have room for more than a book, but you can't run on or the students will revolt at too much reading. I write the text for my class and put together the illustrations. These are posted in a number of lessons. Each lesson contains how-to text as well as step-by-step examples for students to work on. They follow the instructions and create the sample. If they have a question, they post it to the discussion board and I answer it there. Very few digital images are sent in, but this can be done to illustrate a point. This kind of teaching is a step up from putting a book out there and not knowing the reaction, but a step down from a face-to-face workshop."

"Internet learning is the great geographic equalizer," says Sandra Miller-Louden, coordinator of the BizyMom online classes. "No longer are physical miles a deterrent for the wonderful process we call education." A growing number of eBook authors whose how-to home-business books have been published by BizyMoms.com now offer four-week classes on this site. All classes cost $60, and teachers receive 40 percent of the tuition. After registration, students receive weekly lesson handouts via e-mail, which they can study at their convenience. There are no set meeting times for classes, and all questions, comments, and homework are handled by e-mail.

Offering Your Knowledge Through Consulting

The number of consultants has increased dramatically in recent years due to corporate downsizing and company cutbacks, and consultants remain attractive to companies because they can be hired for short periods of time. To become a consultant in any field, you first must have special knowledge about that field and a market willing to pay for it. Don't think that consulting is limited only to laid-off executives, however. Anyone who knows something other people want to know can offer that knowledge through consulting. For example, artists and craftspeople could well find themselves advising museum curators on lost arts

Overcoming Your Fear of Speaking in Public

Not everyone is thrilled about speaking. "I find myself being encouraged by others to branch out into areas I don't feel comfortable in," says a beginning speaker. "My biggest business hurdle so far has been deciding how much speaking I'm willing to do, or how many classes I want to teach. Since I have your basic speaking-in-public phobia, this has been difficult for me. I need to do it to further my business, but I do it with great reservation and raw fear."

I don't know who said it, but I know many will identify with it: "The human brain is a wonderful thing. It starts working the moment you are born and never stops until you stand up to speak in public." If you like the idea of teaching, but are insecure about the idea of "speaking in public," don't think of it as "speaking" but as sharing your enthusiasm for something you love and know others would enjoy. The first time a student comes to you after class and thanks you profusely for all you've taught them, your fears will fall by the wayside, and you will have found a wonderful and profitable new niche for your talents.

and crafts. A homemaker-turned-entrepreneur may be an expert in organizing a home, planning a wedding, or working with children. As an experienced home-business owner, you will find many opportunities to consult beginners in this field in areas of advertising, marketing, publicity, communications, or sales. Pick any field you can think of, and you will find consultants specializing in it. There are even consultants who teach people to become consultants.

Since commerce is now being driven by technology, many businesses now need a new type of consultant, one who specializes in technology and its application to business. Opportunities are open to people both on and off the Web. Some businesses will want you to come to them to solve a particular technological problem or figure out how to accomplish a task they don't have the time or expertise to do themselves. On the Web, consultants are needed to help people get their businesses on line, get a site designed, figure out shopping cart systems, the best merchant account provider for their business, and so on.

As jobs become more specialized, and our technological society becomes

In today's Information Age, economic opportunities for consultants, professional practitioners, trainers, speakers and information product developers/marketers are unprecedented. Nominal capital investment is required to profit in these businesses, which often command daily billing rates of $1,000 a day or more. To augment their services, more and more consultants are developing information products such as manuals, audio tapes, software, books, newsletters and many other products to deliver their knowledge and information. This makes transmitting know-how to clients less expensive and it frees their time for more consulting.

—The late Howard Shenson, author of *Shenson on Consulting—Success Strategies From the Consultant's Consultant*

• • •

Consultants . . . raise to an art form the dissemination of biased information. Their handling of collected data invariably has two results. They find a way to have the finished report coincide with the opinion of the person who hired them. Secondarily, they usually find a way to make the final report become an entree to their being asked back for more consultations.

—from *Infomaniacs—A Brown Paper Bag View of Information Interaction in Corporate America,* by Joseph S. Casciato and Robert M. Vass (Sierra Pub.)

more complex, professions often require one to specialize within a specialty. Herman Holtz, one of my favorite business authors and book contributors through the years, is gone now, but his books on independent consulting probably remain on library shelves and should be read by aspiring consultants. Holtz explained to me that advice is not a regulated business, and anyone can sell advice in any form (except for advice in some regulated or licensed professions). And even in these fields, one is free to sell general advice to the public at large (rather than to individuals) because it is then *information*.

Holtz also emphasized this point: "Any layperson is free to write, lecture, and otherwise render advice in general for fees as long as the advice or information is general and not offered to an individual. For example, you may write or lecture about legal matters in the abstract, but unless you are a licensed attorney, you may not counsel a person in legal matters for a fee."

If you think you have to be an expert in order to sell your advice, you're wrong. "In many cases, simple access to useful information is ample underpinning for selling advice profitably," Holtz told me, adding that consulting is not a business or a profession, but a way of doing business or practicing a profession. "Ergo, anyone with a marketable skill *of any kind* is in a position to become a consultant, teaching others to do what he or she does, solving others' problems, and/or doing work for others on a temporary, permanent, or semi-permanent basis."

Another consultant you would do well to study is Jeffrey Lant. In all his books, he zeros in on what advisers of every kind need to know to launch profitable advice and consulting practices in any field. "The trick to building a practice in its early stages," he says, "is to find a specific service that produces for the client a disproportionate benefit compared to your fee, and to leverage each individual success to get further clients."

Lant's books, all of which he publishes and markets himself, enjoy excellent sales in spite of their high cover prices. "That's as it should be," he says. "I believe that we who assist other people, who do good, should do well in the process. Keep this belief as your credo and you, too, will do well."

 Smart Tip

If you are a consultant or plan to use the services of a consultant, you will benefit by reading "The Consulting Agreement" article on Attorney Ivan Hoffman's Web site at IvanHoffman.com.

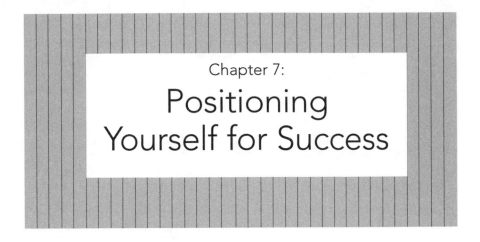

Chapter 7:
Positioning Yourself for Success

The will to prepare to win is more important than the will to win. Preparing usually means doing those kinds of things that failures don't like to do. It means studying and learning. It means reading books, going to seminars. It means not being afraid to corner experts and ask foolish questions.
— Robert G. Allen, from an article in *Creating Wealth*

When they work at home, the British call it "fiddling." Here in America, a lot of people earning money at home are just fiddling, too. They may put in long, hard hours on a moneymaking activity, yet fail to generate a true profit. Some people simply don't know what to do to make more money; others know, yet are reluctant to do anything about it. Some people fear failure; others fear success. Still others simply have their minds set on staying small. But even small, part-time businesses can generate a fair amount of capital and profit if they are properly managed and promoted.

If you'd like to make more money from your small business endeavor, the first thing you need to do is *stop fiddling around*. It's a trap to think small. If you think small, you'll stay small. But if you dare to think big, you have at least a chance of making it big, financially speaking. That's why I encourage you to E-X-P-A-N-D your thinking, S-T-R-E-T-C-H your capabilities, and R-E-A-C-H farther than you have reached before. Accept the fact that you know more than you think you know, and you can do more than you may now believe possible.

To Be Legal or Not—That Is the Question

To successfully position yourself and your business for success, you must develop a professional attitude about business. Do you operate an underground business or think of your income as "money under the table"? This is both an unprofessional attitude and a self-defeating trap. No business can grow if it remains hidden; it needs visibility to survive and prosper. But why should you be legal, especially when so many others are obviously "getting away with it"? Even if you think the chances are pretty good you won't be caught, I think it boils down to whether you want to be an honest or dishonest individual. Do you prefer the feelings of pride and accomplishment that are the rewards for honest actions, or shall you live instead with Fear and Guilt, companions to Dishonesty? As ordinary people, we have enough feelings of guilt in our everyday lives without having to worry about the fact that we're cheating on our taxes and could get caught and be publicly embarrassed—and possibly punished—at any moment. I recall one woman who told me she finally was going to "go legal" simply because she was beginning to wake up in the middle of the night in a cold sweat, convinced the IRS would soon be knocking on her door. Surely no amount of taxes saved could be worth this kind of anxiety.

What too few people realize is that self-employed individuals qualify for many breaks that substantially lower their taxes. You see, once you are "in business," and not just "fiddling around," you'll find you are entitled to many tax deductions that can offset a sizable portion of your annual gross income. In fact, in the early years of a business, it is quite likely you will end up with a business loss, at least on paper, that can be used to offset income from salaries and other income sources, and thus cut taxes. (See "Business Expenses and Tax Deductions" in Section II for more information on allowable home-business deductions.)

"Taxes are the price we pay for a government that guarantees us the freedom to earn enough money to pay our taxes," someone once said. Once you begin business operations, it will not seem at all unusual to the IRS that you need to buy office equipment, a computer, or a new car to advance your business. Lo and behold, a large percentage of such costs can immediately be offset against receipts, or written off (depreciated) over a specified number of years. Once you qualify for the home office deduction, you become entitled to deduct a comparable percentage of your regular living expenses, from rent or mortgage interest to utilities, repairs, and maintenance on your home. Another way to get legal tax deductions is to hire your spouse or children. (For detailed information on the many tax deductions you can take as a self-employed individual, see the books, *Small Time Operator* and *422 Tax Deductions for Businesses and Self-Employed Individuals* by Bernard Kamoroff.)

Who but a fool (and a dishonest fool at that) would continue to hide his or her income and give up all these delicious and perfectly legal tax deductions to which a legitimate home-business owner is entitled? Besides, if you're trying to prove your credit worthiness—possibly to get a business loan or a home mortgage—you will want your gross income (and net profit) to be as high as possible.

Smart Tip

Keep careful records. Make sure your business income and expenses are never mixed with personal income and expenses. This means having a separate checking account for your business and appropriate books that will satisfy the IRS. Failure to do this may cause the IRS to disallow your home-business deductions.

Checking Out Local, State, and Federal Laws

Some people violate a law out of ignorance (an excuse you can't use with this book in hand), but others do it deliberately, perhaps because they feel a law is unfair. It well may be unfair—even unconstitutional in the eyes of many— but the fact remains that ignorance of the law is no excuse, and anyone who deliberately or unknowingly breaks the law must be prepared to suffer the consequences. This might mean the complete stoppage of a business, a stiff fine, back taxes (plus interest), even a jail sentence. In some cases it could mean an expensive lawsuit instigated by your state or federal government, or another business whose rights you may have violated. For information on specific local, state, and federal laws you need to be aware of, see the A-to-Z "Crash Course" in Business Basics in Section II of this book. By following the guidelines you find there, you'll be able to avoid many tax, legal, and financial pitfalls that will catch other business owners unaware.

At one of my workshops, after I had talked for three hours about all the technicalities and legalities of home-business start-up, a small voice in the back asked, "Is it really worth all this effort?" I said I didn't know if it was worth it to her, but it was worth it to me. Only you can answer this question. Just remember that every big job seems intimidating at first, even to a professional. The secret is to make a plan of the big job, then break it into a lot of little jobs. The task then becomes not only less frightening, but easier to do. There is much truth in the old saying, "the only way to eat an elephant is one bite at a time." By putting your plans and ideas on paper and addressing each sticky question or problem as it arises, you will enable yourself to take small business bites that are easy to mentally chew and digest.

Zoning Laws

Zoning is just one of the those "sticky wicket" legal problems homebased entrepreneurs need to address right from the beginning. You could have the world's greatest idea for a profitable home business only to discover it is restricted by your local zoning ordinance (or a restrictive clause in your lease, apartment regulations, or condominium covenants.) Such restrictions do not always stop people from starting or operating a homebased businesses, of course. In fact, many homebased businesses are walking a thin line between being legal in the eyes of the IRS, and illegal in the eyes of their local zoning boards. The problem is now twofold. In some cases, communities still have zoning laws on the books dating back to horse-and-buggy days when no one could have imagined the millions of people who would someday be working in homebased occupations or businesses. In other cases, communities have changed their zoning laws to recognize home occupations, but set impossible-to-comply-with restrictions many business owners are simply ignoring. Of course that means they are also keeping a very low profile by not letting their neighbors know what they're doing, and never advertising or seeking local publicity.

Positioning Yourself for Success

Ordinarily, city officials do not go around checking to see who's violating zoning ordinances, but generally act only when a neighbor complains. Thus, many home business owners who are, in fact, operating illegally, simply keep a low profile, believing that they have a right to do whatever they wish in the privacy of their own home so long as it does not disturb or annoy neighbors in any way. They don't advertise in a way that draws attention to where they live. They avoid making loud noises and do not cause traffic problems. They don't tie up neighborhood parking places, use business signs, or do anything else not in keeping with the character of their residential neighborhood. In fact, they do their best to keep their business a complete secret, especially from busybody neighbors.

If you're thinking about moving to a new community, it would be wise to check local zoning laws first, and consider talking to the neighbors, too. "Before closing on our house, we spoke to the neighbors about what we do and asked if that would bother them," says the owner of a photography business. "We are aware that neighbors could ruin our homebased business, so it has always been our policy to be especially respectful of them so they didn't want us to move. On the plus side, we are home during the day to watch out for their places and many of the neighbors in the ten years we have been here now have a business in their homes too."

In checking a hundred business owners in my network, most of those who said they had no zoning problems were service providers who do not have employees or need to see clients in their home. Many artists, craftspeople, and other product sellers, however, have had serious zoning problems. In many places, zoning ordinances are are simply unfair or ridiculous. Here are some examples:

Receiving Phone Calls and Mail. A business owner in Hollywood, Florida, told me the zoning ordinance in that city prohibited him from receiving incoming business calls to his home telephone number (he had to have a beeper to receive all calls!), and he could not receive business mail to his mailbox. "Neither my phone company nor the postal service cared that I received mail and calls at home," he said, "so I operated a shadow business until I moved to a new location." This same business owner said his city's zoning law required that he display his city and county occupational licenses in a "conspicuous place" even though he couldn't have clients in his office who might view them.

The "Use by Right" Zoning Doctrine

Gary Maxwell, a copywriter in Pennsylvania, explains an interesting zoning doctrine in his state called "Use by right" that may be in effect in your state as well. "The idea is that there are certain things that can be done in a home by virtue of the right to do it," he says. "For instance, as a copywriter, I can write to my heart's content whether or not I make a business out of it. Why? Because I have a right to do so. So, if I wanted to charge for my services, the zoning board could not prevent me from doing so by virtue of the 'Use by right' rule."

Utility Fees. In Milford, Iowa, you'll pay $2 a month more for residential garbage pickup if your business is listed in the phone book—whether your business creates extra garbage or not. In Zumbro Falls, Minnesota, city sewer and water rates are $85 a month for a residence with one or two people living in the household. Businesses are charged an even higher rate, depending on their sewer and water use situation. A basketweaver who lives above her shop was astonished to learn that she was going to be charged for both a residence and a business, simply because the downstairs (homebased) business had a toilet. "I immediately pulled out the toilet and now go upstairs to use the facilities," she says. "The only reason I can still use the downstairs sink in connection with my basketry work is because the washer and dryer for the apartment are downstairs and considered part of the residence fee. This is highway robbery, but what other alternative did I have?"

Where Work Is Performed. This one is outrageous! In Roseville, California, the Home Occupation ordinance states that all home-business activities must be performed indoors, and no activity shall occur outside at any time. Now here's a ruling just begging to be violated. If you're a writer or artist who writes or paints for fun, you can work outdoors . . .but if you do this for money, you have to stay indoors? (See sidebar, "The 'Use by Right' Zoning Doctrine.")

Most people want to do what's right, and they try very hard to operate their business legally. But zoning laws in some areas are literally making criminals out of people who aren't bothering anyone and are merely trying to earn a living. After the city of Topeka, Kansas, changed its zoning ordinance to include a fee to cover inspections required by law, I received this report from the director of the small business development center in that city: "It is unclear what purpose these inspections serve, although they are conducted. It's safe to say that most homebased businesses are either ignoring the law or ignorant of it, although we now make a point of telling folks. The funny part is that the law is almost unenforceable and apparently carries no penalty for non-compliance. In passing a law with no enforcement, and no obvious purpose, the politicians create a class of unwitting criminals."

See "Zoning Laws" in Section II for a detailed discussion of common zoning restrictions you're likely to have to deal with, experiences of other business owners, two possible solutions to zoning problems, and what to do if you get caught operating illegally.

Smart Tip

Thinking about setting up shop in an exterior building on your property? Suppliers of exterior buildings and sheds can be located in the Yellow Pages. But check first with local zoning officials to see what the size limitations are for exterior buildings and ask if a builder's permit is needed for this kind of structure.

Selecting a Business Name

Your business name should tell customers or clients something about you, your products, publications, or services. Here are ten tips on how to select a good name for your business:

1   Don't name your business until you know exactly what you're going to do, and remember that any name you choose may automatically position you badly or beautifully in the eyes of prospective customers or clients.(See sidebar, "Let's Boogie, Jack!")

2   Consider using your own name as your business name if you are known and respected in your community or a particular field of endeavor. If you have a service business, a name such as *Bill Brown's Catering* or *Jim Bradshaw Photographs* will automatically conjure a certain image in the minds of those who know you. I'll never forget the advice a businessman

gave me when I was just starting my book-selling and publishing business. "Don't sell your products," he told me, "sell your good name. Once people know and accept you, they'll also accept your products or services." This message came home to me the day a fellow sent me a letter saying, "When is your next book coming out? I'll read anything you write."

3. Avoid the use of initials. Instead of using their own names, some people merely use initials, such as C & S Associates. While this may have meaning for the owners and even look great in a business logo, it will mean nothing to customers, and it won't give them a clue as to what the business is about—which only makes your marketing job harder.

4. Look at your name and see if there is a way you can combine portions of it to form a new name. For example, writer Dennis E. Hensley incorporated as *Denehen, Inc.*

5. Consider whether you can cleverly tie your last name into a phrase that catches one's interest. For example, Linda Highley named her business *Highley Decorative*, while Trish, Tom, and Chris Powers called their enterprise *The Powers That Be*. Sometimes your product will suggest a business name. Pamela Burns started a business selling artfully decorated denim for infants and toddlers and, playing on the idea of "blue jeans," named it *Injeanious by Pamela Burns*.

6. Try playing with words, using your name in conjunction with ordinary words. With "original" and "primary" in mind, Jane Nichols named her business *Orijanels*, while Mary Prima settled on *PriMary Reflections*. Names like these are much more likely to be remembered than common names such as *Jane's Originals* or *Reflections by Mary*.

7. Try to pick a name that won't tie you down if you later decide to branch out into other areas. I've always like Annie Lang's business name, *Annie Things Possible*. "By choosing a more individual and creative business name, I have not locked myself into a specific artistic style or trend (i.e., Country, Victorian, Crafty)," she says. "It also conveys a creatively positive subliminal message (which happens to be my own personal philosophy in a nutshell) . . . that anything *is* possible."

8 Think about tying your name into a literary work that makes people think they've heard of you before. Tatter Julie Felzien has the perfect name for her needlework business: *The Mad Tatter*, and Elayne Bloom's gift basket business, *Hound of the Basketvilles*, is another good example. I also like *Snow Write Productions*, the name Donna M. Snow picked for her Internet production company, which involves writing. Her e-mail tag line refers to her business as "A charming company offering princely productions."

9 Avoid misspelling names for effect. Some people deliberately misspell words in order to make them go together with their names, but it's wise to avoid a name like *Kathy's Klever Kreations* if you are trying to buy supplies and materials from craft wholesalers. Many will not sell to hobby businesses, and a name like this is a dead giveaway. Having a business letterhead and sales tax number may make no difference. (This is what I meant earlier about how a name can position you badly in the minds of others.)

10 Also avoid a business name with long names or words that are difficult to pronounce or remember. And consider *not* using the word "enterprises." So many beginners have used this word as part of their business name that it has become synonymous with amateur or home-based operations. You probably realize that you cannot use the words, "Limited," "Ltd.," or "Inc." unless you are an incorporated business. But I tip my hat to the people who named their business *Desktop, Ink*. This name is not only appropriate, but it sounds like an incorporated business without being one.

In summary, your business name should not be selected in haste, because your financial future could depend on it. And if you already have named your business and now realize you made a poor choice, change it. The cost of the printed materials you may have to throw out will be insignificant when compared to the probable increase in business a more appropriate name will generate. Times change, and we must change, too, or be left behind. Robert Compton, a Vermont potter, illustrates my point. When he first began to sell, he operated as *The Mad River Potter*, a folksy name that suited the times. As his work improved, however, and his prices increased, he realized the need for a more professional-sounding name, one that would

Let's Boogie, Jack!

After discovering Dennis Gaskill's helpful Web site, BoogieJack.com, I was curious about why he picked this name for his business. "When I first got involved in designing Web graphics, I sent off a few to a site to see if they would be interested in posting them, and they were," he explained. "They asked what name to credit them to, and because my wife was concerned that using my real name might result in something weird happening (we both knew very little about the Internet at that time), I needed an alias. When the e-mail came in asking for a name, a song happened to be playing on the radio, and one of the lines was something like 'but you sure boogie, Jack,' and I simply grabbed the name from that song. By the time I got around to building a Web site, I'd already had my graphics featured in games, software programs, and CD-rom book inserts and was getting a lot of mail from people who knew me as Boogie Jack from the graphics site. So, being just smart enough to realize I had something going with the publicity, I kept the name and used it for my Web site."

offer customers more psychological security. By changing his name to *Robert Compton Ltd.*, he enhanced his professional image, which enabled him to raise prices, which increased profits.

See "Business or Trade Name" in Section II for information on how to register and protect your business name and logo, and what to do if someone tells you to stop using the name you've selected because they are already using it.

Projecting a Professional Image

Many home-business owners complain they lack credibility in the eyes of prospective buyers. One fellow said he had added "References Provided" to his business card after a prospect told him flat out that she would never buy from anyone who worked at home, let alone from a garage, as this person was doing. "Would it help to join a trade organization?" he asked. It might. Some people are impressed by such things. But membership in an organization is not going to give anyone instant credibility.

A professional image does not just happen. You have to create it, then carefully maintain it throughout the life of your business. It involves everything from your business name and logo to good-looking printed and promotional materials, to the way your Web site is designed, to efficient communications and services. Actually, you have two professional images, says Sylvia Ann Blishak, author of *Improving Your Company Image—A Do-It-Yourself Guide* (Crisp Publications). "Your invisible image is the one people hear. Your visible image is your business stationery, order blanks, invoice, business card, brochures or Web site. Being aware of both the visible and invisible images you're projecting, and updating them periodically to make sure you are communicating information that fits the changing nature of your products or services, is an excellent way to appeal to customers, and to make them feel comfortable and confident about dealing with you."

Dealing with Family and Friends

One problem many homebased workers have is getting family or friends to accept the fact they truly are in business and not just playing around with a hobby. If this is your problem, you need a strategy to combat this hobbyist image, and it must begin with your own attitude about yourself and your business. The way you conduct your business influences the way people think of you.

Begin by setting up some ground rules. If your friends and neighbors are used to dropping by for coffee and conversation, tell them how much you're going to miss this contact with them, but ask them to kindly respect your business hours in the future. Emphasize that you are not just "fiddling around," but have started a business, and you need undisturbed periods of time in which to work. Tell them what you are doing and ask them to help you by spreading the word to prospective customers or clients. In the future, arrange to visit friends in the evening, or perhaps on the weekend.

If you have young children, keep them away from the phone. The last thing you want is a child yelling into the ear of a prospective client, "It's for you, Mommie!" The one I especially dislike is the precocious youngster who answers the phone and then insists on knowing your life history before he'll go fetch Mom or Dad, or the child who picks up the phone, then leaves it off the hook without calling the person you want. If your children could ruin the business illusion you are trying to create, a separate business phone or answering machine should be considered.

See Chapter Twelve for more tips on how to successfully blend business into your personal lifestyle.

Smart Tip

Enhance your professional image by leaving a good message on your answering machine or voice mail that tells callers exactly who they have reached and what you want them to do.

Developing a Mindset for Business and Financial Success

Success experts remind us that we can't achieve any goal until that goal is clearly pictured in our mind, so it's important for you to define success before you reach for it. Some people equate success only in terms of dollars, saying, "I want to make lots of money," or "I want to create/make/invent something I can sell for thousands of dollars in mail order catalogs/exclusive shops/chain stores." Such financial goals, however, are neither realistic nor clear-cut, which makes them unachievable. If you set such goals, you will only become discouraged when you don't reach them. So remember this rhyme: *To be achievable, a goal must be believable and conceivable.*

In the beginning, home-business owners need a series of small gains and achievements to keep them going, so it's important to set realistic dollar goals for yourself. For instance, a first year's goal might be: "I'm not going to lose more than $1,000 this year." (A paper loss, we hope.) In that case, you'd feel good at year's end if you lost only $500 because you would have achieved—even exceeded—your goal. Once you meet or better your first-year objective, raise your financial goal the second year to break even or perhaps make a small profit.

Remember, it often takes two years just to work out the kinks in a home business—to refine and improve products or services, test new theories, set up efficient office systems and procedures, locate necessary suppliers, and establish basic marketing channels. By the third year, things will begin to fall

A Four-Step Plan For Success

When we began our literary agency, my husband, Bob, and I sat down and individually did two things: (1) we made a list of all the things we wanted from life—dreaming up everything we could think of, which was quite enjoyable; and (2) we listed what we saw as our own and our spouse's strengths—every kind of positive thing we could think of.

Then we shared our lists with each other and really had a good time evaluating them. Our third step was to together write out our joint goals: business, physical, spiritual, mental, financial, social, home, and family. Only then did we write our business plan (step 4). All of this material went into what we call our "Gold Book," which is a three-ring binder that really is metallic gold in color. At the end of the book, we have an appendix of "axioms," which are inspirational quotes we've gathered from all over.

So, early in our marriage and our business partnership, we made clearly stated goals by analyzing our wishes and desires, ranked these according to their importance, and formulated concrete plans to achieve these goals, both personal and business. We believe in supporting each other in achieving our true potential, and are partners in everything we do.

—Barbara J. Doyen, Doyen Literary Services, Inc.

into place, and a true profit might be realized for the first time. (I say "true profit" because it's not fair to you or your business to say you've made a profit if you've worked all year without a salary, as most home business owners do for two or three years. The employees and all other expenses get paid first, then the owner.)

It's not businesslike, either, to ignore the overhead costs of your business that fall into the area of "home expenses"—such as the rent or mortgage payment, utility bills, telephone, and so on. Whether these costs increase as a result of your business is not really the point. What you need to consider is this: If you build your business on a no-overhead principle, what will happen if you become successful to the point where you must move to outside quarters? In all probability you will not have set your prices high enough to cover the now-unavoidable overhead costs, and you will have to do some fancy figuring to get out of this trap without losing your customers or clients, who by now will be accustomed to your low prices.

"Profit" is another good word for you to define as you develop your mindset for success. It is not always synonymous with cash, of course. New businesses can lose money for several years in a row, yet still be extremely profitable to their owners. For instance, a profitable year might mean valuable business contacts, acquired knowledge and experience, a new understanding of your strengths and weaknesses, or the discovery of a new marketing channel that will pay off big the following year. It can also mean you have made money, but you put it into a retirement plan or simply reinvested every dime into the business, perhaps in the form of computer equipment, larger inventories, new employees, or a Web site.

Even a failed sideline venture can be profitable if it points the way to a better idea that will work, or if it reveals something important in your character that encourages you to go forth in a new direction. Again, failure has its redeeming qualities and you will always learn something from it.

Smart Tip

Pay attention to your professional image. Home-business owners who find resistance from buyers because they're homebased probably need better printed materials, a more appropriate business name, or more professional marketing strategies. If you have a professional business image, no one will care where your office is located.

Chapter 8:
Planning Your Moves

The first management job is planning, a combination of realistic calculations and crystal ball gazing. It is an exercise in arithmetic and imagination, in separating the possible from the impossible.
—from a booklet published by the U.S. Department of Labor

B usiness planning never stops. It is something you must do at the beginning, in the middle, and even at the end of your business. In every business, there is a need for a variety of plans at one time or another, including time plans (short-, medium-, and long-range planning); creative, routine, and problem-solving plans; production plans; marketing plans; and comprehensive business plans.

"People don't plan to *fail*," goes an old saying, "they fail to *plan*." Trying to build a business without any kind of plan is like riding an exercise bike: You do a lot of pedaling, but you don't get anywhere. If you're just getting started in a business, see the handy "Home-Business Start-Up Checklist" in this chapter and take care of those things first. Then, as time allows, address the other topics in this chapter and put all your plans in writing. Ideally, you'll do this on a computer, but if you don't have a computer yet, a notebook will do for starters.

Writing a Business Plan

Few people would try to build a house without a blueprint and some skill as a builder. However, year after year, thousands of people with little or no real business sense try to build a business without any kind of plan. Often, new business owners—particularly home-business owners—begin as dreamers, believing that their good ideas and willingness to work hard will get them through. But that is not enough. Statistics from the U.S. Small Business Administration tell us that between 45 to 48 percent of all businesses fail within the first five years, and about 95 percent of these failures are attributable to poor management. Don't let these statistics frighten you away from your own business, but do let them serve as a constant reminder that certain business and management skills are essential to success in any moneymaking endeavor.

Business experts generally stress the importance of a business plan in connection with getting a loan. Experience has shown, however, that small, home-based businesses seldom qualify for bank loans, at least in the first few years of existence. Generally they are financed with money from personal savings or family loans. So if you're not planning to apply for a loan, and you are the only person who will ever see your business plan, why should you prepare one?

Peace of mind is one answer. "The benefit of a business plan is security in knowing what you need to do, how much it's all going to cost, and where you can go wrong," says one entrepreneur. "Creating a business plan forced me to think specifically about my goals and the path I would take to reach them," says another. "Reviewing your business plan on a regular basis will not only keep you on track, it may also spark new ideas."

No plan is etched in stone, and all plans have to be changed regularly, based on the records of past experience. Planning thus becomes more realistic, and easier, the longer you are in business. A business plan need not follow any set pattern, nor be any set length, but it is important to get as much information on paper as possible. For instance, a business plan might cover thirty pages and contain several elements, including (not necessarily in this order):

- Business history. How, why, and when it came into being.

- Business summary. A definition of your business, plus a description of your business goals, products, and services, including unique features or customer benefits.

- Management information. Who's behind the business, his/her experience, background, qualifications; the legal form business will take.

- Financial plan. Your expected sales and expense figures for one year, cash flow figures for a year, and a balance sheet showing what the business has, what it owes, and the investment of the owner.

- Manufacturing plan (if you are a manufacturer or creator of goods). Description of required equipment and facilities; how and where raw materials will be obtained, their estimated cost; how/where you will store/inventory them; labor and overhead costs involved in the manufacturing process.

- Production plan. How the work will get done; by whom, and at what cost.

- Market research findings. Your market, your customers, your competition.

- Marketing plan. How you are going to reach and sell to your market (distribution), and the anticipated cost of your marketing effort.

If you do not plan to apply for a loan, why should you bother with a written description of the first three elements in the above business plan outline? You'll know the answer to this the first time you have an opportunity for publicity because these are the points of most interest to many interviewers, reporters, and editors who may give your business publicity in a feature article. Thinking them through in the beginning not only will make you feel good about yourself, but actually will give you ideas on how and where to get publicity once your business is rolling. News releases are often "hooked" on news pegs like these.

If you're a manufacturer, you will need to incorporate a manufacturing plan into your overall business plan. (Anyone who makes anything—by hand or by machinery—is a manufacturer, so when this word is used in later places in the book, remember that it applies to you even if you make only one-of-a-kind, handcrafted wares.)

An important consideration in a small, one-person manufacturing company is who eventually will make the goods when demand for a product increases beyond the owner's ability to produce it. At this point, many business owners turn to independent contractors for assistance, forming small cottage industries that involve a number of homeworkers in one's community. Before you decide on the direction your growing company will take, however, be sure you are well versed in all the legal and tax aspects of using independent contractors vs. employees, a tricky gray area for today's entrepreneurs and a topic discussed at length in this book's companion marketing guide, *HOMEMADE MONEY: Bringing in the Bucks.*

On the SBA's Web site at www.sba.gov/starting/indexbusplans.html, you'll find a good outline for a business plan that you can use as a model when developing a business plan for your business.

Smart Tip

Keep good records so your business plan will contain the kind of details you need to analyze various aspects of your business. Review your plan each year, adding annual updates as needed. Use your plan as both a guide and a goal to work toward, one step at a time.

Your Financial Plan

You may hate the idea of having to prepare a written financial plan, but it can be critical to the success of your endeavor, whether financing is being sought or not. You simply must know, in advance, how much everything is going to cost, and where you are going to get the money you need. (See "Business Loans and Other Money Sources" in Section II.) So many businesses start in a whirlwind of activity only to falter a few months down the line because there is not enough money to keep going.

If you're already in business, it's not difficult to estimate the next year's sales and expenses. But how do you do this if you are just starting? It takes a lot of assumptions, to be sure. You are the only one who can project sales for the first year, and this projection can be based only on what you believe to be the salability of your product or service, and your ability to market it. Much also depends on the time you're going to give your business. If you are a manufacturer, you probably can determine an estimated number of units that might be produced in a year, based on how long it takes to make one, and the number of hours you plan to devote to production each week. By setting a suggested retail price for each unit, you can estimate the revenue that would be generated if certain quantities were sold to certain markets at certain discounts.

If you offer a service, figure out the price you're going to receive for it and estimate the number of customers or clients you could reasonably expect to get as a result of your planned marketing efforts.

Planning Your Moves

If you have difficulty thinking of all the expenses you might possibly incur in the first year, refer to the checklists of tax deductions and other business expenses in Section II and use them to prepare an estimated expenses worksheet.

"Wise planners will take a somewhat conservative view of what is realistic when estimating what can be accomplished with any given level of staff and other resources," notes the Department of Labor in one of its booklets. "It is a disastrous mistake to assume that everything will go according to an ideal utilization of these resources, with no allowance for breakdowns of machinery, delayed deliveries, sickness, and other disturbances of the perfect plan. You must build in a generous contingency factor in any plan—slippage is part of the human condition."

Slippage? You bet. The most important thing I have learned in over three decades of working at home is that nothing is as simple as it seems, everything takes longer than expected, and unexpected happenings will always force us to change our well-laid plans. There is so much more to running a business at home than just taking care of the business details involved in it. In addition to business, there is life, with its infinite variety of large and small crises—family problems, accidents, illness, death, divorce, fires, flooded basements, and what have you. Experience has taught me to build a disaster element into all my plans. Given the unpredictability of life in general, and home businesses in particular, it's wise to anticipate the worst possible thing that could happen to your plans. (Remember Murphy's Law.) Once the worst has been imagined, you can plan around it—or "build in a generous contingency factor," as the Department of Labor suggests. Quick decisions, on the other hand, can be disastrous.

I recall a newspaper publisher who set her subscriber rates according to her print costs. She was working with the least-expensive printer in town, and when he went bankrupt, she found she could not afford the higher rates of other printers. After publishing only a few issues, she was forced out of business. *No matter what your business, always have an option in reserve. Never leave yourself without an escape route.*

 Smart Tip

Plot deadline dates and income expectations on a monthly calendar to help you complete projects by scheduled deadline dates and avoid late-payment charges on bills.

The Many Hats of Business

If you are like most home-business owners, you'll end up doing all the work for awhile, so you may chuckle a bit when you get to the production plan. Still, it's important for you to figure out, in advance, exactly how you are going to get everything done in the time available to you. Stop and think about all the business hats you may have to wear for awhile, and be realistic about your ability to do all the work that may be involved. Following is a list of the many different people you may have to be at one time or another:

- **General Manager.** You get the worrisome jobs simply because you're the decision maker and risk taker. You also get to write all the business plans and read a wide variety of business publications and electronic newsletters to stay informed.

- **Marketing Manager.** You get the job of figuring out who customers might be, where they are, and how you can sell to them. You, too, must read a variety of business and marketing publications (print and electronic) to stay abreast of what's happening in your industry and which marketing strategies are likely to work for you.

- **Advertising Manager.** You work closely with the marketing manager to decide when and where to place ads, and what type (classified or display) to place. It's your job to send for rate cards and sample magazines (and media kits) and explore electronic advertising options on the Web.

- **Publicity Director.** When there is not enough money for paid advertising, your job is to figure out how and where to get free advertising (publicity) for the business, and to develop a good media list for mailings.

- **Copywriter.** Since you must write the copy that goes into the company's sales brochures, flyers, catalogs, advertisements, and news releases, you will need to constantly hone your writing skills by studying the finer points of copywriting shared by experts in books, magazines, and ezines.

- **Graphic Artist and Printer Liaison.** You must work closely with the copywriter to achieve the right blend of copy and art on all printed materials, and you get the job of putting everything together for the printer, as well as following through to the completion of each job.

- **Production Manager.** You get to make the work schedules and determine the quality control standards of your product line.

- **Production Worker** (maybe the whole line). You must complete the work on schedule while meeting the above-mentioned quality control standards.

- **Mail List Supervisor.** You're the one who sets up and maintains the company's mailing lists (customers, prospects, PR list, and other important business contacts) adding and deleting names or making address corrections, etc.

- **Bulk Mail Expert.** If your business involves direct mail advertising of any kind, you get the job of figuring out the post office requirements for bulk mailings and redoing the entire mailing when the post office says you've sorted everything incorrectly.

- **Order Fulfillment Clerk.** You get to process orders and prepare the necessary order forms and shipping labels.

- **Shipping Clerk.** In addition to receiving shipments of raw materials for the manufacturing of products, you get to pack for shipment all outgoing orders, plus take a physical inventory at the end of the year for tax purposes. (You will be greatly relieved when you can afford to hire an outside fulfillment center to handle all orders.)

- **Secretary and Customer Relations Service.** You get to order office supplies, sign for packages, compose and type the business letters, handle customer complaints, and acquire all information needed by management.

- **File Clerk.** You get the job of figuring out what to do with the mountain of paperwork everyone else in the company is generating every day!

- **Bookkeeper.** You will keep inventory records and post all income and expense figures to the company's journals and ledgers—after you have set them up, of course. You will also approve and pay bills, balance the checkbook, and organize and file all receipts for tax purposes.

- **Accountant.** You will analyze the books and handle whatever the bookkeeper can't do, such as fill out government forms for tax deposits or payments, do paperwork related to employees, and prepare quarterly and annual financial reports and tax returns. You must also stay abreast of changes in tax laws that might affect your business.

- **Computer Expert.** One of you guys is also going to have to become the computer expert if you hope to long survive in business. If your business needs to be on the Web, you'll have to spend hundreds of hours learning how to navigate the Web, do business electronically, and set up and maintain a Web site. (Let's give all this work to the general manager, who started this whole thing.)

Whew! Some list, isn't it? Early in her business, speaker, columnist, and consultant Patricia Katz (PatKatz.com), took a humorous approach to this topic by creating special cards for her entire family. She came up with some categories I hadn't thought of, such as manager of the humor department, cheerleader, and captain of the "Knock 'Em Dead" squad. The awesome list above still isn't complete because we've yet to add family and home responsibilities. Since there is a limit to what one person can do alone, it's wise to acknowledge your limits and plan early to find outside help, particularly within your own family. Include all possibilities for assistance, and think of creative ways you might pay for it, including bartering of services or products with business acquaintances, sales commission plans for people who might help you market your product or service, and family bribes, if necessary.

You may be thinking it's impossible for any one person to do all the individual jobs listed above; yet, that's exactly what you'll have to do if you are a sole proprietor with no money to hire outside help. Now do you understand why so many new businesses fail? Too many people start with no idea of all the work that must be done, let alone the special skills or experience some jobs require. As you can see, there are many individual and important jobs to be done, even in the smallest business, and your main job now is to decide which ones you are capable of doing—or learning to do—and which ones you'll have to get help with.

Setting Up Your Office or Workplace

Since whole books have been written on how to set up an office at home, emphasis here must be limited to the importance of creating a space that's entirely your own, one that's comfortable, efficient, and pleasant. Where you locate your home office may depend on whether you will be receiving clients or not. If so, your professional image will be greatly enhanced if clients can be brought into your office through a private entry or impressive front room. If you're the only one who will see your work area, spot yourself in the quietest part of your home, away from family gatherings.

Ideally, your office will be located away from main family activity, such as downstairs in a family room, or a spare bedroom that doesn't have a lot of traffic. In one of her columns, Erma Bombeck once advised readers never to locate their office outside a bathroom door: "We're talking freeway traffic here, plus outbursts of steam, singing and gargling," she warned.

If your work involves considerable detail, pay particular attention to the lighting in your work area because the wrong lighting not only causes visual discomfort, but can also lower productivity. For minimum eye strain, vary the intensity and type of lighting used in your work. "Opt for fluorescent or halogen lamps over incandescent bulbs," advises a spokesperson for an office lighting manufacturer. "Fluorescent or halogen light produces a light that is brighter and whiter than that from incandescent bulbs. This type of light reduces glare, and subsequently reduces eye strain. Also establish two different light intensities because your eyes will get tired if lighting remains at the same intensity level all day long. Ideally, your office will have an overhead light for general office work, and a task light source for specific work areas."

Except for the final preparation of tax forms (which I hate and never intend to do), I have learned to do every job on this list. But I've become familiar with every facet of the tax forms and monitor them like a hawk to make sure my accountant hasn't made a mistake. Although I do not have a college education, I've been working and studying all my life, always believing I could do exactly what I wanted to do. So far I've been able to learn everything I've needed to know, and attained every goal I've set for myself. I believe you can do the same with time and perseverance.

Remember, there are how-to books for everything you can imagine, and your self-education can be reinforced with free information and assistance on the Internet and from government agencies, as well as with seminars and workshops or outside consultants. True, it may take the next five years for you to learn what you need to know, but if self-sufficiency is your ultimate goal, what's five years in the scheme of things? Keep reminding yourself of what I emphasized in the beginning of this book: *Each new thing learned broadens your economic base, and each new skill increases your income potential.* Go for it!

Smart Tip

Put all your goals in written form since they will automatically become a plan. Keep them large enough to motivate you to go forward, yet small enough to be easily achieved.

Doing Market Research

Before you can successfully launch a business, you need to do market research to identify, describe, and categorize the current and future market for a particular product or service. This research is concerned with the customer, the product or service, the competition, and outside forces (like the economy) that might affect one's business. It is interesting detective work and a critical part of your marketing plan.

Too many sellers make the mistake of offering a product or service that pleases them, rather than one that people may want to buy. This is backward thinking. You will find it is a lot easier to fill an existing need than it is to create your own market. (See sidebar, "People's Needs vs. Wants.") The following questions will help you define the market for any new product or service:

People's Needs vs. Wants

What's the difference between selling something people need, as opposed to that which they may only want? Here's how a family income development report, issued by Michigan State University, answered this question:

Most items produced by home industries . . . represent wants (discretionary purchases) on the part of the final consumer, not needs or necessities. The closer an item is to a necessity, and the farther the market extends beyond the local community, the greater the potential for success of the business.

- What, *exactly*, am I trying to sell? (If you can't define your product or service in 50 words or less, you will have a hard time trying to publicize or advertise it.)

- Why do I think my product or service will sell?

- Is my product or service something people want, or need? What are its benefits to buyers?

- If it's something people do not need, why might they want to buy it anyway? (As a gift? For leisure time enjoyment? Business convenience? To save time, money, aggravation? To beautify their home, enrich their life, or satisfy a nostalgic desire?)

- Who is my ideal customer or client? (Male? Female? Young, middle-aged, older? A white-collar worker? Blue-collar worker? Corporate executive? Homebased business person? Professional or technical worker, homemaker, consumer . . . who, exactly?)

- Where do my clients or customers live or work? (In the community, my county, my state, a specific geographic region, or nationwide? Worldwide, perhaps?)

- How can I connect with these people? What trade or consumer periodicals, ezines, organizations, trade shows, directories, or mailing lists are available? What established networks exist for my clients or customers?

- Is my product or service available elsewhere in stores or by mail? At retail or wholesale prices? Can I compete pricewise?

- Is there currently a strong demand for my product or service? Why? Is it related to the economy? Is demand likely to increase, or decrease, with a change in the economy? Is the current demand a fad, or is it likely to endure for a long time? If a fad, can I move quickly to capitalize on it before it dies?

- Is the market for my product or service likely to expand slowly, quickly, or not at all? Is my product or service closely tied to some other, similar product or service for which the market could expand—or collapse—very quickly?

- Is my entry into the marketplace more dependent on price than on quality? If so, can I successfully compete in this type of market?

- What kind of competition will I/do I have . . . locally, regionally, nationally?

- Is my product or service newer, better, different from that of my competition? Does it offer higher quality? Longer life? More speed or efficiency? (The very fact that competition exists proves a demand, or at least a *need* for what you offer. In the end, your competition may become your marketing strength, provided you work with it and not against it.)

- How does my competition publicize and sell? Will the same techniques work for me? What can I offer, say, and do that they can't?

- Is the competition overlooking a segment of the market I can reach? (Larger companies often ignore smaller markets because they are not worth their time and trouble, but such markets may be perfect niche markets for homebased entrepreneurs.

- If there is no competition, why? (Maybe the need for your product or service is being satisfied in some other way, or maybe it simply is not a profitable idea to begin with—or maybe your idea is so new and unique, no one has thought of it yet.)

Smart Tip

To take the mystery out of marketing, look for clues to who your customers or clients might be, where they are located, and how you might reach them with publicity, advertising, or sales calls. It's not enough to know that a market exists for what you offer. *What is important is that you know—in advance—exactly how you're going to connect with it, promote to it, and sell to it.*

Outline for a Simple Marketing Plan

Once you have answered the market research questions posed above, it should be easy for you to write a marketing plan, even if the only marketing you've ever done before was shop for groceries. Here's an outline to help you tighten your focus and draft a plan that will enable you to develop successful strategies for your business:

- **What do I do?** (Write a description of your business in 25 words or less.)

- **How does my product or service benefit buyers?** (Buyers do not buy products or services per se, but rather the *benefits* offered by those products or services.)

- **How do I want to be perceived by my buyers or clients?** (Your positioning and core concept statements—see sidebar on this topic.)

- **What are the characteristics of my target audience?** (Indicate age, income, lifestyle, geographic location, etc., along with whatever your market research information to date tells you about the total number of potential customers in your target area, the share of the market you expect to capture, and why.)

- **Who is my competition?** (Write a description of your competitors, what you think their share of the market is, what you think their strengths and weaknesses are, what they might do to take business away from you, and how you'd fight back.)

Your Positioning and Core Concept Statements

"Positioning" is a common marketing strategy even the smallest business can employ. It is not something you do to your business so much as what you do to the minds of your prospects to make them perceive you in a particular way.

In creating a "positioning statement," you need to consider what business you're in, your primary goal, what you feel your strengths and weaknesses are as compared to those of your competition, and how you see the need for your product or service in today's marketplace. In short, you need to be able to state *why your product or service has value, and why it should be purchased.* No product or service can be all things to all people, and if you do not deliberately position your products, services, and your business itself, you may find they have been positioned by circumstances you do not control, and not always to your advantage.

Once you've written a positioning statement, try to create a "core concept" statement as well—a tight seven-word summarization of your positioning statement. Remember that what you do isn't exactly what you *do.* Consider, for example, this positioning statement of a homebased beauty shop owner who doesn't just "do women's hair."

"No," she says, "I satisfy the need for physical enhancement among working women in my town who don't have much time."

To translate this positioning statement into a seven-word "core statement," she might say, "I make busy working women look good!"

- **How will I market my product or service?** (Will you sell to the private sector or to the business community, and will you deal with buyers or clients directly or indirectly; retail or wholesale, market by mail, through reps, trade shows, on the Internet, and so on.

- **How will I advertise, and where?** (Display ads or classifieds in local papers or national magazines? Distribution of flyers? Direct marketing methods? Trade ads, shows and conventions? Electronic bulletin boards, mailing lists, or Web sites? And don't forget your publicity opportunities!)

Planning Your Moves

- **What are my selling policies?** (You'll need to establish standard credit terms, guaranties, customer discounts, returns policy, shipping or delivery charges, etc.)

- **Is my pricing okay?** (Is it in line with industry standards? Does the present economy in your market area justify higher or lower prices for certain products or services in your line? How do your prices compare to those of your competitors? If lower, are you sure you can make a profit after all costs are considered, and do you really want to accept anything less than what your competition gets? If your prices are higher, can you justify them by offering something special your competition does not? Why might your prospects gladly pay a higher price for what you offer? Again, think of the *benefits* you can offer.)

You've got the idea now. After creating your first rough-draft marketing plan, you'll have something to build on. And, as you gain additional marketing information and expertise, you will begin to fully understand how better marketing automatically leads to greater income.

"A sound marketing plan," says one marketing expert, "is a prophecy of coming events. It contains the specific steps designed to make the prophecy come true." Like a business plan, a marketing plan will always be changing, based on sales results and the results of any special tests you may run. Marketing is something you must do throughout the entire life of your business, so don't think you can rest on your laurels once you have come up with a good marketing plan. It may work beautifully for awhile, but you cannot expect to stay ahead of your competition unless you constantly test new markets, new marketing methods, and new advertising and promotional ideas. Nothing stays the same, least of all business, so be aware of changes taking place that may affect your business.

In time, you may find it necessary to change your prices, your product or business name, your packaging, designs or colors, your marketing outlets, the function of your product or service, even the entire image or personality of your business. You will know when it's time to make changes, too, because your sales will level off or begin to drop for no apparent reason. By doing a little planning before the worst happens, you'll be prepared to take off quickly in a new and more profitable direction.

Homemade Money

Here's a handy reminder checklist of the tax and legal matters you need to take care of as you begin a new business. Detailed information about each task will be found in Section II, under the topic heading shown in parenthesis after each listing.

1 Call or visit city hall or county clerk
- ____ to check on local zoning laws (see "Zoning Laws").
- ____ for information about a license or permit (see "Licenses and Permits").
- ____ to register your business name (see "Business or Trade Name/Fictitious Name Statement").

2 Call state capital
- ____ to register your business name on the state level (see "Business or Trade Name").
- ____ about a resale tax number if you plan to sell taxable products (see "Resale Tax Number").

3 Call local financial institutions
- ____ to compare cost of a business checking account (see "Business Checking Account").
- ____ about a safe deposit box for storage of valuable business papers or computer disks.

4 Call insurance agents
- ____ about business rider on house insurance, or need for separate in-home insurance policy (see "Insurance/Homeowner's or Renter's Insurance Policies").
- ____ about benefits of an umbrella policy for extra liability insurance (see "Insurance/Personal Liability Insurance").
- ____ about car insurance/use for business (see "Insurance/Vehicle Insurance").
- ____ about product liability insurance if you are wholesaling products of any kind (see "Insurance/Product Liability Insurance").

Planning Your Moves

5   Call friends for the names of a good accountant or attorney if you
    think you need one (see "Accountant" and "Attorney/Lawyer").

6   Get free information from these government agencies:
    ____ Internal Revenue Service (see "Taxes Businesses Must Pay").
    ____ Consumer Product Safety Commission (see "Consumer Safety
         Laws").
    ____ Bureau of Consumer Protection (see "Consumer Safety Laws").
    ____ Federal Trade Commission (see "Federal Trade Commission").
    ____ Copyright Office (see "Copyrights").
    ____ Patent and Trademark Office (see "Trademarks").

Chapter 9

Developing Necessary Printed Materials

Your printed materials represent you and your business. Make sure they convey the image you want your clients or customers to have.
—Anon.

One way to make your business look successful, even when it's not, is to have classy printed materials—a well-designed business card, a good letterhead and matching envelopes printed on quality stock, and a brochure. It's nice, but not necessary, to have your card match your letterhead. As your business grows, you may need a number of other printed materials, including promotional flyers, a catalog, price lists, order forms, news releases, postcards, and so on.

Many beginners in business fail to grasp the direct relationship between good printing and more sales or business. It's tough for any homebased business to succeed if its professional image isn't comparable to that of its competitors. No matter how professional you may be in your business dealings, you must be concerned with *the buying attitudes of prospective customers*. A few will always buy, regardless of a seller's image, simply because they really want or need the

167

advertised product or service. But to long survive in business, you must eventually *sell* all those other prospects whose interest has only been piqued. If such prospects are also being solicited by the competition, a buying decision is likely to rest on the professionalism of one's marketing approach and printed materials. (The same logic applies to businesses being run exclusively on the Web.)

If you create art or crafts, convey your professionalism by designing an "artist card" that speaks of your experience or shares the story behind your art or craftwork. Such cards will make your products seem more valuable to customers and enable you to get higher prices for everything you sell.

Designing Your Own Printed Materials

If you have a computer and inkjet or laser printer, you can easily design and print outstanding stationery, business cards, and brochures using regular paper or some of the exciting preprinted and scored papers available. These papers are not inexpensive, but when you really want to make an impression on a few prospective clients or customers, they do the job beautifully. The best thing is that you can print as few or as many as you wish, buying stock in boxes of about a hundred sheets at a time. For larger quantities of printed materials, you will save money by working with a local copy center or "quick printer."

Request free samples from the following companies. Both offer colorful preprinted papers for stationery, flyers, business cards, postcards, presentation folders, labels, and much more: Great Papers, 1-800-287-8163, www.PaperShowcase.com, and Paper Direct, 1-800-A-Papers, www.PaperDirect.com.

If you don't have a computer, or you feel uncomfortable about designing your own printed materials, discuss your needs with an artist (check with the art department of your local high school or college), or call printers in your area. If you can use a computer, but just don't have one yet, check out local print shops or service centers such as the franchised Kinko's Copy Centers, which offer do-it-yourself services that include the use of their computers and software and whatever assistance you may need. Some entrepreneurs use these centers almost like a temporary office at nights or on weekends. (Most Kinko's shops are open 24 hours a day.) Or, if you don't want to do it yourself, you can bring in copy on disk with a sketch of what you want, specify the fonts and design elements you like, then turn the job over to an expert.

When it comes to a decision between price and quality, only you can decide what's essential for your business. Just remember that your customer is likely to judge you, your product, and your service on the quality of your printed materials. Superior printing isn't always necessary for promotional flyers, price lists, and certain other printed materials such as inner-office forms and order blanks. But your brochure or catalog—the piece that really carries your business—*that* has to look not just good, but great. So should your stationery, business cards, and catalog sheets for wholesale buyers. (You don't apologize for your products or your service; neither should you have to apologize for the printed materials that describe them.) If you have a salable product or service to begin with, the cost of better brochures and other promotional printed materials will always be offset by greater sales and profits.

Business Card Design and Copy Tips

An originally designed card (which may not cost any more than a standard raised-letter business card) can speak volumes about you and the quality of your business, product, or service. The kind and color of card stock you select, the ink, the artwork—all these things convey to your customers or clients an image of you and your business. Think twice about the image you want them to have.

Types of Cards

Standard-sized cards are most likely to be saved in regular business card files, but odd-size cards have their place, particularly when they serve an extra purpose. Some people use oversized cards so they can print a map on the back to direct customers to their out-of-the-way business. (I recall one craft shop owner who got his business cards paid for by tying the location of his crafts gallery to that of a hotel in his area.) Others suggest that their card can double as a bookmark, or they add special information on the back to turn the card into a promotional freebie.

Folded cards may also be appropriate and impressive, especially if you want to include more than the usual amount of information about you or your business. In fact, this kind of card can be an effective mini-brochure. Now that photo cards have become more affordable, many small businesses are using them with great success. Photo cards may include a picture of you or more of your products—which makes them especially valuable to crafts sellers who lack color flyers. Such cards are an excellent visual marketing tool—a mini-billboard—likely to be kept longer than regular business cards. Printed messages may be included on the front or back, or both.

Copy Guidelines

In creating the copy to be used on your card, include your name as well as your business name, plus a line that describes your business specialty, your products, or your service. Add your logo or business motto if you have one. (Example: A chimney sweep's card reads, "Satisfaction guaranteed or double your soot back!") In listing your telephone number, be sure to include the area code since there are now many different area codes in the same region. (Note that use of your home telephone number as a business number is prohibited by telephone company regulations. For more information on this topic, see "Telephone" in Section II of this book.)

If you have a business e-mail address or Web site, this information should be prominently displayed on the card. Unless it's absolutely necessary to get business, however, *do not* include your home address on your business card. This will not only help protect your privacy, but will discourage would-be thieves and possibly avoid problems with local officials as well. (After ordering her business cards, one of my readers in El Paso learned it was a violation of local regulations to print a home address on a business card.) If you sell anything by mail, rent a post office box for your business mail.

Business Card Design Tips
by Diana Ratliff, BusinessCardDesigns.com

Here are some tips for designing business cards that will work as hard as *you* do:

1. Visualize your typical customer, or the typical situation in which a customer will use your card, and design your card to match. Do you market to senior citizens? Use large type. Is your card pulled out in emergencies (the toilet is overflowing)? Make sure your phone number is highlighted. An address is not essential on every card.

2. If it's not evident from your company name, be sure to add a tagline or slogan describing what you do and who you do it for.

3. Add color. Using colored ink (such as brown or maroon) or colored card stock is an inexpensive way to make standard cards more visually appealing. There are many printers (particularly online) who print in full color for very reasonable prices.

4. Use the back side of your card to add testimonials, give directions, cite your guarantee, describe product benefits, and so on. Don't drop the font size so you can cram everything onto the front. (According to printers, overcrowding a card is the single biggest design mistake.)

5. Create more than one card for use in different situations. Create a "personal networking card" for times you'd prefer not to reveal a company affiliation. Have general and specific cards made. (*Example:* one saying "Attorney at Law" and the other stating your specialty, "Personal Injury Specialist.") For some industries, a "fun" card is acceptable as well.

In my experience, printing your own cards from paper you buy at the office supply store is a false economy for most businesses. You're seen as unprofessional and unwilling to invest in your company. Your business card is a reflection of you, sending a statement to recipients about your personality and professionalism. Make sure you're proud to give it!

Brochure Design Considerations

Your brochure should be a handy reminder of what you offer customers or clients. It should focus on the benefits of your product or service, include some customer testimonials, and convey your overall professionalism.

Paper and Color Considerations

Paper does make a difference. There are soft, velvety papers, dozens of different kinds of textured stock, papers in light colors, bright colors, *electric* colors! Feel the paper. . . let it speak to you. When you select a paper that matches the mood of whatever you're selling, your customers and prospects will take notice.

The right color has much to do with order response. For example, older buyers who have difficulty in reading may automatically toss mailers that are printed with black ink on red or dark blue paper, not to mention type that is too small to read. While men may hate pink, women tend to love it. Once when I changed the color of one of my standard follow-up mailers from a sedate ivory to a shocking yellow, I received an amazing 8 percent order response when 3 percent would have been the norm. I never used ivory for that group of prospects again. Experiment, experiment!

Photographs and Line Drawings

A picture of you on your brochure could make a difference in the response you get. Silvana Clark, who offers innovative presentations for seminars, workshops, and banquets, says the inclusion of a picture of her dressed in a safari suit has made a big difference in getting jobs. "I frequently get calls from people who say the picture on my brochure (and on my Web site) makes me look like an entertaining speaker. Spending the extra money to get good quality paper has made me proud to leave my brochure with groups I speak for."

When selling my books and reports by mail, I always used my photograph on mail pieces because people often commented that my "smiling face" made them feel comfortable about ordering from me, even though they'd never heard of me before. I also used line drawings of myself on other items such as promotional newsletters and follow-up postcards to prospects who earlier received my mailings.

Artists will generally do a line drawing for about $35–$75, but here's how to do your own: Lay a smooth piece of clear plastic that will accept ink over a head-shot photo of yourself, then carefully trace the picture onto the plastic overlay using a fine-point black pen. Using your scanner or photocopy machine that offers reduction/enlargement capabilities, create the number and size of line drawings needed. Product sellers could do the same thing to create illustrations of certain products. (Long before we had inexpensive scanners, a craftsman told me he created line drawings by first taking close-up slides of his products, then projecting them onto white paper hung on a wall so he could trace the image.)

Do You Really Need a Brochure?
by Ilise Benun, author of *Self Promotion Online*
SelfPromotionOnline.com

Just because someone says, "send me your brochure," doesn't mean that's what you have to send. What they really mean is, "I want to know more about your business. Send me some information." Don't let the fact that you don't have an official "brochure" prevent you from getting that important information to your potential clients in a timely manner.

Brochures are valuable because they give your prospects something tangible in your absence and can convey stability or reliability. But the creation of a brochure is often a long and expensive process and, depending on the nature of your business, may be unnecessary. Letters and postcards are viable options that offer you flexibility and are considerably more cost-efficient.

Even if you have a Web site, you still need something tangible— something your prospects can put in a pile and then act on when they're ready. Send a letter, postcard, brochure or press clipping to follow up with a prospect who isn't quite ready to sign on the dotted line or to remind a past client of their interest in you and your services or products.

Proofing Copy. If you've done all the writing, typing, and proofreading of your brochure copy, ask someone else to proof the piece before printing. I've learned from experience that it's impossible for the creator of such work to spot all the errors in it because the mind tends to "see" what it knows is supposed to be there, whether it's there or not.

Smart Tip

Be sure to check the weight of a sample piece before printing to make sure it can be mailed at the rate you desire (brochures under one ounce, for instance). Also make sure the size of your mail piece is standard, according to postal regulations, or you will incur a penalty charge on each piece mailed.

A Crash Course in Working with Printers

At some time in the future, you may need a specialty printer instead of an offset printer like the quick-print shops now found in even the smallest of towns. Because specialty printers specialize in printing only envelopes, package inserts, business forms, catalogs, or bound books, their prices are generally lower than other "general printers." Such printers can work with you by mail, and you can find them by searching the Web or reading ads in trade magazines or books on mail order or self-publishing.

Getting Printing Quotes

It's always a good idea to get quotes from more than one printer, and samples of their work, too, because the type of equipment they use, and the size of their presses, will dictate the prices they can give. In working with a variety of printers over the years, I found that the local printer who did my postcards and self-mailers couldn't begin to compete, pricewise, with the printer in Minnesota who printed my newsletter and 12-page catalog. And neither of those printers could compete with the printer in Michigan who did all my book printing. In requesting a quote for any print job, put your specifications in writing, and ask for quotes on different stocks and weights of paper. Sometimes paper alone can double or triple the cost of a job, and sometimes it also throws the weight of your printed piece into a different postage bracket. The use of colored stock will normally add 15 to 20 percent to the cost of any print job, and each color of ink used in addition to the basic color (usually black) adds to your cost, too, because the press has to be washed after each color is used.

Ask for quotes on different quantities, too, such as 500, 1,000, and 2,500 for small press runs, and 5,000, 7,500 and 10,000 for larger runs. The first 500 copies cost the most, due to the printer's expenses in preparing negatives and plates and setting up the presses. After that, the primary expense will be paper and press time only, which is nominal in comparison to other costs mentioned. Don't make the mistake, however, of ordering more printing than you can use on the notion that you're saving money.

Printing Terms

When ordering stationery, business forms, brochures, and other printing, communication with the printer will be easier if you are familiar with the following printing terms:

- Bleed—is when the printed image or a color screen extends to the trim edge of the page.
- Color Proof—is something you should get before authorizing a large print run of a brochure. (This costs a little extra, but it gives you a chance to spot any errors before the job is printed.)
- Color Separation—is the process of separating full color illustrations into the primary printing colors in negative or positive form.
- Matte Finish—is dull paper finish without a gloss, often used on photographs.
- Mechanical—is a term for artwork that is all pasted up and camera-ready. (All type, photos, line art, etc. are positioned on one piece of artboard.)
- Ream—500 sheets of paper. (Stationery is often ordered by the ream.)

—An excerpt from *The Crafts Business Answer Book & Resource Guide* by Barbara Brabec (M. Evans)

Quick Printing vs. Metal Plates

The quick-printing process uses paper plates that are discarded after use. Whenever you need a print run of a thousand pieces or more, or if your job incorporates more than one color of ink, or you think you'll need to reprint the same piece later on, the printer will make negatives and metal plates for printing. Once you've paid for the print job, the corresponding negatives belong to you. The printer will be happy to store them for possible future use, but there may be a limit on the length of time such materials are retained for customers, so be sure to check this point. (You never know when you might need to change printers.)

A good printer will take the time to help you with your printing problems and will answer your questions because the more you know, the easier his job will be. Also, the better your camera-ready artwork, the better the finished job, and the happier you'll be. Always put your printing instructions in writing, one copy for you, one for the printer. All kinds of things can go wrong in a print shop, and if the error is the printer's, you will want to be able to show it with your written instructions. Good printers will always do a job over at no charge if they've made the mistake.

Smart Tip

For everyone's protection, especially yours, ask to see a "blue line" before final plates are made for a long press-run job. Better to find typographic errors and other problems at this point than to end up with 5,000 catalogs or brochures that have something wrong with them.

In summary, good printed materials make a difference to buyers. If you have no printed materials at all, you are telling the world you're an amateur. If your printed materials are of poor design or print quality, prospective customers or clients will question the quality of your products or services. Thus, attractive printed materials enhance your professional image, make you feel good about your business, and enable you to charge higher prices than the competition.

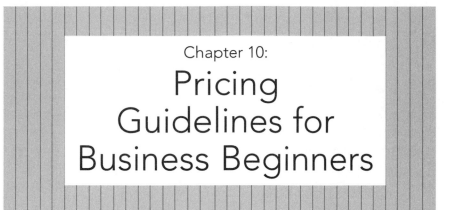

Chapter 10:

Pricing Guidelines for Business Beginners

Never charge a client what you think you're worth; charge what you think *he's* worth.
  —Anon.

Pricing can make or break your business. That's why it must be your first marketing consideration. As one expert put it, "If your price is wrong, it hardly matters whether you do everything else right."

Unless you are involved in a product business where the retail price of the merchandise you sell already has been set or suggested by someone else, you are going to have pricing problems of one kind or another throughout the life of your business.

Product and service sellers alike need to be concerned with the same basic pricing factors; the value of one's time, profit, overhead, labor costs, and so on. In addition, there are a number of intangible factors to consider, such as market trends, the way price affects one's image (and thus the growth of a business), and the preconceived notions buyers have about the worth of certain things. Product makers (manufacturers) have yet another major factor to consider: the cost of raw materials and their availability at wholesale prices.

Finding Supply Sources

One of the easiest ways to find the special suppliers you need—from raw materials to service providers—is to obtain copies of the Yellow Pages from large cities such as Chicago, New York, and Los Angeles. Call your telephone office for information on how to obtain the directories you need.

Many other suppliers can be found simply by searching the Web, but you may also want to thumb through library directories such as the *Thomas Register of American Manufacturers* and annual directories published by trade magazines. (The *Thomas Register* is also on the Web at www.ThomasRegister.com, where you can do a search of more than 170,000 manufacturers by product, company, or brand name.)

Another way to find the special suppliers you need is to network with others in your industry, either on the Internet or through membership in professional or business organizations, as well as through subscriptions to newsletters and trade periodicals. Sometimes members of an organization band together to buy supplies on a cooperative basis—something you might want to explore.

As a consumer with a lifetime of shopping experience behind you, it's only natural to ask yourself how much you would be willing to pay for your product or service if you were the buyer instead of the seller. This kind of common sense logic in evaluating the prices you set is fine if you happen to be selling to a market of buyers much like yourself. But unless you're rich, or at least a "free spender," you may find it hard to believe that some people might actually pay the price you need to make a profit on whatever it is you are selling. People in this category tend to keep their prices low because they are afraid no one will buy at a higher price.

This is just one of the little traps sellers sometimes fall into. Time and again I have heard people say, "But no one will pay more than this for what I offer." Sometimes that's true, but often this statement is based on belief, not fact, and such belief is directly tied to one's own spending habits. While fearful sellers sit around complaining that no one will pay more, smart entrepreneurs come along and offer the same kind of products and services at two or three times the price—and get it. Why? Because they know some things fearful sellers do not. They know their marketplace, they have marketing savvy, and they know exactly what it takes to get people to part with their money.

One thing you should never do is apologize for working at home. Instead, stress this benefit: *You provide a quality product or service at a more reasonable price because you are a homebased business without a retailer's overhead expenses—and customer service is your specialty*. Be careful never to say your prices are *cheaper*. The fact that you work at home is no excuse for lowering prices. Even when your prices are the same as a retail competitor, your pricing edge is the fact that you are able to give your customers more individual attention and personal service than the average retailer can.

Smart Tip

Don't lower your prices—*improve* your product or service! Price is rarely the most important reason for lack of sales. More often than not, the fault lies with the product or service itself and the fact that people just don't need or want it.

The Value of Your Time

Few people seem willing to set a price on the worth of their own time, yet everyone in business must do this, and soon. Most people who work at home don't have enough time to begin with. As their home-business workload increases, each hour seems more precious and fleeting.

The decision as to what one's time is worth is quite personal. It is influenced by many factors, including one's education or degree of skill, age, professional reputation (if any), amount of salaried job experience, level of confidence, and degree of boldness or nerve. Where a person lives also has much to do with the pricing of a product or service, as does a person's need for money or lack of need for it.

Homemakers-turned-business-owners often feel as though their time has no real value, particularly if they lack salaried job experience. But it is not job experience that determines the worth of one's time in a business, it is what one does with the time that counts. It's what you know, and what you know you are capable of doing. Don't sell yourself short. Your time is worth as much as anyone else's.

People with full-time jobs naturally equate the value of their time to their present salary, while others may decide on an hourly rate by asking themselves what they could earn if they went out and got a job. This is a good place to start, but Kate Kelly, author of *How to Set Your Fees and Get Them*, (KateKelly.com) reminds us that self-employed people should multiply the hourly rate they receive in a salaried job by at least 2.5. In her book, she explains:

> *Let's suppose that you're making $16,000 per year on staff. That means you earn approximately $308 per week; $62 per day, and $8 per hour. To arrive at a starting figure for your hourly rate once you are self-employed, multiply $8 by 2.5 (some even say by 2.8 or 3). This means that you would use $20 an hour for your initial estimate as to what you might charge. The true reason for the multiple figure is overhead.*

I can just hear some of you product makers hollering, "But I can't charge $20/hour for my time. That would put the price of my products totally out of reason." If you're making all the products you sell, you may be right. But this only emphasizes the fact that it is difficult, if not impossible, to make a large amount of money when you—the business owner—are also the entire labor force. In that case, maybe what you ought to do is set several different hourly rates for the various jobs you do; perhaps $20/hour for design time or marketing, and a lower rate for labor (based on whatever you would have to pay to hire a production worker).

Remember that while owners of product businesses can make a profit from the individual items they sell, owners of service businesses must include in their hourly price whatever profit they hope to realize at year's end. In truth, the only product they have to sell is their time and expertise, and it must be valued accordingly.

In this light, then, $20/hour isn't much money at all, especially when one considers what professionals in many fields currently receive. I think one problem here is that many of us are still living in the past (particularly if we have been out of the job market for some time), before inflation took its toll and dramatically increased the price of everything. Many professionals who work at home command and get $50–$100 an hour and more for their services, but hourly rates like these are generally based on special skills, knowledge, or years of experience in a particular field. You may have a long way to go before you reach this point, or you may be there now and just don't know it. One thing is sure: No matter how much an hour we are finally able to get, there will always be someone else who can get more, and all we can do is shake our heads in wonder. I felt terrific when I was finally able to get

Hourly Rate Pricing Formula

Before any pricing formula will work, you have to come up with some kind of hourly rate for your time or labor. Here is one of the most sensible formulas[1] I have ever found. It can be applied to any kind of business.

Desired annual net income ÷ number of working hours per year + annual expenses ÷ number of working hours per year = hourly rate needed to realize desired annual net income.

Here, the hourly rate is determined through a calculation based on time and expenses. Decide how much you would like to net for the year, then estimate the number of working hours per week and multiply this figure by 50 weeks (giving yourself two weeks' vacation). Then add your fixed, variable, and selling expenses for the year and divide by the number of working hours per year. Add this hourly figure to the first hourly figure to get the final hourly rate you will need to charge to realize your desired net income at year's end.

Example: Let's say you desire $30,000 net income, and you work full time 40 hours per week × 50 weeks, or 2,000 work hours per year. Divide net income by 2,000 work hours to get a $15 hourly rate for your time. Now add up expenses for the year. Let's assume they are $38,249. Divide this expense figure by 2,000 hours to get an hourly expense rate of $19.13. Add this to the $15 figure to get a total of $34.13, or the amount you must charge per hour to realize $30,000 net income at year's end.

---

[1] Libby Platus's Pricing Principle, as noted in *The Crafts Report.*

$1,000 a day as a speaker . . . until I met a fellow who said he charged $1,000 *an hour* for his business advice. But as my husband has so often said, "Charging that much—and getting it—are two different things entirely."

Smart Tip

Set up a daily work schedule for yourself that is right for your personality, lifestyle and family responsibilities, and try to develop a routine that is normal for you (even if others think it's weird). Be firm about having private time for yourself, and set specific times for family activities or visits with friends.

Buying Materials Wholesale

Next to labor, the cost of materials is the most important consideration in setting the price on any product. Small manufacturers and other individuals who create a limited number of products for sale each year often run into trouble when it comes to obtaining wholesale prices. Manufacturers and distributors in certain industries (the crafts industry, in particular) often will not sell to anyone who lacks a storefront. (It doesn't matter whether a buyer can meet their minimum quantity order requirements or not.)

In other industries, suppliers don't care where one works; mostly they want evidence that you are a legitimate business and not a hobby buyer, have a resale tax number, and can meet their minimum order requirements. (Small budgets, however, sometimes make this impossible. And whenever any material used in the production of goods for sale has to be bought at retail prices, a lot of the maker's profit goes down the drain.)

Some manufacturers sell to dealers, bypassing wholesalers and distributors entirely, while others sell only through wholesalers and distributors. When you find a manufacturer who will sell to you at dealer prices, but whose minimum quantity requirements are too high, ask for the name of the distributor nearest you. If you cannot meet the distributor's minimum quantity requirement, the next thing to try is to approach a dealer who carries the materials you want. Ask for a 20 percent "professional discount," but if this is a retail store, don't do it in earshot of customers or you'll get a fast turndown. Instead, telephone for an appointment to discuss your situation and explain the benefits to the retailer. (Your orders from a small retail store might enable the owner to buy in greater quantity and thus get a greater discount on the material or item in question. This strategy has often worked for fabric buyers.)

With supplier catalogs in hand, your next job will be to convince them you are entitled to wholesale prices—a legitimate business. Do this by having a professional letterhead, and send well-typed letters requesting catalogs. Don't give explanations. Just say, "Will you please send me a copy of your current catalog? Thank you." The businesslike appearance of your letter should do the rest. (If you don't know the proper format for typing a business letter, obtain a secretarial how-to book from the library.)

When you receive a catalog and decide to order, be prepared to meet the company's minimum quantity requirements without question. If you are concerned that you might not qualify in their eyes as a legitimate dealer, send your first order on a purchase order (get them at any office supply store), include your resale tax number (See "Resale Tax Number" in Section II), and enclose a check for the total amount of the order. (Few companies will turn away an order with a check attached.) You might also send a cover letter saying you are enclosing payment because you need the materials quickly. If you plan to continue ordering from this company, ask for a credit application at this time so you can be invoiced the next time around.

Finding reliable and affordable suppliers is a major challenge for all business owners regardless of size or type. It's a job you must do for yourself, and it may take a couple of years before you finally solve your particular supplier problems. (See sidebar, "Finding Supply Sources.")

Smart Tip

Never build a business around a product that's available from only one source because you'll be out of business if that source ever dries up. Keep looking for alternative sources of supply you can tap in an emergency.

Bringing Overhead into the Picture

As emphasized above, overhead is an important factor in pricing products and services alike. Overhead includes all the operating costs of a business that are not directly related to the production of a specific product or service. Such costs are generally fixed, monthly expenses. Even when a business is generating zero income, overhead costs will be adding up. (See nearby sidebar for list of typical overhead costs.)

If you have been in business for at least a year, it will be fairly easy for you to pull all these overhead figures together to arrive at an average monthly cost. If you are just starting, you can do some fancy guessing and estimating. (You might start with a figure that is 8 to 10 percent of anticipated gross sales.)

To illustrate how overhead figures fit into the pricing picture, let's assume your annual business overhead costs are $3,000, and you're working 1,000 hours per year on your business. That means your hourly overhead rate is $3 per hour. You can either add this hourly figure to the one you arrived at earlier for your time, or, if you make goods for sale, you can apply it proportionally to each product on a percentage basis.

Assume for example a $3 per hour overhead cost. If you can make three of something per hour, you would add $1 to the labor and materials cost for each of those three products. Or, if it takes two hours to make a product, you would add $6 in overhead costs to each product.

Some production workers use a different method based on the total cost of labor plus materials. For example, if you spend $15,500 to produce your goods in a year, and you have $3,000 in overhead costs, you would divide $3,000 by $15,500 to get a percentage of 19.4 percent overhead to production. That translates to $.19, the amount that should be added to every dollar of production costs on an item.

> **Example:** An item costs $10.39 in labor and materials. Add 19 percent of this figure ($1.97), increasing total cost to $12.36.

Start now to document all the overhead costs that will affect the profitability of your business in the months and years to come. At the beginning of each new business year, refer to these figures to see how much your overhead costs have increased because of inflation and other expense factors, then increase your prices if necessary.

How to Quote a Job

You'll recall Kate Kelly's pricing advice earlier in this chapter. In quoting a job, Kate stresses giving yourself plenty of time to figure the price you need. "No matter when the subject of money comes up," she says, "make it a practice of getting back later with a figure. Unless you're simply quoting an hourly or daily rate which you've set in advance, or if it's a fee on a propos-

A Checklist of Overhead Items

General Office Expenses
Telephone and fax
Internet Service Provider (ISP) fee
Office and computer supplies
Stationery and other printed materials
Postage and postal fees
Bank charges
Legal and professional expenses
Subscriptions, memberships, conference fees

Home Office Expenses (a portion of)
Rent or mortgage expense
Taxes
Utilities
Insurance

Selling Costs
Show fees and display expenses
Sales commissions
Photography
Packaging
Shipping and freight charges
Samples
Advertising
Promotional mailings
Cost of merchant card service
Web site hosting fee
Web site development/maintenance costs

Other Expenses
Travel and auto expenses
Equipment purchases
Maintenance and depreciation
Employee or independent contractor expense
Cleaning and repairs
Business interest expense
All other costs related to the overall operation of a business

al you've written (when you've had ample time to consider how much work is involved), then it's too early to talk money."

Different jobs will require different rate structures. You will need to consider quoting by the hour, versus by the day, per head or per project. Some jobs lend themselves to a flat rate charge, while others need to be charged on a retainer or contingency fee basis. (See sidebar, "Hourly Rate Pricing Formula.")

In Chapter Six, I shared some fee guidelines for teachers, speakers, and consultants. Some professionals charge by the hour when their services are required for only an hour or two, and offer a more economical hourly rate for a full day's work. In setting a daily rate, much has to do with the amount of preparation time required, not to mention time lost to travel. When I first began as a speaker, I thought I was doing well to get $250, then $500 a day plus expenses. But reality soon set in when I considered that this "daily fee" actually had to cover at least four days of my time: a full day of preparation (planning the program, gathering handout materials, packing, etc.); a day of traveling (often to rural areas with poor plane connections and possibly a long car ride once I landed); the day of the workshop; and another long trip home the following day. In addition, such trips wore me out physically and emotionally (fifty workshop students picking your brain is mentally exhausting), so I didn't accomplish much the next day back at my desk. I suspect many other people who sell their services are making the same kind of mistake I made in the early years of my business and will eventually make adjustments in their pricing or stop offering certain services because they aren't profitable enough to continue.

Some jobs are better quoted by the project, particularly if the job is one you know you can do easily and quickly, but is one that may seem difficult to the client. As Kate points out, people often react poorly to knowing how much she earns an hour. "When they compute and compare their hourly staff pay with mine, they tend to forget that I must pay for my own insurance, set aside my own pension benefits, and budget for any vacation time I take. What's more, I couldn't possibly bill out forty hours a week, so my overall income is almost surely less than they expect."

In setting fees of any kind, consider your overall experience and expertise. Just because you may be able to do a job in a day doesn't mean someone else could do it that quickly, or as well as you. The client, after all, is buying *your* experience and expertise. You are not obligated to tell him how quickly you have done the job. There are definite advantages in not delivering a job too quickly, lest the client thinks he has, indeed, been overcharged. As Kate confirms, "I once billed

The Profit Factor

"Profit" and "wages" are not the same thing, though many who work at home tend to forget this fact. After all expenses (including owner's salary) have been deducted, the idea is that there still should be something left over as profit for the owner or company. But there won't be if you forget to include profit in your pricing formula.

As emphasized earlier, service providers must include in their hourly price whatever profit they hope to realize at year's end because the only "product" they have to sell is their time and expertise, and it must be valued accordingly. Product sellers, on the other hand, need to learn how to make a profit on all the individual items they sell. It can be an expensive mistake to set the retail and wholesale price of a product based only on the cost of materials, labor, and overhead. The following example illustrates what happens when you add a 10 percent or 20 percent profit factor to your pricing formula:

10 percent profit: $18 wholesale price × 10 percent = $1.80 + $18.00 = $19.80 adjusted wholesale

20 percent profit: $18 wholesale price × 20 percent = $3.60 + $18.00 = $21.60 adjusted wholesale

While this small hike in the wholesale price may mean little or nothing to the buyer, it can mean a lot to you. For example, if you sell 500 units of this item in a year, look what happens:

10 percent profit: $1.80 × 500 units = $900 profit for you
20 percent profit: $3.60 × 500 units = $1,800 profit for you.

And while you are thinking about that, here's another thought to ponder: if you work on a 10 percent profit margin, you will have to sell $1,000 worth of goods to offset a $100 loss; but at a 20 percent profit margin, you must sell only $500 worth of goods to offset the same $100 loss.

$1,200 for a project due in seven days' time, and the client never knew whether I polished it off in a day or burned the midnight oil for a week, though I feel quite certain that he preferred to think the latter."

Setting fees and quoting on specific jobs is both an art and a skill most business professionals acquire gradually with time and experience. But sometimes you just luck into higher prices when you least expect it, as I did the time I was asked to speak in Canada. Remembering the awful experience I'd had going through customs on my first speaking trip to Canada, and recalling how tired the trip made me, I figured the easiest way to say no was to double my prices. "That will be fine," I was told, and the job was mine whether I wanted it or not. Stunned by the simplicity of this experience, I quoted that same price to the next three prospects and was astonished when each one said yes. So the next time you want to test your wings, and you're presented with a job proposal you really don't want, you have little to lose and perhaps a lot to gain by simply asking twice your normal fee. In the process, you may accidentally discover, as I did, a whole new market that's prepared to pay you what you think you're worth.

"Don't be sheepish about your fees," says master marketer, consultant, and author Jeffrey Lant. "Your ability to deliver success to your clients—a disproportionate benefit compared to fee—entitles you to raise your prices. A client is not merely paying for your current time, but all the years, the effort, the intense mental concentration, the innovation, the creativity and patient practice and determination it took you to get to this point."

Pricing Formulas for Product Sellers

Classic Formula for Manufacturers

Cost of labor + materials for one unit × number of units to be produced in a year + estimated annual overhead costs + desired annual profit ÷ number of units to be produced in a year = wholesale cost per unit × 2 = retail price.

Here, the idea is to get into the price of each item not only all the costs and expenses, but the profit as well. Whether you are planning to produce several thousand units per year, or a limited edition of 250 handmade items, this formula clearly shows any pricing problems you are going to have.

Pricing Guidelines

Example: Let's assume you're going to make laminated walnut-and-pine breadboards. Based on the time it takes you to make one, you figure you can make 800 a year. Let's then assume that you will have to invest a total of two hours' time in each breadboard, and you want at least $10/hour for your labor. Materials cost will be $2.85 per board (you have a good source for scrap lumber). That gives us a total labor + materials cost of $22.85/unit.

Let's also assume that you will have $3,000 overhead costs for the year, and you would like at least $2,500 annual profit from your money-making enterprise. Here's how the figures would work out:

$22.85 × 800 units = $18,280 + $3,000 + $2,500 = $23,780 ÷ 800 units = $29.73 (wholesale price) × 2 = $59.45 (retail price).

Logic tells us that $59.45 is too high a price for a breadboard, even one that is to be offered as an exclusive handmade item in a gourmet catalog. What this exercise has done, then, is point out that you will have to be satisfied with either a lower hourly labor rate or less profit. It's clear you would not be able to reduce your materials cost much, if at all. On the other hand, if you could produce this item in half the time, the figures would change considerably, as follows:

$12.85 (labor + materials) × 800 units/year = $10,280 + $3,000 + $2,500 = $15,780 ÷ 800 units = $19.73 (wholesale price) × 2 = $39.45 (retail price)—more reasonable price, but still high.

When your recalculated price is still too high, you must consider your options: to sacrifice profit, trim your overhead costs, do something to the product itself to give it a higher worth in the customer's mind, or make something else that will be more profitable.

If you want to work with this formula, but have no idea what overhead costs and profit might be, simply begin with what you know a product will cost you in labor and materials, then estimate how many you can produce and sell. The difference will be what's left to cover overhead and profit.

Example: Let's suppose you want to write and publish a simple book, and you plan to do the writing and the page layout on a computer. You find from a printer's estimate that it will cost you $988.55 to print 1,000 copies of a 64-page, perfect bound book, or $.99 each. To this per-book print cost, you should add production costs (art and cover design, $250), and something for the hours you will spend actually doing page layout or paste-up for the printer—let's say 40 hours at $15/hour or $600. Production costs thus add up to $850, or $.85 cents per book. Add this to the per-book print cost to get a total book cost of $1.84.

Now let's assume you can sell 1,000 copies of this book on the retail level for $6.95. Multiply that figure times 1,000 books for a gross income of $6,950. Deduct your costs of $1.84 per book, or $1,840, and you have $5,110 left. Now ask yourself if this is enough to cover your time in writing the book, plus the overhead costs connected with your endeavor. Don't forget your marketing costs and time that will be required to advertise and sell the book. The arithmetic looks like this:

(a) $988.55 ÷ 1,000 books = $ .99 per book (print cost)
(b) $250.00—art and design
$600.00—labor
$850.00 ÷ 1,000 books = $.85 per book (production cost)
(c) $ .99 print cost + $.85 production cost = $1.84 total book cost
(d) $6.95 (suggested retail price) × 1,000 books = $6,950.00 gross income
(e) -1,840.00 ($1.84 x 1,000 books)
(f) $5,110.00 left.

Is it enough? I would say so, because a book, once written and printed, can produce income for years and may require only minor updating from time to time. But now assume you want to write a larger book of 200 to 300 pages. Your investment of time to write it will be considerably larger, as will production costs. The higher these costs, the higher the retail price. (Trade book publishers generally figure that the retail price of a book needs to be from 6 to 8 times the total production cost to make it a profitable title, but self-publishers rarely are able to set prices more than 3 to 4 times their production costs because their print quantities tend to be so low. This leaves too little room in the pricing formula to allow for wholesale prices, which limits marketing options. (Now you can see why so many self-publishers today are moving from print books to electronic books.)

Three Pricing Formulas for Product Makers

Craftsellers and makers of other products often use simple pricing formulas like the ones that follow, but only as a general guideline. In the end, they know a thing is worth only what it can be sold for, and a pricing formula is worthless whenever it yields an unrealistic retail price. But just for fun, let's apply the same basic figures to each of the three formulas below, to see how they work.

Without identifying the object we are making, let's assume that our materials cost is going to be $1.50, we can make three units an hour, and we want $10/hour for our labor. (Labor cost per unit, then, will be $3.33.) In the last formula, we also will add 20 cents for overhead and a 20 percent profit based on the wholesale price.

A. Materials × 3 + Labor = Wholesale price × 2 = Retail price
$1.50 × 3 = $4.50 + $3.33 = $7.83 × 2 = $15.66

B. Materials + Labor × 3 = Wholesale price × 2 = Retail price
$1.50 + $3.33 × 3 = $14.49 × 2 = $28.98

C. Materials + Labor + Overhead + Profit = Wholesale Price × 2 = Retail Price
$1.50 + $3.33 + $ .20 + $1.01 = $6.04 × 2 = $12.08
($1.50 + $3.33 + $.20 = $5.03 × 20% = $1.01)

Interesting, isn't it? Now if the item we were making happened to be a piece of jewelry, all three prices would be realistic since jewelry runs the gamut in both price and style. However, if the item happened to be a Christmas ornament or a ceramic coffee mug, all prices would be high, although certain mugs and ornaments might sell for $12–$16 in exclusive shops. The point I'm trying to make is that formulas are fun, but they often are impractical, and the retail price still has to be adjusted to whatever consumer market one is trying to reach.

Here, for comic relief, is my favorite pricing formula, from Raymond Martell, a jeweler in New Jersey:

Cost of materials + labor (at the rate it would cost to pay someone to replace owner at the bench) + 40% of the labor-plus-materials figure + 10% of the labor-plus-materials figure for overhead × 2 = retail price. "Then," quips Ray, "I throw the whole thing out and figure what I can get."

In the end, common sense must take over and the retail price must be set by the maker based on what the market will bear. If the maker cannot realize a profit in addition to his or her wages, perhaps the product should be dropped from the line.

Industry Pricing Guidelines

When trying to set the best selling price, keep industry guidelines in mind. For example, if you are in catering, you may learn from a book, as I did, that caterers all over the country just sigh when asked how they figure prices. Many say the question is too hard to answer concretely, but they do use a couple of "rule-of-thumb" formulas. In large cities like New York, caterers simply multiply the cost of ingredients by four or five, which amount is said to allow for all overhead, profit, and labor costs. Other caterers, in smaller cities, multiply the cost of ingredients by three, then divide that figure by the total number of guests the client plans to invite to come up with a per-guest cost figure for the client.

Similar guidelines for other professions and industries will be found in one small business book or another. You don't have to work in the dark; you just have to do a little research and reading.

While the cost of supplies is always important to your pricing formula, the Department of Labor cautions that costs alone are insufficient to fix a price. "Expenses must tell the entrepreneur one important fact: the price below which he is losing money. Costs only set a floor. Consumer demand will set the ceiling. In between, the business person must fix a cost-competitive price. In the last analysis, your price must lie somewhere between a product's cost and the ability of the buyer to get it somewhere else."

Finally, a note about setting the last two digits of a price for a product. "Some researchers believe that there exists some magic in ending a price in six, seven, or nine," says marketing professor Donald W. Caudill. "Seven, as you know, is a lucky number; six and nine double and triple the powerful and mystical three. Others suggest pricing on the even dollar because buyers automatically round up to the nearest round figure."

Before deciding on the last two digits of your price, check to see how others in your industry are pricing. For example, if you're selling quality hand-crafted products or art, avoid the $5.98, $10.99 type of prices found in discount stores; if you're selling a book, set figures that end in $.95 or $.99 like most other publishers; if offering a service, use round figures like $35 an hour, and so on. The use of weird prices in an industry that traditionally uses a certain type of pricing will only mark you as an amateur.

For more information on how to increase profits and get higher prices for everything you sell, see this book's companion marketing guide, *HOMEMADE MONEY: Bringing in the Bucks.*

Smart Tip

At least once a year, analyze your business reports and check your profit margins. Too many business owners set prices and then never change them, but everything is going up these days, and when your expenses increase, your prices for products and services must also increase. Have the courage to raise prices when it's necessary because people *will* pay higher prices if they really want what you offer.

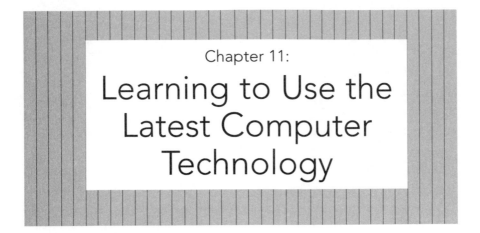

Chapter 11:

Learning to Use the Latest Computer Technology

No two factors are more responsible for the vitality of the home business sector than Internet and computer use.
—*Home Business* magazine

To excel in business in the 1980s and early 1990s, we self-employed individuals and home-business owners generally learned one thing after another through research, self-study, and hands-on experience until we eventually became expert in all areas important to the success of our business. As we continued to hone our business management and marketing skills, most of us felt we had all our ducks in a row. But late in the twentieth century, advanced computer technology began to change everything, from the way products and services were designed and manufactured, to the way we communicated, to the way we managed our business and marketed our products and services. Suddenly, with the incredible growth of the Internet in the last decade of the century, we all had to start learning how to do business all over again.

By late 1999, I was feeling so overwhelmed by all the new technology and what was happening on the Web that, after nearly thirty years of self-employment at home, I was seriously thinking about getting off the high-tech road and letting the rest of the world pass me by. I figured I'd just curl up in my little office cocoon and keep writing books on my old computer. But life has a funny way of throwing surprising and interesting challenges in our face when we least expect them. I was literally dragged onto the Internet early in 2000 when I accepted an exciting job offer to provide Web content for a new e-commerce crafts site.

Prior to this—because my computer was too slow for use on the Internet—I had signed up for WebTV thinking that would be sufficient for my simple needs. I was comfortable surfing the Web and sending e-mail this way, and I even had a Web site, designed and maintained by a friend. I figured that was all I'd ever need. *How wrong I was.* Accepting the e-commerce job offer meant I had to buy a new computer system so I could send my articles electronically. And—horrors!—it also meant I finally had to learn the Windows operating system, something I had successfully avoided for years.

"If it ain't broke, don't fix it," I steadfastly maintained throughout the 1990s, but that logic no longer applies in a world where perfectly functional computer systems and other electronic products are being dumped simply because they aren't big enough, fast enough or new enough. Frankly, this is a hard attitude shift for a frugal person like me who thought the world was perfect the way it was back in the 1950s. Now, with even faster computers, more complex software that is constantly being updated, and one new technological gadget after another begging for our attention, it seems we must all look forward to an endless cycle of learning and the acquisition of new skills and know-how that will serve us only until the technology changes and we have to repeat the learning cycle all over again.

In a way, it's funny. I was a computer dummy when I sat down at my first computer in 1986 but, over the years as I upgraded my system, I became quite accomplished in using the DOS-based software I needed to run my writing/publishing/mail order business. Yet, at the turn of the century when I found myself in front of my new Gateway computer with its Windows operating system, all new software, and a microprocessor that offered more power than ten writers like me would ever need, there I was—a computer dummy all over again. This is progress?

The Computer's Role in Your Business

While many homebased businesses can be successfully launched without a computer, sooner or later you must become computer literate and add this technology to your business if you hope to stay abreast of your competition or merely in control of your business. Everyone in business today needs a computer to handle business correspondence, record keeping, and accounting, if only to speed up routine work and be better organized. Not every business needs a Web site, however (at least not yet), but with few exceptions, every business owner needs access to the Internet for e-mail, research, and learning purposes. About half the adults in the United States. now use e-mail. At the rate people around the world are coming online (currently about a hundred million a year), it won't be long before the whole civilized world will be online, and you'll need to be there, too.

Smart Tip

In deciding whether you must have e-mail for business communications or a Web site for selling right now, ask yourself whether the particular clients or customers you are targeting will expect you to have e-mail or be on the Web. If so, or if your competition is operating this way, then you need to operate this way, too.

In interviewing dozens of business owners for this book, I found only one business owner who truly does not need e-mail at this time. Yvonne Conway, now seventy, provides in-home beauty services to an elderly clientele, including many people in nursing homes. Since few of her customers have computers or e-mail, all she needs to serve them is a telephone to set up appointments. "I attended several computer classes to see what I was missing," she says, "and decided I really don't need the World Wide Web or e-mail at this time. That does not rule it out in the future, however. For now, I know I won't miss the viruses, porn, spam and scams that automatically come with e-mail. My old word processor, telephone and fax machine will do for now."

Although most everyone with an interest in business today realizes the importance of computers in business, a few of this book's readers may figure they really can get along without a computer. After all, people did business for years before personal computers existed, right? In fact, I earned a nice living at home for fifteen years before buying my first computer in 1986, but what that first computer did for me was almost magical. I had launched my present publishing and mail order business five years earlier with nothing more than an IBM Selectric typewriter, secretarial desk, and comfortable chair. Three years later, with a mailing list of 20,000 names and a 24-page newsletter being done entirely on typewriter, my business was wildly out of control and I was making myself a nervous wreck trying to get all this work done while also generating the unending supply of printed materials needed to sell my publications by direct mail. Yet, lacking $5,000 for what a com-

Write Your Own Computer Manual

As you begin a new computer-learning experience, the smartest thing you can do is to write your own computer manual as you go. As long as you're doing the same thing day in and day out, it's easy enough to remember how-to details, but if you use a lot of different programs, and don't use all of them all of the time, you'll find it difficult to remember all the thousands of little details related to the operation of each of them.

Set up a word processing folder with a chapter for each software program you use—including your computer's operating system. Every time you learn a new command or solve a particular problem, put it in your manual in language you can understand. In particular, include notes on how to set up your computer programs again when your computer crashes—which it will, eventually. Include the special set-up commands and preferences you've entered for each of your software programs, particularly the preference and connection codes for your e-mail program. Also document all the serial numbers and passwords related to each program you use and print out this information for reference. (Don't keep it on your computer where hackers can access it.) List all the phone numbers you'll need for technical support, and so on. The important thing to remember here is that memory alone will not serve where computers are concerned. The more you learn, the more there is to remember, thus the more to forget. Software reference manuals, how-to books, and monthly computer magazines are great—but your own computer manual will give you a sense of control you cannot obtain in any other way.

puter system cost in those days and reluctant to go into debt, I struggled along for another two years, at which time prices finally dropped to where I felt I could afford to buy. It took only a few days for me to realize that buying a computer was the smartest move I'd ever made—and the dumbest move I'd made to that point was in waiting so long.

Without computer technology, I could not have continued to manage my ever-growing mailing lists; expand my direct mail efforts; continue publishing my newsletter; stay on top of my bookkeeping, tax, and financial records; develop and maintain the growing number of database and word processing files necessary to the advancement of my business; create all the printed promotional materials needed to market my business, or write new books. More important, if I hadn't incorporated computer technology into my home-business life when I did, upgraded my equipment in later years, and continued to learn right up to this minute, my competitors would have run me over and I would have been out of business years ago.

While it's true that most of the jobs businesses are doing today were once done without benefit of computer technology, just think how much longer it took, and how many employees such work required! To me, the real wonder of a computer is that it enables the average individual to successfully operate a business single-handedly, doing a job that years ago might have required half a dozen employees or, in my case, several outside services. In this light, then, a computer daily saves the average business owner enough time to do twice or three times the amount of work that once was done without such technology.

To reiterate, even though you may be able to operate your new home business without computer technology, you won't be able to do it as well, as efficiently, as quickly, or as economically as you can when you have computer power! More important, you may not be able to successfully compete with others in your field if you aren't doing business the same way everyone else is doing it.

Learning Later in Life

It's easy to learn new things when you're young; much harder when you're older and more fixed in your ways. Prior to learning how to set up her own Web site, art teacher Alberta S. Johnson (K6ArtLessonPlans.com) told me how intimidated she felt initially by the whole learning process.

"The fear of just starting nearly stopped me cold," she said. "Technology seems to be harder on you if you're introduced to it at a later stage in life. You worry about whether or not you'll understand it, or whether you'll ruin the computer if you hit the wrong keys. Children don't care if they break it—they keep right on going no matter what happens. They aren't afraid of it, which is why they learn it so quickly. If something breaks or freezes, they'll find the nearest adult to fix it. When some adults run into a freeze, however, they panic. 'What happened? Now what will I do?' is a common refrain. We need to be more open to the possibilities, like kids."

When the new millennium rolled in, I felt like I had a foot planted in each century, and I wasn't sure which one I preferred. The nostalgic part of me was longing for the comfort and security of the old century while the part of me that is a competitive businessperson was literally shouting, "Wake up, Barbara! You can reminisce about the past when you're *old*. Right now, there's a whole new world out there you can explore." It would have been so easy and comfortable to keep doing things the way I had always done them in the past, but as I began my new career on the Web in 2000, I decided to opt for "difficult and uncomfortable."

Vowing to finally "get with it" technologically speaking, I decided to make that year *my year* for personal growth and development. In looking back, I can hardly believe how many new tricks this old dog was able to learn in just a few months of intense study and experimentation, and how that new knowledge quickly began to lead me in exciting new directions. Now, as I continue to write and develop my graphic and Web site design skills, I'm also exploring my options in electronic publishing and teaching. All of this learning has brightened my personal life, brought me a host of new friends and readers, greatly expanded my professional horizons, and made me feel many years younger than I am. (The knees are creaking, but the brain is working just fine!)

It's always hard to leave our comfort zone to explore new territory, but every time I've had the courage to do this, I've reaped benefits galore. As I've learned from experience—and as you will learn, too—the real secret to success is wanting to do a particular thing and having a good reason for doing it. Once you get to that point, you're halfway there. Change doesn't come easy and, without a major shift in your attitude, it cannot even be accepted as a possibility. You must first embrace the idea of change, and then accept with a positive attitude the stress that is likely to accompany any intense period of learning. Take it from one who's "been there, done that." It *is* worth the effort.

Learning to Use Computer Technology

Smart Tip

Welcome change because each shift you make in the way you work or manage your business may reposition you for something else that wouldn't have come your way if you hadn't moved in the first place.

Your Computer Learning Options

A survey of my readers in the late 1980s revealed four reasons why users had delayed their purchase of a computer, in this order: they didn't think they could afford exactly what they wanted, they were not convinced a computer would do that much for them, they didn't think they had enough time to learn to use a computer because their business kept them so busy, and they were concerned about their ability to learn to use a computer.

Today, most people in business realize they need computer technology, and those who are about to enter the computer age aren't as concerned about price or their ability to learn as much as they are concerned about being able to find the time to learn. I won't kid you here—it can take a hundred hours or more to master some complicated software programs, and even then, you may be utilizing only 25 percent of the software's total capabilities. On the other hand, this expenditure of time is often spread over several months as you learn a little bit at a time. Because today's computers and software programs are much easier to understand and use than they were back in the 80s, most people are up and running in a jiffy, after which time the learning process becomes a natural and continuing part of their daily lives.

Local Learning Centers. If you are not yet computer literate, I suggest you take a general computer class at a local community college or adult education center. This could be more important than you now imagine. "Computer technology is seeping into every aspect of our lives," says publisher LaVerne Herren. "Very soon now, a computer-illiterate person will have the same disadvantage as the non-reader of the past decade."

Depending on the kind of computer power you need for your particular business, you may also want to take a class to learn how to use a particular software program or the latest Windows operating system. If you have an interest in learning how to market on the Web, or want to design your own Web site, a wealth of how-to information awaits you on the Web. (See "Other Resources" for a few of my favorite computer learning sites.)

Magazines. There are several computer magazines to choose from, but the one that helped me the most when I was struggling to learn Windows 98 and all the other new software that came with my new computer was *Smart Computing*. Everything is written in plain English and I particularly like the fact that each topic is neatly covered on full pages so you can tear out the pages applicable to your particular needs and file them in folders or a notebook for easy reference.

Learning on the Web. Have you ever wondered how all those people on the Web learned how to do all that "high-tech stuff"? Actually, the easiest way to learn new technical skills is to just get *on* the Web and look for the special how-to information you need. Much of it is free for the taking, but the real inside information is more likely to be found in one or more of the hundreds of eBooks now being offered by Web experts.

Many people now making money on the Web had high-tech skills to begin with, but what if you're just an average Jane or Joe who doesn't have computer or technology skills of any kind? Is there hope for you? Yes, but only if you're willing to put in the time and effort it will take to learn such skills. Take Dennis Gaskill for example.

He used to earn his living working 48 hours or more a week in a factory job that was taking its toll on him physically, emotionally, and spiritually. "I saw the job as a kind of poison that was slowly killing me," he says. Dennis bought his first computer in 1995 and discovered the Internet a few months later. Deciding he wanted to be a part of it, he began to work an extra 40 hours a week teaching himself computer skills.

"I worked harder during that period than I had ever worked in my life, often logging over a hundred hours a week," he recalls. "Because my lack of higher education had boxed me in for so long, I saw this as my best bet out of the factory. I taught myself how to create Web sites, design graphics, do accounting, marketing, cost ratios and everything else I thought I needed to know to find a place on the professional side of the Internet."

Dennis started a hobby site in 1997, turned it into a part-time business the next year, and has been working full time at home since 1999. He now supports himself and his family entirely from the Internet and sales of his book, *Web Design Made Easy* (Morton Publishing). "My book is now a teaching text in colleges from Alaska to Zimbabwe," he says, "and it came

Surge Protectors

The average office or household receives 100 power surges of as much as 1,000 volts each month. These may be caused by nearby electrical storms, or merely by the on-and-off switching of air conditioners, refrigerators, and other equipment. Such sudden increases in voltage can internally damage or destroy computers, fax machines, telephones, TVs, VCRs, stereos, and microwave ovens unless they're protected by a surge protector.

The less voltage that gets through a surge protector, the more effective the protection. Surge protectors are now rated by joules, the higher the better. (For more information on this topic, type "surge protectors" into your browser's search engine, and check out the new joule technology circuitry that absorbs and reroutes surge energy to ground, or, in the event of a catastrophic surge, completely disconnects the power.) When buying a new surge protector, look for one that offers a manufacturer's warranty that includes not only replacement of damaged surge protectors, but of damaged hardware caused by a power surge.

Don't count on a surge protector to save your computer in the event of a direct lightning strike. To dramatically cut your chances of loss here, avoid using your computer during storms and unplug the system until the lightning stops. Although your backup tapes or disks may be current, it could take you a couple of weeks to replace your computer system and get back to work, so what's a couple of hours' downtime during a storm?

about because of my Internet doings. A publisher found my site and called me out of the blue, asking me to write a book on Web design."

Dennis urges others to set goals for themselves and keep at it, even when the situation seems hopeless. "That kind of drive and perseverance almost always pays off," he says. "Except for the inspiration and wisdom gained by reading the words of others, and because of the patience and understanding of my wife who became a "computer widow" for a while, I pretty much got it all going on my own, although many have helped with publicity along the way." Many people will identify with Dennis's triumphs and find inspiration from his words and perspective shared on his site at BoogieJack.com and in his free ezine, which contains a balance of both business and life advice written straight from the heart—messages Dennis hopes someday to put in a book for others who are struggling to achieve special life goals. He adds, "I've learned you can't separate who you are and who you're becoming from your business activities and aspirations because you will always think and act from within your character. To fully succeed, your character needs to be tuned in to the success foundations of life."

Analyzing Your Current Computer System

Do you have an older computer you're thinking of using in your business? More than half the homes in America now have personal computers, but not all of them are new enough or fast enough to be effective for use in business. However, an older computer can be a valuable office tool when used for accounting purposes, record keeping, mail list management, and word processing.

For example, I'd be lost without a fast computer for e-mail, Web research, graphic design and Web site design and maintenance, but I much prefer my trusty old 486 DOS-based computer for all my serious writing and bookkeeping. When all I want to do is write, my productivity soars by moving back to my old computer with its programmable keyboard and function keys on the left side (very difficult to find these days). Here, I can perform all keyboard functions with only my left hand, move more quickly between documents, and never have to lift my hands from the keyboard to use the mouse. I have WordPerfect 6.1 installed here, and this version is far superior to later versions with all their extra "bells and whistles." (The only reason I bought WordPerfect 10 for my new computer was for its ability to convert eBooks to PDF format.)

A primary reason for using an older computer is whether its software is useful to your business. If so, it can serve a double purpose by being both a useful office machine and an emergency backup system in case your main computer crashes. (Whenever I'm working on a book, I keep my files on both machines as well as on floppy disks to make sure I don't lose a word in case of a computer crash.)

Loss of data due to failure to back up files remains the greatest error most beginners (and even experienced business owners) make. It's not a matter of *if* your computer's hard disk is going to crash, but *when*. The reasons are too many and varied to discuss here, but your insurance against a crash is a good backup system. All hard disks eventually wear out or develop bad sectors. The trick is to operate on the assumption that your computer could crash at any time *and always will when you least expect it*. Probably the greatest risk we all face these days is a computer crash caused by a virus. To protect against this, you'll need a good virus program such as Norton or McAfee that is regularly updated. (See "Other Resources" to find Web sites that will give you an education on viruses and antivirus software.)

There are different types of backup systems available, and you will need to explore your options here. If you're using an old computer, remember that back-up systems, like computer hardware, also go out of date. Make sure your present computer's backup system is compatible with any new computer you might buy. (For example, the efficient tape backup system on my 486 is not compatible with today's computers.) Whenever you're working on an important project, make frequent backups to a floppy disk during the day. If you do a lot of work in several programs every day, daily backups of all your files are essential. Store daily backups in a small fireproof safe in your office, and for protection against loss by fire, flood, tornado, etc., periodically store complete backups in a location away from your home office. (See also sidebar, "Surge Protectors.")

Smart Tip

Keep your cat away from your computer keyboard. The static electricity from a cat's coat could discharge into the terminal and blow a computer chip. If cat hair is sucked into the computer through the floppy disk drive, it could cause overheating and loss of data. If your cat likes to lie on your computer monitor, make sure it doesn't block air vents and cause overheating.

Parallel or Serial?

Here's a chuckle from an old issue of *WordPerfect* Report. The editor shared a sampling of the variety of calls they answer daily, from users in The White House to Stephen King to a woman in San Francisco who called because her computer wouldn't boot up after it had fallen off her desk during an earthquake. Then there was the lady who, when asked if her printer was parallel or serial said, "Well, I think it must be parallel because it's sitting right next to my computer."

Software Considerations

There are literally hundreds of software programs that can be used to manage a small business, and any new computer purchase you make will probably include more Microsoft software than you need (or care to learn), including word processing and office management programs as well as some kind of graphics program.

Most businesses need some kind of database software to create sales reports or labels for customer and prospect mailings. If all you need are labels, any simple database or mailing list program will do the job, including shareware you can access through the Internet. John Schulte, chairman of the National Mail Order Association (NMOA.org), says the simplest database program he has found is Microsoft Access, which is bundled with some versions of Microsoft Office (or available separately). "Some people have this software and don't know its capabilities, but it's easy to learn," he says. "It includes a Database Wizard that does all the work for you. Just click here and there to build an address book, order entry files or a dozen other types of database files. If you need only labels, Microsoft Access is all you need, but if you want to send personalized letters to your customers, then you'll also want Microsoft Word."

A survey of many businesses in my network attests to the popularity of QuickBooks, a program designed to accommodate the small-business owner who needs to do invoicing, inventory management, and accounting tasks. Dodie Eisenhauer, who wholesales a line of craft products through sales reps and trade shows, says this software is perfect for her needs: "This is my whole accounting and record-keeping system. When I type in customers' names and data, I include information on where I acquired them and who the rep is so I can sort my mailing list by category. If I want to send something to everyone who came to a particular trade show, I can sort on that data field; or I could contact all the customers generated by a particular sales rep or in a particular area of the country. Mailing lists may also be sorted by zip code or alphabetically by name. At the end of each year, I print a directory of accounts so I can see if I have accounts in a particular state without going to the computer."

The following list will serve as a reminder for what you'd like a computer to do for you. Once you've checked your needs, chat with friends about their favorite programs for these jobs and also research the Web for discussion lists and bulletin boards where you can post questions on this topic and get feedback from experts.

Learning to Use Computer Technology

Word Processing
___ Correspondence
___ Newsletters
___ Articles or books
___ Creation of printed materials
___ Word files of all kinds

Database Files
___ Mail list management
___ Inventory control
___ Charts and worksheets
___ Sales reports

Financial Management
___ Accounting
___ Invoices and statements
___ Check writing
___ Sales analyses
___ Cash flow projections
___ Income tax preparation

Publishing
___ Desktop publishing
___ Web site design and management
___ eBook design
___ Ezine list management

Designing
___ Projects for books and magazines
___ Art or craft patterns
___ Needlework charts
___ Blueprints and spec sheets
___ Web site graphics
___ Photo-enhancement software

Other Software
___ E-mail
___ Computer backups
___ Virus-prevention
___ Electronic organizer
___ Multimedia program
___ Presentations (overhead transparencies)

The Personal Benefits of Computer Ownership

In closing, I'd like to bring attention to some additional, less obvious personal benefits of computer ownership. In surveying 75 computer users in my network for an earlier edition of *Homemade Money*, I received considerable evidence of how taming a computer affects one's feelings of self-worth and confidence. You may relate to some of their remarks:

● "I have this feeling that I am hedging against the aging process. I think one way to feel like you are not growing old is to keep up with current technology. I have two sons, one in middle school. When he talks ROM and RAM, I at least know they aren't obscure mythical beasts in the *Odyssey* that I have forgotten. In fact, I have conquered my own mythical beast by learning how to use this machine to do me some good, and that is a major confidence-builder for me. It means the brain cells will still accept new concepts and skills, and that's pretty exciting for an entrepreneurial housewife."

—Marion Boyer

● "The computer cured me of a lifetime sense of inadequacy regarding machines and anything too mathematical. It took only the initial leap of faith to make me realize that a computer is only as smart as what I put into it, and it took only a smidgeon longer to realize that one tames a computer with logic and not math skills. Naturally, fine-tuning your logical skills to solve computer problems carries over to everything else you do in life."

—Elyse Sommer

● "I never realized how much I could teach myself and how proficient I could become in a subject all on my own. In just two years, I moved from being 'just a housewife' to someone who converses with university-trained programmers and systems people who are amazed by how much I've been able to do and learn. If anyone had told me I could do all this without going back to college, I would have thought them crazy. I did this because I just had to. The computer at my husband's office wasn't working, and someone had to figure out why. I just read, studied, experimented, tried, failed, and eventually succeeded."

—Susan Anderson

Learning to Use Computer Technology

● "For me, the computer unlocked creativity and new ideas. When I took typing in school, I was barely able to get a grade of D. My mind and fingers just didn't seem to function at the same speed. Add terrible spelling to that and you have a real writing problem. I didn't realize until after I got the computer that all sorts of ideas were waiting to emerge on paper, but my typing problem had been keeping them locked in. The word processor was thus the key to my writing."

—Liz DeCleene

● "I wanted to be an artist when I was young, but due to my family's financial situation I wasn't able to pursue this. In operating a mail order business and playing around with my Macintosh computer, I not only discovered my creative streak but released my sense of humor by publishing a book of business cartoons drawn on the Mac."

—Janet Hansen

Chapter 12:
Maintaining Control

The great advantage of a hotel is that it's a refuge from a home-based business.

—Beverly Neuer Feldman

This chapter offers practical suggestions on how to blend business into your personal life, work around or with your children, and control the extra stress that is sure to result when you're running a business at or from home base. Because stress management is so closely connected to one's organizational and time management skills, extra emphasis has also been given to these topics, along with some motivational tips and extra encouragement to help you keep pursuing your goals.

Remember that this book represents only *half* of all the home-business advice my readers and I want to share with you. While this book was designed to help you select and start your business, its companion guide, *HOMEMADE MONEY: Bringing in the Bucks*, takes you by the hand and shows you how to generate new business through advertising, publicity, and smart marketing strategies; resell existing accounts; diversify into new areas; do business on the Web; and much more. (See last page of this book for detailed content information.)

Blending Business into Your Personal Lifestyle

One of the first problems facing the typical home business owner is where to set up shop, do the work involved, and store related merchandise, supplies, or files. It's not so bad if you have a four-bedroom home, but it takes real skill and ingenuity to run a business out of a small apartment, house trailer, or recreational vehicle—something more and more people are doing these days. Initially, a business may be confined to one room or area of one's home but, like weeds that creep into a garden, it soon consumes all unoccupied space. "Ours is the only home in the neighborhood with three toll-free telephones in the living room," says one diversified business owner. "Actually, we don't run the business out of our home—we run the home out of our business."

Even when there is plenty of space in which to work, a complete separation of business from one's private life is an impossibility for most of us. Thus we never have the sense of quitting at five o'clock to go home. After a while, this can have a disturbing psychological effect. That's why people devise all kinds of little tricks to help them mentally "quit work and go home." One woman says she carries her purse into the office in the morning, and takes it with her when she leaves at night. Another says she dresses in business clothes while she's in the office, and changes to jeans when her workday is done. A fellow says when he's through for the day, he goes out into the garage, comes in, slams the door and hollers, "Hi, honey, I'm home."

Even when you've mentally quit for the day, your customers or clients may intrude on your privacy unless you make plans to control such interruptions. Some home-business owners assume that, because they are working late in the evenings or on weekends, everyone else is, too. And people who telephone the offices of home-business owners often have little regard for regular business hours or time-zone differences.

Smart Tip

Don't let your customers or clients rule your personal life. Work late or start early if you like, but inform your customers and clients early on that you keep "regular office hours" and your answering machine or voice mail will catch all calls at other times of the day.

Quick! The Chocolate Chips

One day, in a telephone conversation with Silvana Clark, we were talking about how some mothers manage young children when they're on the telephone, and I said I'd read somewhere about a woman who tossed her child a jelly bean to keep him quiet each time the phone rang.

"I can top that," said Silvana. "I was on the phone in the kitchen one day when my two-year-old toddled into the room, mouth open, all set to vocalize. I quickly grabbed a nearby package of chocolate chips and threw a handful on the floor. Entranced, my daughter began to pick them up, eating them one by one. And I kept on throwing handfuls of chips until I was able to complete the important contractual agreement I was then negotiating."

Because you can't walk away from your homebased business at five o'clock, it's very easy to become a workaholic. Business naturally spills over into the home, so you gradually lose a clear separation of living and work spaces. This creates a different kind of stress than that associated with working for someone else, and it can adversely affect your life or family relations if not properly handled. To put it less mildly, and to quote Michael Gerber, a speaker I once heard at a conference, "Some people start a business to get rid of a boss," he said, "but they end up working for a lunatic—themselves!"

Although it may be impossible to make a complete physical and mental separation of business from your home life, strive to attain some kind of psychological separation from time to time. Although vacations may seem a luxury you don't have time for, or can't afford, some time away from the place where all the work is waiting is essential to your mental and physical well-being. (And the longer you're in business, the more important this will become.) Remember: The more important you are to the continuity of your business, the more important it is for you to put your own health (mental as well as physical) first. Otherwise you may not be able to run your business at all.

Working Around—and with—Your Children

Some people think it's impossible to successfully work at home with kids underfoot, but I know many individuals who do it well. The trick lies in being flexible. As one mother told me, "I won't postpone my creative instincts until my children are adults. I've simply changed my perception of work, altered my view of distractions and interruptions, and adjusted my work schedule to accommodate the needs of my children. This means, of course, that clients must be chosen carefully. We think about the kinds of jobs we can handle and those we can't." Here are several other successful strategies used by mothers in my network.

Share Your Business Success With Your Children. "Keep your children informed of what you are doing and share your business successes with them," advises Angela Allen, who offers small and home-based business consulting and virtual assistance services at CumberlanDunes.com. "My own sons, prodded by questions from friends, had to ask me what I did all day at home," she says. "I should have had the forethought to tell them! All they knew was that I worked on the computer. Make sure your children understand, in simple terms, what you do and why so they will be comfortable answering questions from their peers."

When Angela told her boys about her first contract, they gave her ecstatic "high-fives" and then began to check regularly to see if she had any more clients or prospects. "Now they are always interested in my current project's progress," she says. "Talk about built-in external motivation!"

Once involved in your business, your children may be of more help than you might imagine. One day as Angela's 13-year-old son listened to her complain about her inability to relay to an online graphic artist exactly what she wanted in a logo design, he asked her to sketch it. Then he opened a paint program on the computer and created a great logo for her that required only a little touching up by the designer. "It's the one I use today," says Angela, "and my son and I are quite proud of that fact."

If constant interruptions by your children are wearing you down, try teaching by example, as Angela did with her 11-year old boy. "When he became frustrated because I could not be interrupted while doing creative work on product descriptions for a Web site, I decided to show him why I needed the uninterrupted time," says Angela. "He loves writing poetry, so I asked him to

Quick Tips for Working Around Children

- Develop a series of hand signals you can use to communicate with young children when you're on the telephone with a client.

- Preserve your professionalism by using an answering machine to take messages when children are being unruly, and don't let children answer your business line until they're educated in the proper way to do it.

- If your child will be at home under someone else's care during your uninterrupted time, choose for your workspace an area of the house where you aren't in sight. At the appointed hour, close the door and try not to listen. (This gets easier with practice, says one mother.)

- Set time aside for children's activities so they don't become resentful of the homebased business. To avoid missing anything important, keep a calendar for each child showing all ball games, practices, meetings and other appointments so the whole family has a clear view of what's happening each day.

write a poem for me. Once he started, I kept calling him for this or that reason—all nonessential interruptions—until he became quite frustrated. Then I sat down with him and asked him what was wrong. He told me he was angry because I kept interrupting him. He said he would start to write something, and before he could get it down, I'd interrupt him and he would lose his train of thought. About then, he looked at me and a lightbulb went on. I asked him if he now understood why I became frustrated when he interrupted me. He smiled and nodded. Since that little 'exercise,' he has been much more thoughtful about unnecessary interruptions."

Give Young Children Their Own Little Office. While certain types of professional service businesses can't be run with young children causing a ruckus, dozens of other homebased businesses seem to function quite well when structured around the needs of a family. A strategy some mothers use is to give their daughters a tiny corner of their office or workroom so they can "play with mother" all day long. When Shirley Sigmund and her husband were operating Marrakech Express Printing out of their home, Shirley gave her daughter her own little desk; toy typewriter; an old, defunct telephone; and lots of blank paper, pens, pencils, crayons, paints, and markers. "Except for my desk and files, everything in the house was made accessible to Dana," says Shirley. "All breakable, fine or dangerous items were put away or out of reach so I didn't always have to be saying 'no, don't touch.' Because Dana was free to touch and play with everything she could reach—except the papers on my desk—she learned to respect this at a very young age. By the time she was four, she was extremely bright and artistic, confident, and secure, owing greatly, I feel, to the fact that I was always with her during her formative years."

Dana is now nineteen and at college, but Shirley's advice remains timely for all moms with young children. Marrakech now serves customers all around the world from its Web site at Marrak.com, producing books and publications in a plant in Tarpon Springs, Florida. Technology has made it a breeze to work anywhere, and Shirley still works at home whenever she can.

Hire a Babysitter or Mother's Helper. Many at-home working mothers eventually resort to hiring a babysitter or mother's helper for a certain period each week so they know they will have the time to get their work done. When her daughter began to walk, Shirley Sigmund used mother's helpers of various ages to play with Dana while she worked. Author Kate Kelly also told me how well this strategy worked for her.

"In almost all cases, your sitter should be given the authority to handle whatever comes up," says Kate. "With time, your uninterrupted time will be increasingly productive. If you teach your child that certain disturbances will bring you out, you can be guaranteed a lot of them. While there will be difficult days when you feel pulled in too many directions (like the day your child is running a high fever and your biggest client is expecting a delivery), you'll probably still find that the effort is worth it. When it's time to return to the children, you will feel all the better for the time you had for your own interests."

Make Your Children Partners in Your Business. Instead of simply working around their children, many parents put them to work in the business, often paying them a small salary. More important than the tax advantage of this strategy is that an involvement in your business will give your children greater respect for it, and may even spark entrepreneurial efforts of their own. Here is advice from two women whose businesses I've followed for more than twenty years. Beginning at home, working around young children, both went on to build large, successful companies outside the home with their children following in their business footsteps.

Years ago when Dottie Walters was just starting in business, her children were adding to her stress by yelling and making noise while she tried to work. "They felt left out of the business," she recalls, "so I gave each child a title, made little business cards for them on the copy machine, and paid them for their work in the company. My husband told the oldest, our son, that when he figured out a way to do a job faster and better, he would get a raise. Within a week, our boy had an improvement for our business and his work. He learned to use not only his hands but his brain. We were amazed when each of the younger children also thought of a better way to do their jobs. They got raises, too. We praised and rewarded them constantly, and listed them on our letterhead."

By involving her children in her business, Dottie gave them a tremendous platform on which to build their own professional lives. The son mentioned above is now an attorney. Daughter Lilly, now an author like her mother, is in charge of Walters International Speakers Bureau (Walters-Intl.com). Another daughter is a speech and communication teacher, and grandson Michael is the advertising manager of Dottie's newsmagazine, *Sharing Ideas*.

When Cindy Groom-Harry launched a little business at home back in the 1980s, she had no idea she would one day be running a company in partnership with her husband, Lee, serving a variety of corporate clients in the crafts industry. In those early years, she wasn't thinking about the employees she would one day manage; only how she could manage her growing design and consulting business at home around two growing daughters who also had busy lives of their own. In time, as the business grew and had to be relocated outside the home, Cindy and Lee incorporated as Craft Marketing Connections, Inc., and the children blossomed right along with the business.

"The girls grew up knowing that a ringing telephone meant that the TV or stereo or most recent fight over a toy or article of clothing went off immediately," Cindy recalls, "and they learned hand signals early on. One signal indicated business (when they were expected to disappear into another part of the house); another indicated they could play nearby quietly."

Like Dottie's children, Cindy's daughters followed in her footsteps. As preschoolers, they ran errands, licked stamps, and monitored the door when she was on the phone, receiving wages equivalent to an allowance. In their teens, they attended trade shows with Cindy and Lee, assisting with sales work and receiving adult wages. "This encouraged their ability to manage money and grow their college funds," says Cindy. "At trade shows, where they met clients informally and followed the business meetings we conducted, they learned about the world outside a small business in a small town and how large companies operate."

Today, Cindy's daughters—now in their twenties—have maturity and poise beyond their years. Although they have careers in education and public relations, they periodically return to assist Cindy and Lee with special client events.

Time Management Tips

Time management experts say the first principle of time management is to do one thing at a time and finish it before starting another. That's fine if you happen to be talking about task consolidation, but all the successful businesspeople I know say their time-management secret is to do two things at once. Ideally, it would be terrific to have to think about only one thing at a time, but so often one thing is dependent upon another, and what you do in one area automatically requires some kind of counter-action in another area of the business. (Anyone who has a business knows exactly what I'm talking about. The rest of you will learn soon enough.)

Successful entrepreneurs quickly learn to do two things at once. The woman rocking her baby may actually be composing her next press release in her head or trying to figure out how she's going to generate enough cash to pay a supplier, while the fellow who's mowing the lawn or driving the kids to soccer practice may be mentally rehearsing his speech to the banker or planning his cold-calling approach. In airports or in a doctor's office, we do business reading or planning while we wait. At home, we often will find ourselves in the position of rushing to complete a job or meet a deadline while also preparing to entertain guests for the weekend. At all times, entrepreneurs are *thinking* while doing something else and trying to get their ideas down on paper before they forget them.

"When I'm feeling overwhelmed by work, the first thing I do is write down everything that needs to be done," says literary agent Barbara Doyen.

"Then I prioritize, setting time deadlines for each individual job. Then I put the whole list out of my mind and concentrate on the *now* and the *one item* that has to be done first, then second, etc. You can't worry about the whole or you'll go crazy."

"We all have 24 hours a day," says Dottie Walters, international speaker, author, consultant, and publisher of *Sharing Ideas* newsmagazine. "An important key to time management is to do all the things in one direction together." Dottie is one of the busiest and most productive people I know, and she practices the advice given by Kipling, who said, "Fill every unforgiving minute with 60 seconds worth of distance run."

To do this, you have to look at everything you do—production, paperwork, mail handling, etc.—with an eye to grouping certain jobs that require similar physical movements, tools, supplies, or a particular mindset. You lose time each time you have to change mental gears or physical position, so any time you can do a large block of work that takes a certain kind of mental concentration or physical movement, you will save time.

If you make a product, you will find that you'll greatly increase output if you do the same step on at least two dozen items (one craftswoman says she does 100) at a time, then move on to the second step and do that on those same items, etc. For example, imagine that you're making a sawed-out, hand-painted toy. First you would transfer the pattern to the wood for 24 items, then cut out (saw) 24 items, then sand them, and so on. If your painted design involved six colors of paint, you would add the first color to 24 items, then the second color, and so on. *Every unnecessary movement you can eliminate will save time and speed production.*

Production techniques like this can be applied to every part of your daily and business life, resulting in the saving of many precious minutes each day that can be put to better use. Start thinking now about things you can do to give yourself the extra hours you are going to need for your business.

Organizational and Stress Management Strategies

Like many readers of *The Crafts Report*, I got a chuckle from a cartoon that appeared in one of its issues. It showed a woman sitting in a messy work room, and the caption said, "The advantage to being disorganized is that if a burglar breaks in, he won't be able to find anything either."

We may joke about being disorganized, but most of us would be less stressed and more productive in a well-organized workplace. "Everyone has the ability to be organized," says Stephanie Winston, author of *Getting Organized* (Warner Books). "If you can manage to cross Columbus Circle in New York, an intersection of eight streets, you have the potential to be organized. It's simply a matter of negotiation."

It's hard to separate the topics of organization, time management, and stress because they are so closely related and connected to one another. For example, if your filing system is disorganized, you'll waste time every time you look for something that isn't where it ought to be, and this will automatically increase your stress. If you don't have an organized area in which to work, you'll waste time moving from one place to another, once again increasing your stress. Thus, learning how to manage the extra stress that automatically comes with being in business is as important as learning how to manage and market your business.

When I launched my present business in 1981, my office was a small pantry off the kitchen with floor-to-ceiling shelves on both sides and a board across to hold my typewriter. It got pretty hot in the summertime, not to mention claustrophobic. I was greatly hampered by the fact that this particular house had no other suitable place to work, and with my business supplies and files scattered in three closets, one corner of the bedroom, and the basement, I was constantly irritated by the time I wasted running back and forth from one place to the other. How my productivity and satisfaction level increased when we moved, and I was finally able to have an entire room to myself! As time passed, I bought new furniture, good chairs, and added atmosphere with nice carpeting, good lighting, lovely plants, and fine art. The nicer my office has become, the more productive I've become, and I'm also less stressed because I'm so satisfied with my surroundings. I can't think of a better place to put your early business profits than into your office, studio, or other workspace.

Jot It Down

Do you tend to be forgetful? No wonder! As home-business owners, we live simultaneously in two worlds: a personal world that may include a spouse or partner, children, aging parents, and a host of community or personal responsibilities; and the business world we have created in some part of our home. If we forget to do something, some may think we're absent-minded. But that's not it at all. It's simply that our brains are so full of ideas and so fragmented by the weight of our many two-world responsibilities that we sometimes get our mental wires crossed. Experts advise us to hire out the housecleaning, get a baby-sitter, and stick to business, but the reality in the homes of most of the home-business owners I know is that individuals generally do it all. If it's not a matter of money, it may simply be a matter of choice.

Smart Tip

No matter where you are when the muse strikes, it's important to get your ideas on paper as quickly as possible since the force of all the other things on your mind will soon push your great ideas aside and they may be lost forever.

Entrepreneurial-minded folks are never out of reach of paper and pen for jotting down brainstorms in the kitchen, on the night stand in the bedroom, and even in the bathroom where, it is rumored, some of the most creative home-business thinking and learning takes place. Diane Wolverton once wrote a marvelous editorial for her newsletter (now out of print) about the "power of the shower." "A shower," she said, "provides the right conditions to get your creative mind into full gear. First, it's relaxing and soothing. Second, it's private time—no phones, no kids, no clients, no pressure to be anything but yourself. And third, the running water is full of negative ions, which have a positive influence on us."

In checking with other writers and businesspeople, Diane learned she wasn't the only one who got bursts of inspiration in the shower. Instead of waiting for those bursts of inspiration, she began to schedule them, taking her problems into the shower for resolution. In a "Nekkid Notes Notebook" kept in the bathroom, she began to record all her great ideas, solutions, and brainstorms that came out of her little steam room.

"My shower is my own private idea-generating chamber," she reported. "I've written poems in there, organized conferences, planned meetings, written chapters for my book, rehearsed important conversations and scampered out dripping and cold to jot down just the perfect headline for an ad."

Can you, too, do some of your best work stark naked? "Try it," Diane urges. "You'll be amazed."

Organized Chaos

A record of how you spend your time will automatically help you to get organized, but if disorganization is a problem for you, I suggest you read a book or two on this topic, any lengthy discussion of which is beyond the scope of this book. I do wish to emphasize, however, that being organized is not the same as being neat. When I began my secretarial career out of high school, one of my favorite bosses, then co-owner of a direct mail advertising firm in Chicago, had a desk I couldn't believe. It was always loaded with foot-high stacks of one kind of paper or another, and I longed to organize it. But on my first day in the office, Bob warned me sharply, "Don't ever touch a thing on my desk. It may look a mess, but I know where everything is." And he did. Often when I would ask him for a certain file, he'd run his fingers down a stack of material and, to my astonishment, pull out exactly what I needed.

Now that my office looks just like Bob's, I know why he worked this way. Out of sight, out of mind. I worry about things I can't see, and if I file something that requires any kind of later action, I forget about it because I have too many things on my mind all the time. So the best way for me to remember what has to be done is to actually see the work stacked somewhere, begging my attention. Thus, my desk is loaded with racks of manila file folders, mail-holding trays, spindles of notes, and other piles of "to do" work. It doesn't look beautiful, but I know where everything is. If you work like this, and are criticized for it, tell your critics this is one of your time-saving devices. (If you can manage to keep the entire surface of your desk covered with paper, you'll never have to dust it.)

It's not that I'm disorganized, it's merely that I cannot seem to do my kind of work in any other manner. Or, as Harold S. Geneen said in his book, *Managing*, "If you are on the firing line with the leadership of several projects, you are going to have 89 things on your desk, ten others on the floor beside you, and eight others on the credenza behind you."

Designer Judy Mahlstedt used to feel guilty about the way she worked until she read that people who are dominated by the right half of the brain (as the majority of creative people are) often function better in controlled chaos than they do in an organized environment. "Right brain people are stimulated by working on several projects at once," she told me. "We need to be surrounded by the tools of our trade. We think better when we are facing a deadline and will often put our action off until the last moment, although our minds are constantly hashing over the problem for days or weeks in advance. We can actually sabotage our creativity by attempting to follow the suggestions of well-meaning left-brain people who can't resist trying to physically organize us." Judy closed her letter by saying she naturally could not find the magazine in which the article appeared because she was trying to get organized by discarding her reading material as soon as she finished it.

After writing about this topic in my newsletter, several subscribers wrote to say they were greatly relieved to know there was a term ("organized chaos") for their style of working, and that they weren't disorganized slobs after all. One reader found the perfect sign for this situation, but said there wasn't room to put it on her desk: *Neat desk—empty mind. Cluttered desk—genius at work!*

Talking To Yourself

Many people get through life, I'm convinced, simply because they have a sense of humor. And when you work for yourself at home, it's essential for survival. I consider my sense of humor one of the greatest gifts received from my parents. They instilled in me and my two sisters the belief that, no matter how bad things might get, they could always be worse; and we should always look for whatever good we could find in a situation and try to laugh our troubles away. I guess that's why, when the freezer thawed, I thought how lucky we were that we had not just put in half a beef. And the green peppers were still growing, so I could replace them. The beans? In spite of warnings not to refreeze food, I refroze some of them anyway, and although they were a little mushy, they tasted fine.

Throughout my life, I have tried to maintain a positive attitude about everything, and it has never failed to benefit me. Some people look at a partially filled bottle and say, "It's half gone," but I say, "There's still half a bottle left." I try to apply the same kind of thinking to the daily happenings of my life and business. When things go wrong, or get out of control, I may not be able to do anything about the situation at that particular moment, but I can do something for myself immediately, and I do. I find something positive to think about. You must learn to do the same.

In the end, each of us has a choice about how we perceive our experiences in life, and how our bodies will react to them. You have heard about the power of positive thinking and what it can do for you; where stress is concerned, positive thinking can make all the difference in the world. When you think negatively about anything, your body also responds negatively because the power of suggestion definitely affects the nervous system. But if you force yourself to think in positive terms, your body will respond accordingly.

Remember: your subconscious mind has the ability to accept as real any impression that reaches it, whether positive or negative, constructive or destructive. That's why it is vital to your mental and physical well-being to protect your mind from undesirable influences and suggestions that can bring you down. The next time you find yourself thinking negative thoughts that begin with "I can't," go to the mirror and give yourself a pep talk. Look yourself in the eye and say "*I can!*" You will then be sending a clear signal to your subconscious mind and planting a seed that will grow in strength and eventually help you find the answer to the "how" part of your problem.

I was delighted the day I received a review copy of a book titled *What to Say When You Talk to Yourself* by Shad Helmstetter (Grindle Press). On reading it, I was even more delighted to learn I had been saying all the right things to myself. This book confirmed what I had been telling my readers for years: that our minds are like computers that accept all the information we and others pour into it, good and bad alike. If we don't like what we're getting back, we simply have to change the programming.

"Imagine what you could do if you could override the programs in your subconscious mind, those that still work against you, and replace them with a refreshing new program of absolute belief?" Helmstetter states in his book. "How successful you will be at anything is inexorably tied to the words and beliefs about yourself that you have stored in your subconscious mind. You will become what you think about most; your success or failure in anything, large or small, will depend on your programming—what you accept from others, and what you say when you talk to yourself."

Sources of Help and Encouragement

Homebased workers often feel a sense of isolation that in itself can be depressing and thus stressful. But contact of any kind with others who understand what you are going through—and are there to lend emotional support and encouragement when needed—is often worth more than gold.

Networking

One secret to staying motivated and encouraged lies in communication with your peers and those you are selling to, working with, or otherwise trying to serve. Here, little things mean a lot. A supportive phone call from a business pal or a note of thanks from a satisfied customer can literally make your day. No one ever does it all alone, and even when success is assured, we all have a constant need for positive feedback from our peers.

Thanks to e-mail and the Internet, it's now easy to build a network of business supporters. All you have to do is join a few discussion lists and start reading the bulletin boards of home-business Web sites until you find a couple of places that feel like home to you. You must be selective, however, as involvement in too many lists and bulletin boards will take too much time away from your business. Soon you'll have more e-mail friends than you can count.

Electronic networking is great, but there's nothing like face-to-face contact with others who have dreams and goals similar to yours. If a local home-business network doesn't exist, consider starting one yourself with an announcement in the paper. (Your library or school can offer a room for this kind of meeting.) Join some organizations related to your field, and don't just read their newsletters, but attend annual conferences to make important business contacts and maximize your networking power.

Self-Encouragement

When you aren't getting enough feedback from others, encourage yourself by listening to motivational tapes or reading uplifting books and magazines. Put your dreams and goals in writing and keep a journal of your accomplishments, rereading it periodically for encouragement. Pat yourself on the back if there is no one else around to do it for you, and consider all temporary setbacks merely "profitable learning experiences." Above all, refuse to listen to discouraging talk of any kind. Ironically (and many people have confirmed this to me), our closest friends and family members are often the ones who discourage us most. They may tell us we're wasting our time, we are never going to make money doing this or that, or we are attempting something we "have no business doing." The problem, you see, is that others do not share our secret dreams, nor do they have any real understanding of how important something might be to us, or how hard we are willing to work to make our dream a reality.

Prayer

Finally, let me share a lesson it took me far too many years to learn. Until the age of 58, I had always taken great pride in the fact that I could "do it myself." Always feeling self-sufficient, I never asked anyone for help, even when I needed it. But the day finally came, after nearly twenty years of self-employment, when I had used the last ounce of my personal strength resources and didn't know how to replenish them. A good friend in my network had the answer: "Have you tried praying?" she asked. "To get help, you must ask for it."

Until then, I'd never thought of asking God for help with my business because He was surely too busy with the important things of the world to be concerned about my little problems. Since this is a business book, I'll spare you the details of what happened when I finally went to my knees in prayer and turned my life and business over to God, but you'll find them on my Web site at BarbaraBrabec.com if you're interested. Suffice it to say that my whole life and the direction of my work began to change in exciting ways as soon as I plugged myself into God's power. Things happened that I never could have imagined or accomplished through my own doing. As new doors of opportunity opened, some doors I had struggled to keep open for years slammed shut immediately, totally changing the way I would earn my living five years later.

This was when I finally saw that we can go a long way under our own steam and much farther when others are behind us offering motivational support and encouragement. But sooner or later, with or without emotional and motivation support, we're all going to run out of ourselves someday. The problem is that there are so many books and so many humanists out there saying "You can do it! All you have to do is believe in yourself." While I still believe this kind of positive thinking is important to a well-balanced life, I now know it's not nearly enough. Some day you, too, will discover there is a limit to the number of times you can pull yourself up by your bootstraps. Unless you plug into a source of power greater than yourself, one day you may discover, as I did, that, without God, you're as dead and useless as a lightbulb without electricity.

Do you remember what I said earlier about what you could do if you could override the bad programs in your subconscious mind—those that are working against you—and replace them with a refreshing new program of absolute belief? That's what I did, and that's what a simple prayer to God might do for you right now, if you will simply allow yourself to be open to the possibilities.

As you pursue your home-business endeavors, thank God for all the talents and abilities He has given you, ask for His guidance in selecting the business that's right for you, and don't hesitate to lean on the Lord whenever you need help or encouragement in either your personal or home-business life. From experience, I have learned that if we will simply open ourselves to God's spirit, He will lead us in surprising new directions and reveal wondrous things we never could have discovered on our own. As the Bible confirms, "Commit to the Lord whatever you do, and your plans will succeed" (Proverbs 16:3, NIV).

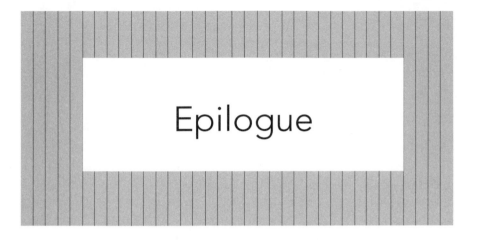

Epilogue

A good book remains one of life's true miracles . . . a remarkable value. What you are getting for the money is the result of several years of work on an author's part, and a lifetime of learning. In some cases, a man or woman struggles for most of his or her life to produce one book. All the experiences of that lifetime, all the encounters and conversations, may have gone into the wisdom that produced the book.

—Bob Green, syndicated columnist and author

"Life is short, and life without books is much too small," says Garrison Keillor. "Books are what change our lives, and a person has to feel sorry for people who say they don't have time to read. It's like not having time to dream."

I see books as natural beginnings to all kinds of wonderful things. It was a book, after all, that led me to start my first small home business. That book, *You Can Whittle and Carve*, released a stream of creativity in me that has yet to cease. I never made much money selling my woodcarvings, but oh, what I learned in the process.

A few years later, another book, *On Writing Well*, by William Zinsser, changed my life because it changed the way I thought about myself. It convinced me I could be a professional writer if I chose to be one. Many other books have taught me additional things and propelled me in exciting new directions, as I hope this book will do for you.

In the process of writing my first book (*Creative Cash*), I learned something about dreams and goals I want to share with you. After finishing that first book, I told myself I was going to write another one. Someday. When I had more time. I dreamed about that book for five years. For a long time, I used the excuse that I was overwhelmed by work and couldn't possibly find time to write another book. In time, I came to realize that part of my reluctance to start a new book was my fear that I would not be able to write a second book that would measure up to my first. (I think a lot of new authors must feel this way. You have done it once . . . but can you do it again?)

Thanks to a publisher who kept nudging me, I finally stopped dreaming about my second book (*Homemade Money*) and made plans to write it. Believe me, there is nothing like a written contract with a firm deadline to spur one onward! Curiously, while the dream of a second book had seemed an impossibility for five years, the book—as a clearly defined goal—suddenly seemed achievable. There can be no doubt about it. We do not make gains by dreaming about things. We must set firm goals and then work like the dickens to achieve them, else they will remain dreams forever.

When I finished the first edition of *Homemade Money* in 1984, I thought, "Whew! What a big job. Am I glad it's finished." I did not realize then that I had written what would soon become a classic in its field, not to mention a book that had to be updated often if new readers were to be well served. Nor did I realize that each of these updates would take hundreds of additional hours of my time, actually preventing me from writing other books. But with each new edition, I felt a special kind of satisfaction in knowing I had done what was necessary at the time. My books are like children to me, and like children, they have required my constant care and attention as they (and I) have matured.

When *Homemade Money* was acquired by a new publisher in 1992, I invested nearly a thousand hours more into a product many said was already the best of its kind. Still more time went into later revisions, and when the fifth revised edition was published I was *certain* this would be the last rewrite of the book. But I hadn't counted on the Internet. *Homemade Money* was totally out of date

Epilogue

by the turn of the century, and my publisher wasn't interested in a new edition. The book would have died at that point if not for another publisher's longtime interest in this title. So, once again, I signed a contract to deliver an all-new edition of *Homemade Money*, this time as two totally new books.

Once again, I've invested nearly a year of my life into a work I once thought I'd finished nearly twenty years ago. Now you can understand why I relate to Bob Greene's remark in the opening quote of this chapter:

"What you are getting for the money is the result of several years of work on an author's part, and a lifetime of learning."

I could have taken an easier route for *Homemade Money* than I did, but age has taught me there is always room for improvement, even in the best products and services, and we must never become lazy and think we can rest on our laurels. ("If you rest on your laurels, all you'll end up with is a leafy design on your behind," say authors Esther Blumenfeld and Lynne Alpern.) My husband has never understood why I can't leave well enough alone, but Norman Vincent Peale explained it when he said, "We are self-made victims of mediocrity. We make ourselves content. But no one should ever be satisfied with a performance less than the best. Every human being has top quality built in. We are born to be achievers."

I am always exhausted by the time I've finished a new book or a rewrite of an old one, but there is also enormous satisfaction from having done the job right. It will be that way for you, too. The hard work and extra hours you put into your business, now or in the future, are going to cause problems or work pile-ups in your day-to-day life. It definitely will add to your stress level, and it positively will exhaust you time and again. But, oh, the exhilaration of it all! There is nothing quite so satisfying as the achievement of a goal that's important to you.

That's why I urge you to stop dreaming about the things you want to do, and start making plans to do them before another season passes. Set firm, written goals and then get to work. It's absolutely amazing what you can accomplish once you begin. As you continue to learn, remember it will take time for everything to gel into a cohesive whole. Take heart, those of you who are just beginning, those who are fearful of the unknown, those who are struggling against opposition from friends and family. It's not easy to build a business, but even when it's hard, it's satisfying. Even when it's financially unprofitable, it's rewarding. Take comfort in the fact that you are not alone.

Homemade Money

Like salmon swimming upstream, some home-business owners make it, some don't. There are no sure bets in this game, but one thing is certain: It *is* a game worth playing. Even those who fail as businesspeople will succeed as individuals. It takes gumption and guts to start and operate a business of any kind, and anyone who does it, even for a little while, is a winner in my book. I firmly believe it is better to have bossed and lost than never to have bossed at all.

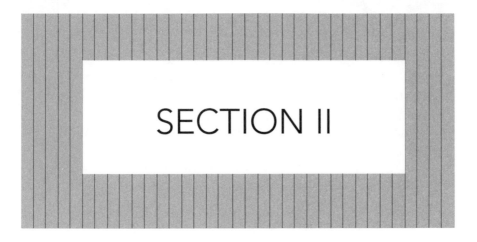

SECTION II

Much of the material in this section is in such "professional service" categories as legalities, taxes, and accounting. While this information has been carefully researched and is accurate to the best of the author's knowledge as this book goes to press, it is not the business of either the author or publisher to render such professional services. Readers are therefore asked to exercise normal good judgment in determining when the services of a lawyer or other professional would be appropriate to their needs.

An A-to-Z "Crash Course" in Business Basics

This section of the book offers answers to hundreds of questions related to home-business start-up. It incorporates tax, legal, and financial information from several experts in my network along with the shared experiences of my readers and lessons I've learned from a lifetime of self-employment. In particular, I would like to thank the following individuals for their help in double-checking the accuracy of my information on accounting, taxes, copyrights, and trademarks:

● Bernard Kamoroff is a CPA and the author of *Small Time Operator—How to Start Your Own Business, Keep Your Books, Pay Your Taxes, and Stay Out of Trouble* (Bell Springs Pub.). This small business classic is now in its 27th edition with over 640,000 copies in print. Kamoroff's publishing company, Bell Springs Publishing, is located in Willits, California, and is on the Web at www.BellSprings.com.

● Mary Helen Sears has been in private law practice in Washington, D.C., since 1961. The M. H. Sears Law Firm is mainly devoted to patents, copyrights, trademarks, and related matters.

The in-depth information in this chapter—material that will not be found in any other home-business guide—is possible only because hundreds of caring readers have shared their experiences with me through the years in hopes of helping others avoid problems they encountered. Because laws and regulations can change at any time, however, I do ask that you accept all the technical and legal information in this section with the proverbial grain of salt. My primary goal is to familiarize you with important areas of concern for homebased business owners and enable you to ask the right questions *when you double-check my information with your own tax adviser, accountant, attorney, or other professional.*

Note: Information in this section is presented alphabetically in logical topic categories, but since different aspects of some of these topics are also discussed in the text, check the index to make sure you have all the information you need on any given subject. Mail addresses have been provided only when a company, agency, or organization does not have an 800-number or Web site. If you need an e-mail address, simply visit the Web site in question for contact information.

Section II

Contents
A-to-Z Business Basics

Section II

Accountant

(See also *Accounting Methods*)

Contrary to the usual advice given to all new businesspeople, an accountant is not needed at the beginning of a business *if* it is small and you are capable of setting up the necessary record-keeping system to operate it. But unless you happen to be thoroughly acquainted with the tax code, you'll need an accountant, enrolled agent, or highly qualified tax preparer when tax time rolls around. Look for someone who is thoroughly familiar with the many special deductions to which a home-business owner is entitled. (Not every accountant is comfortable in this area.)

Certified Public Accountant (CPA)

Not all accountants are certified. CPAs charge more than noncertified accountants and are more likely to specialize in larger businesses. Although you may prefer to use a CPA, the average small home business does not require one. More important than the title is the fact that the accountant you pick should have knowledge of your particular occupation or type of business, and be willing to work with you. Avoid accountants who handle only corporate work; you want someone who understands *small* business. To find a good accountant, get recommendations from other business owners like yourself or some other business professional whose advice you trust.

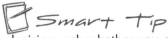 Smart Tip

Before you make a decision, ask whether you can come in for a short, no-charge discussion about your needs. Ask the accountant to furnish the names of clients who are in occupations similar to yours. Since there are several ways to bill for services, be sure you understand the firm's fee structure.

Enrolled Agents

An enrolled agent is one who is approved by the Internal Revenue Service to represent taxpayers before the IRS. Such agents have completed a comprehensive IRS-administered examination in federal taxation and related subjects, and must complete a minimum number of credit hours each year of continuing education. Enrolled agents may work as independent consultants or practice in a firm that includes both CPAs and attorneys engaged in tax preparation. Their cost may be higher than a tax preparer but less than a CPA. To find an enrolled agent near you, call the National Association of Enrolled Agents, 1-800-424-4339; www.NAEA.org.

Tax Preparers

Tax preparers generally work only with the figures a taxpayer gives them; they are not trained to handle the more complicated tax reports of self-employed individuals. Unless you are knowledgeable about every business deduction to which you're entitled, and can prepare all the necessary figures for your annual tax return, you'll be wise to use an accountant or enrolled agent instead of a tax preparer. (You'll probably save more money in taxes than you'll spend for their fee, which is tax deductible.)

Accounting Methods

(See also *Accountant; Business Deductions Checklist for Home-Business Owners*)

Some small business owners consult with bookkeepers for help in setting up their books while others hire them to do all their bookkeeping. However, Bernard Kamoroff, a CPA and author of *Small Time Operator*, says all business owners should keep their own books for at least a year, just to learn how to read and use the books once they've been posted.

Some home businesses use single-entry bookkeeping systems that keep paperwork, figurework, and headaches to a minimum while still providing all the information needed to properly manage a business and prepare tax returns. Others do their bookkeeping on a computer, using one of the many accounting packages now available. For a sole proprietorship, however, a simple system consisting of a business checkbook, a cash receipts journal, a cash disbursements journal, and a petty cash fund is quite sufficient. An important first consideration in setting up your bookkeeping system is whether you will operate on a cash or accrual basis:

- **Cash Method.** All income is taxable in the year it's received, and expenses are generally deductible when paid, with some important exceptions an accountant can explain.

● **Accrual Method.** Tax must be paid on earned income, whether it has been collected or not; expenses may be deducted when they have been incurred, whether they have been paid or not. Some businesses are required by law to use the accrual accounting method.

Note: A recent change in IRS policy has enabled many business owners to switch from the accrual method of accounting to the cash method, but some businesses are prohibited from using it, and you should check with an accountant to see if yours is one of them.

● **"Hybrid System."** A mix of the above types of accounting systems. For example, a small business might use the accrual system for inventory purchases and the cash method to record all income and expenses. (Inventory is expensed only when sold.) An accountant will help you decide which method is best for you.

 Smart Tip

The IRS prescribes no specific accounting records, documents, or systems. It merely requires that taxpayers maintain a set of records adequate enough to prepare an accurate tax return. Since the burden of proof lies with the taxpayer, make sure your records reflect all income *and* expenses.

Attorney/Lawyer

(See also *Contracts; Legal Forms of Business*)

Contrary to popular belief, you do not need a lawyer to start a simple home business. Many small businesses have never used a lawyer, and never intend to. Of course, if you need someone to hold your hand through the start-up process, a lawyer will be happy to do it, while giving you a big bill for fast answers to your questions. With this book in hand, you're getting the same thing for a lot less money. As your business grows, and various legal questions come to mind, you'll often be able to answer them yourself by reading books and periodicals or doing research on the Internet.

There are times, however, when you should hire a lawyer even if you're strapped for funds, because the alternative might cost far more than your legal fees. If you lack a good layman's understanding of the kind of legalese normally found in contracts, it could be an expensive mistake to sign one without the advice of legal counsel. Also of concern should be long-term agreements such as partnerships, cooperatives, exclusive dealer or distributor agreements, licensing or franchise arrangements, and royalty contracts. And *never* purchase property or buy a business without the guidance of a lawyer who will make sure you're not placing yourself in an uncomfortable legal or tax situation. (Of course, your accountant or CPA can also advise you on tax matters. Not all lawyers are tax experts, just as all tax lawyers are not authorities on contract law.)

Smart Tip

If your business is the type that may require regular legal advice, consider membership in one of the many prepaid legal plans now available. Often, these plans are included as part of the membership benefits of some small business organizations, but you can also join them as an individual. A search on the Web will turn up such services.

Do you need a lawyer to incorporate your business? It is entirely possible, and quite legal (in some, but not all states), to incorporate without the services of a lawyer, but this is not something a business novice should attempt. One lawyer pointed out to me that it will cost more to unincorporate yourself than to incorporate, so you don't want to make the wrong decision. This is just one more reason to seek professional advice.

At times, your business may also require the help of an attorney who specializes in a particular field, such as labor law, taxes, patents, trademarks, or copyrights. You do not need an attorney to get a copyright, however. (Some business novices have told me they've paid attorneys $100 to do something they could have easily done themselves for just $30—fill out a form. See "Copyrights" elsewhere in this section.)

If you have a legal question you want answered free of charge, check this Web site: www.LawGuru.com. Here, a network of over 2,000 attorneys and law firms in over 35 countries answer questions online *free of charge*, and the Web site's database now includes answers to 35,000 FAQs in 45 legal categories.

Bonded Service

Bonding is a form of insurance you buy to give your customers peace of mind—assurance that you are trustworthy and reliable, and that they're fully protected against loss. Some services can be sold more easily if they're bonded, such as house-sitting or vacation services where you would have access into people's homes during their absence. Another example would be a delivery service that normally handles valuable documents or expensive objects—jewelry, art, etc., or possibly a photographer who is taking pictures for insurance purposes. Bonding companies are listed in the Yellow Pages. Call one of them for more information about procedures and costs.

Business Checking Account

(See also *Business Loans and Other Money Sources*; *Checks and Money Orders*; *Credit/Credit Cards*)

Do *not* use your personal checking account to conduct the transactions of your business. A separate business checking account is essential for accurate record keeping and substantiation of business deductions for tax purposes.

In selecting a bank for your business, be sure to ask if it offers a business line of credit, small business loans, or merchant account services. (You will find that "savings banks," which used to be called "savings and loan associations," do not.) Get a listing of all bank charges, too, since these can vary dramatically from one bank to another. Call several banks in your area and note the following charges on a chart:

● Is there a charge for *each deposit made?*

● Is there a charge for *each check deposited?* (Some banks make a charge for each deposit, while others charge for each out-of-state check deposited—very costly for mail order businesses.)

● Is there a charge for *each check written*, or are checks purchased in quantity for a flat fee?

- How much is the charge for *bounced* checks?

- Is *interest* paid on the checking account balance?

When you have these figures, fictionalize a typical month's banking activity and compare one bank's charges to another to find the one best suited to your needs.

Smart Tip

If you're a married woman with a home business, be sure to open your business checking account in your name only. If you add your husband's name, it becomes a joint account with credit history going automatically to his file.

Check Writing Tips

1. If your checking account pays interest, hang on to your money as long as possible. Bills paid later in the week take longer to clear because of the weekend.

2. When writing the dollar amount of a check, always place figures close to the printed dollar sign on the check to make it impossible for anyone to add another figure between your figure and the dollar sign.
   Example: $9.85 (Correct) $[blank space] 9.85 (Dangerous)

3. When spelling out the dollar amount on the second line of a check, take the same kind of precaution, filling the entire line. Example:
   Nine and 85/100————————————————————————-Dollars

Business Expenses and Tax Deductions

(See nearby *Business Deductions Checklist* and *Checklist of Home-Related Tax-Deductible Expenses*)

Tax evasion can lead to a stay in the slammer; tax avoidance, however, is the right of every taxpayer. If you operate a business at home, a wide variety of expenses becomes deductible, provided you can show that the expenses are

Business Expenses and Tax Deductions

ordinary, necessary, and somehow connected with the operation and potential profit of your business. A detailed discussion of taxes is beyond the scope of this book, but this kind of information is readily available to you in books such as *Small Time Operator* by Bernard Kamoroff.

A nearby chart gives you a master checklist of deductible expenses available to business owners. Note that this list includes some expenses (marked with a footnote reference) that are deductible only in certain instances. Not everything one spends in connection with a business can be "expended," or deducted, at the time the money is spent. Some purchases must be depreciated over a specified number of years while others, such as inventory purchases (anything bought for resale), are expensed only when actually sold. (Example: You buy $1,000 worth of inventory but sell only $700 in the year of purchase; you deduct $700 of inventory costs and carry the remaining $300 worth of inventory to the next year's tax report.)

Business assets, such as equipment, office furnishings, and other major purchases connected with your business, are generally expensed through depreciation, a complicated tax area that may require professional help. Depreciation must be taken in the year in which it is sustained. (You cannot deduct in any one year the allowable depreciation that you failed to take in a prior year.) Business owners have another option, however, called "expensing." They may completely write off a certain dollar amount of new equipment that would normally be depreciated—an excellent strategy to use in years when your income takes a jump while regular expenses remain the same. The amount you can expense is scheduled to increase to a maximum of $25,000 in 2003. Your accountant can help you decide whether expensing or depreciation is best for you in any given year.

☑ Smart Tip

When you need extra deductions, here's a year-end tax strategy to remember: IRS considers that payment has been made on the date of a credit card transaction, not when one actually pays the bill. Thus, business items charged to credit cards are deductible in the year of purchase even when a balance remains on the credit card. The only catch is that you must use a third-party credit card such as MasterCard or Visa—not a card issued by the company that supplies the deductible goods or services, such as a department store purchase on that store's credit card.

Business Use of Personal Property

What happens when you start a business and begin to use personal property that may already be paid for, or in the process of being paid for? You can depreciate this equipment on either a cost or market value basis, whichever is less, says Bernard Kamoroff. But how do you determine a fair market value? "Pick a figure and hope you don't have to prove it," he quips, adding that, in his experience, the IRS seldom questions any reasonable amount.

Business Deductions Checklist for Home-Business Owners

Generally speaking, all money spent in connection with the operation of your business is tax deductible. Following is a checklist of business deductions that may be applicable to your homebased business. Note that these deductions are *in addition* to the other tax deductions listed on the chart, "Checklist of Home-Related Tax-Deductible Expenses for Home-Business Owners." Since tax laws are constantly changing, always verify the legality of a questionable business deduction with your accountant or other tax authority.

____ Accounting or bookkeeping services
____ Advertising and promotional expenses
____ Bad debts/bounced checks[1]
____ Bank charges
____ Books and periodicals (business related)
____ Briefcase or samples case
____ Business development expenses[2]
____ Business gifts
____ Business seminars
____ Christmas cards (for business associates)
____ Cleaning services (office, business, uniforms, equipment)
____ Collection agency fees
____ Computer software
____ Consulting fees
____ Conventions and trade show expense
____ Copyright fees[6]
____ Delivery charges

Business Expenses and Tax Deductions

____ Donations

____ Dues/membership fees, professional

____ Educational expense[7]

____ Entertainment expenses[3]

____ Equipment lease/rental costs

____ Equipment purchases[2]

____ Freight and shipping charges

____ Insurance premiums[8]

____ Interest on business loans or late tax payments

____ IRA or Keogh account deposits[4]

____ Labor costs (independent contractors)

____ Legal and professional fees[2]

____ Licenses and permits

____ Mail list development/maintenance

____ Maintenance contracts (office equipment) and repairs

____ Office supplies

____ Postage

____ Product displays, exhibiting expenses

____ Professional services (artists, designers, copywriters, Web services, etc.)

____ Refunds to customers

____ Research and development (R&D) expense[2]

____ Safe Deposit Box[9]

____ Sales Commissions

____ Sales and Use Tax

____ Start-up/organizational expenses[2]

____ Stationery and printing

____ Subscriptions to business periodicals

____ Supplies and materials

____ Tax preparation fees

____ Telephone, fax, modem expense

____ Tools of your trade

____ Trademark expenses[6]

____ Travel expenses[5]

____ Uniforms or special costumes used only in trade or profession

____ Union dues (related to home-based business or profession)

____ Wages to employees, including those paid to spouse or children

Footnotes

1. If you use the accrual method to report income, you are entitled to a deduction for bad debts (bounced checks and other uncollectible accounts) because they were previously counted as reportable income. If you use the cash method, however, you cannot deduct an uncollectible account because the payment was not previously counted as reportable income.

2. Start-up expenses are deductible only when one is already in business. As a general rule, you are not entitled to a deduction for legal and accounting advice you obtain before you start a business. This is considered an organizational expense. Therefore, it would be tax-advantageous if you were to legally establish your business before you hired any legal or accounting advice. (The same rule applies to start-up expenses and research and development costs.)

3. Deductions for entertainment are a touchy area; ask an accountant for help in taking such deductions because they could trigger an audit.

4. Under current law, deductions for IRAs are primarily limited to those who do not participate in the pension plans of their employers.

5. Travel expenses (meals and lodging, airfare, train, bus, taxi, auto expenses, tips, tolls, etc. are fully deductible, but deductions for business-related meals and travel expenses are currently limited to 50 percent. Spousal travel deductions are allowed only when the spouse is an employee of the company.

6. Previously nondeductible until they were sold, trademarks, as well as copyrights and patents, can now be deducted over a fifteen-year period.

7. If your business is established, the cost of business education (seminars, conferences, workshops, book purchases, etc.) is fully deductible. Such expenditures prior to business start-up would not be deductible. (See point 2 above.)

8. Most insurance premiums related to your business—product liability,

home-office policy or special rider on homeowner's policy, computer insurance, etc.—are fully deductible. Premiums on your house insurance and car are deductible in part, as explained on the "Checklist of Home-Related Tax-Deductible Expenses for Home-Business Owners."

9. Safe deposit box rental is deductible only if the box holds documents related to production of income or business documents, computer back-up disks/tapes, etc.

Checklist of Home-Related Tax-Deductible Expenses for Home-Business Owners

Once you've tallied all your regular business expenses (see "Business Deductions Checklist for Home-Business Owners"), begin the special calculations that determine home-related deductions.

Direct Expenses.

Those that benefit only the business part of your home. You may deduct all costs of direct expenses, which include:

___ **Decorating or remodeling costs/expenses** (that do not result in capital improvements); painting or repairs made to the specific area or room used exclusively for business; or repairs done to change an ordinary room into a place of business, such as rewiring, plumbing changes, walls or flooring, etc.

___ **Certain room furnishings.** Larger purchases, such as office furniture and equipment, must be depreciated, as a general rule. Inexpensive items, like an office bulletin board, for example, could be deducted under office supplies and materials.

Indirect Expenses

Those that benefit both the business and personal parts of your home. Only the business part is deductible as a business expense (on Form 8829, "Expenses for Business Use of Your Home"—known as the "Home Office

Deduction"):

_____ **Rent** (on percentage of home used for business)

_____ **Mortgage interest** (percentage related to use of home for business; balance of interest is deductible on the personal portion of your tax return)

_____ **Insurance premiums on home**

_____ **Depreciation of home** (not the land, however. Ask your accountant to explain the tax problem that can occur if you take a deduction for depreciation of your home, and then sell it at a profit.

_____ **Utilities** (gas, electric, oil)

_____ **Services** (trash removal, snow removal, yard maintenance). The latter two may be questionable unless clients or customers normally visit your home.

_____ **Home repairs**, plus related labor and suppliers (furnace, roof, etc.)

Other Expenses

_____ **Personal Computer.** If you use one computer both for personal and business usage, you need to document one or the other with a time log so you can calculate a percentage related to business that may be used to figure your business deduction. You may depreciate the business percentage of the computer's cost and also deduct related supplies and materials.

_____ **Personal Telephone.** Fully deductible are all business-related long-distance telephone calls and all extra charges for business extensions or services, such as call forwarding, call holding, Internet, etc. However, homebased business owners may not deduct a percentage of the basic monthly charge for the first phone line coming into the home.

_____ **Family Automobile.** All business-related mileage or actual operating expenses related to business use is deductible, provided you document such expenses for the IRS with some kind of log or diary. Note the odometer reading at the beginning and end of each year and log each business-related trip you make.

You may find that your deductions for business use of your vehicle will be larger if you calculate on the basis of total operating costs. In this case, you would add up all expenses for the year, including gas, oil, supplies, repairs, maintenance, parking and tolls, towing, washing, tires, garage expenses, license tags, inspection fees, taxes, insurance, depreciation, even Motor Club memberships. Take total miles driven for business and divide by total miles driven for the year to get a percentage of business use. Multiply total car costs by this percentage figure to get your business-related, tax-deductible automobile expenses for the year.

_____ **Child Care Expenses.** If you are self-employed and you pay someone to care for your child (or an invalid parent or spouse) so you can work, a portion of the cost may be deductible on the personal portion of your tax return.

Business Forms and Terms

(See also *Invoicing Terms*)

Standard business forms can be purchased in office supply stores or ordered by mail from many companies. Here are six forms used by most businesses:

● **Sales Order Form.** Needed when dealing with wholesale buyers. If you do not wish to use a sales order book, simply write an order on your business letterhead, making a copy for the buyer. If buyers want to give you their own purchase order, make sure it is signed by the buyer, and that he or she agrees to all your terms and conditions as stated on your price list.

● **Purchase Order.** You may receive purchase orders as well as send them. A purchase order received from a shop or store should be acknowledged either with immediate shipment of the order, or by an order confirmation that indicates when later shipment may be expected. When you use a purchase order for your own suppliers, it signifies that you are a businessperson, not a hobby business, which is why the use of this form may help you in getting wholesale prices or credit. Purchase order forms are also helpful inner-office records that enable you to keep track of incoming supplies, invoices that must be paid, and the volume of business you are giving each of your suppliers.

- **Price List.** Do not place retail and wholesale prices on the same sheet, but print individual price sheets for each, adding them to your sales brochure. Your wholesale price list should state your conditions for new customers (your need for credit references or check with first order, etc.), your guarantee (if one is offered), and your shipping charge policy. (Some sellers charge the actual postage or shipping costs incurred while others work on a certain percentage of the order—from 5 to 10 percent depending on size of item—which few buyers would question. The latter charge probably would help offset your overhead costs in packing orders.)

- **Packing List.** Product buyers need some kind of checklist when they are unpacking a shipment. The packing list serves this purpose by describing the contents of each box or carton in the shipment. The packing list must agree in description and number with the information shown on the invoice, which is why some standard invoice forms include a packing list as one of the copies in the form. Obviously, this saves time by eliminating the typing of a second business form.

- **Invoice.** Standard invoice forms are available in three, four, or five-part sets but many business owners create their own computer-generated invoices. An invoice should include the following information: seller's name and address; buyer's name and address; ship-to address (if different from sold-to address); date of invoice; date of shipment; method of shipment (parcel post, truck line, UPS, etc.); invoice number; customer's purchase order number; terms of payment (net 30 days, etc.); quantity and description of items shipped, their unit price, and total amount; plus shipping charges. (See also "Statement" under "Invoicing Terms.")

Business Loans and Other Money Sources

(See also *Credit/Credit Cards*)

Bank Loans

Once your business is established, you may have no difficulty in getting a bank loan to advance your growing business, but forget about start-up money because banks do not give loans to new home-business owners. The blunt truth is that many banks consider homebased entrepreneurs a poor business risk. In fact, one of my reader sent a list of businesses considered high-risk by her particular bank. It included mail/telephone order merchants, insurance agents, self-improvement courses, homebased businesses, limousine services, travel agencies, and house party plans . . . right along with massage parlors, used car dealers and phone sex merchants.

On the other hand, banks love to loan money to consumers for worthwhile things like vacations, new cars, and home improvement. A personal loan may be the answer if you have a good credit rating or can offer the kind of collateral the bank requires, such as a savings account, equity in your home, or cash surrender value of an insurance policy. Years ago when Leila Peltosaari needed money to print her sewing books, the bank considered her venture too risky and refused the loan request. "But it was easy to get credit to buy a car and take a vacation, so we told our bank we needed a new car and wanted to make a trip to see our parents in Europe, and then we used the money to print the books. With the profits from book sales, we then bought a car, a house, a swimming pool, and trailer tent, made a fabulous European trip and invested in our retirement, too. I understood that banks had no confidence in our intentions, so we just played their game and it all worked out fine."

Home equity loans are now common, but you may not know that home equity *lines of credit* are now available from many lenders, and you might be able to figure out how to use this kind of money to start or advance your business. In the end, many new entrepreneurs decide it's easier to borrow from their own savings account, or perhaps a relative (see tip below). Others figure out how to raise their own venture capital through a variety of entrepreneurial activities such as having a garage sale or selling a bunch of personal items on eBay.

Homemade Money

✓ Smart Tip

If you have a friend or relative who has money in savings but is not keen on just lending it to you outright, he or she could move these savings to your financial institution and let you use the savings passbook as collateral for a loan. Although your friend or relative could not spend the money in this account so long as your loan was outstanding, no interest would be lost. As you paid back the loan, you would free up that amount of funds in the savings account. Stocks, bonds, and notes receivable may also qualify as collateral for this type of loan. As you repay the loan, you would be establishing a valuable credit history that could make future business loans easier to get.

Life Insurance Loans

Don't overlook this possibility for start-up capital. If you have an insurance policy with cash value, you may be able to borrow on it at a much lower rate than a regular loan. (Some smart investors borrow on life insurance policies even when they don't need the money simply to reinvest the loan money in higher interest-bearing investments such as government securities or money-market funds.)

Credit Card Loans

A study in 1999 by the SBA revealed that almost half of all small business owners with ten or fewer employees used credit cards as a financing source. Although credit cards remain a time-honored source of quick money for established business owners, be very cautious about launching a new business with a credit card loan until you're reasonably sure that you'll have enough business to repay the loan in a timely manner. (See "Credit/Credit Cards" for tips on getting a low-interest credit card.).

SBA Loans

The U.S. Small Business Administration has a Microloan Program that offers loans from $200 to $35,000 to budding entrepreneurs. More information can be obtained from an SBA or SCORE office near you (see listing of "Government Agencies" in this section). Some *Direct Loans* are available to handicapped persons and disabled vets. *Guarantee Loans* are also available to certain new/young businesses when a local bank will not provide a loan without additional backing. Before the SBA can process this type of loan, however, it needs the signature of the local zoning officer to verify the business is operating legally—a fact that would automatically eliminate many homebased business owners from consideration.

Although state and federal governments have an assortment of programs to assist economic development through financing new business, the processing of applications for government loans or loan guarantees is a lengthy procedure. It may be better to consider government assistance as an additional or secondary source of financing once the business is under way, rather than as a source for start-up funding.

Other Sources of Money

Your membership in certain organizations—particularly those that focus on women, minorities, and other underrepresented sectors of the population—may give you access to small business loans or venture capital. To find such organizations, read business magazines and newsletters or search the Web. Also see "Other Resources" for books such as *Government Giveaways for Entrepreneurs* that list grant opportunities and sources of private, state, federal, and corporate money.

Some states now have business enterprise programs whereby would-be entrepreneurs can collect unemployment insurance benefits while they're trying to get a new business off the ground, with income from the business not counting against benefits. If you've recently lost your job, be sure to inquire if such a program is available in your state. If you are on welfare, note that most states now have self-employment programs that permit one to use welfare benefits to start a business.

Business or Trade Name

(See also *Licenses and Permits; Trademarks*)

After you've picked your business name—but *before* you order stationery and cards—check with your city or county clerk to make sure no one else is using the name you've selected. It's also a good idea to do a search to see if someone has trademarked that name. (See "Trademarks" in this section.) Otherwise, the name you think is completely original may be challenged by someone else.

> **Note:** Banks often use the abbreviation of "d/b/a" in their records to connect a depositor to his or her fictitious name. This stands for "doing business as." *Example:* Jack Robinson, d/b/a Antiques Galore.

Fictitious Name Statement

If you are using an assumed name, you must file a *Fictitious Name Statement* with your county clerk and publish a specially worded notice in the legal section of a local newspaper of general circulation (see special tip below). The purpose of such registration and notice is to give the public information about your identity. A fictitious name has to be connected to the name of a person who can be held responsible for the actions of a business.

Prior to registering your name, you need to find out if anyone else is using it. Check with your county clerk to see if you can do an online search of its database to determine this or whether you must go to the office where such records are kept. (To find your county's Web site, check the National Association of Counties Web site at www.Naco.org.)

Your assumed business or trade name should be registered with the state, too, to prevent its use by any corporate entity. Of course, your name must be free of conflict from corporate names already registered. (If it isn't, you'll be notified.)

> **Note:** Some states require registration even when one's real name is part of the business name, so you'll need to check this on your own. If you want to protect your business name from being used by a corporate entity in your state, you must register it with your state. To protect your name and business logo on a national level, see "Trademarks."

Smart Tip

If you don't want your neighbors to know you're running a business at home (for personal reasons or concern about local zoning laws), the ad you run does *not* have to be placed in your hometown paper, but can be run in any newspaper in your *county*. Also, be sure to find out when you have to renew your local business name registration. You won't be notified about this, and you wouldn't want to lose the name over such a technicality.

Many small businesses do not bother to register their names with local officials, but if you're investing time and money into the development of a business, you'll be smart to protect your business name. I once heard about an unscrupulous entrepreneur who went through county records checking on whether certain local businesses had registered their names. He then filed fictitious name statements for all the unregistered businesses he found, approached each business one by one, and told them they either had to stop doing business under that name (because he now owned it), or pay him a stiff fee to buy it back. Since registration of your name is a simple and inexpensive matter, take care of it today, even if you've been in business for some time. (The form you have to complete doesn't ask for the date your business was started, so no one will be the wiser about your delay in registering.)

Checks and Money Orders

(See also *Merchant Accounts*)

Although the world is quickly moving to a cashless society, payment by check is still the choice of many today. In accepting checks for your products or services, your primary concern will always be to avoid bad checks. The SBA recommends never accepting checks that are undated, postdated, or more than thirty days old, adding that checks should be written and signed legibly in ink, with no erasures or written-over amounts. Look twice at checks with signatures you can't decipher, as well as those without a printed address or sequence number. (Although such checks are common and certainly legal, experts say that checks with sequence numbers below 300 are more likely to bounce than those with higher numbers.)

Accepting Checks at Shows

In taking checks from buyers at consumer fairs or shows, try to feel a transaction as it is being made. That uncomfortable sale will most likely be the one that results in a bad check. When you feel uncomfortable, ask more questions of the customer and get complete information. In addition to identification, obtain the individual's place of employment and phone. Also look closely at the picture on a buyer's driver's license and jot down the license number on the check.

Checks in the Mail

If you have a mail order business and you receive a check that looks suspicious, remember that you have thirty days' time in which to ship the order without violating Federal Trade Commission (FTC) rules. Thus, you may wish to deposit the check, wait a couple of weeks (if a check is going to bounce, you'll know it by then), and then ship the order. Some mail order businesses follow this procedure as a matter of general practice, viewing all personal checks as suspicious, a practice I do not recommend, however. In nearly thirty years of selling books and other information by mail, I rarely received more than two or three bad checks a year, and these usually cleared when deposited a second time. (Checks bounce for a lot of reasons. Once, when I got a bad check for $62 from a buyer in California, I called to see what she planned to do about this problem. She had the best excuse I've ever heard: Her bank had been bombed!)

If a check is large, and you're doubtful about it for any reason, you can also call the bank that issued the check and ask if there are sufficient funds in the account to cover it. (While this does not ensure that other checks won't be presented before yours, it will relieve your concern to get a "yes" answer.)

 Smart Tip

An ex-con gone straight once appeared on television with tips on how to avoid bad checks. He said that real checks are perforated on at least one side while phony checks are usually smooth on all four sides. He also suggested checking the routing number in the lower left-hand corner, adding that real checks have a magnetic ink that doesn't reflect light. This number on a phony check will look shiny and slightly raised because of the copying process used. If you're really suspicious about a check, dampen your finger and rub it across the background color on the front of the check to see if it runs.

Consignment Laws

Canadian Orders, Payment Options

U.S. businesses who sell to Canadians must decide whether they will ask Canadians to remit in U.S. funds (a move that may diminish response), or calculate the higher prices in terms of Canadian dollars and accept Canadian checks (a move that may create problems when depositing checks). Many U.S. banks are not equipped to handle foreign checks, and such deposits may incur high handling charges.

Canadians, on the other hand, are happy to accept U.S. dollar equivalents because the higher exchange rate helps offset their extra postage charges in shipping goods into the United States. Of course, U.S. postage costs to Canada are also higher, and because all mail, except postcards, must be sent in envelopes, this often adds an extra ounce to the package. Bulk mail is not acceptable at all.

Note that a bounced check from a Canadian buyer can be expensive since the costs of manually handling a returned check through international channels can amount to $20 or more. One reader who reported this problem was told by the Canadian bank in question that this problem could be avoided by requesting a money order or certified check from customers. In all my years of selling books to Canadians, I never got a bad check from one of them, so think twice before you establish a money-order policy for your Canadian consumer mail order buyers. This might cost more in lost orders than one or two bad checks a year.

If you're shipping a large order to a company whose credit you have not yet verified, a money order or certified check with first order seems only prudent.

Smart Tip

If you offer customers a charge card service, this will neatly avoid the problems associated with checks from a customer in a foreign country. The charge card company will automatically calculate the correct amount in U.S. or Canadian dollars, based on that day's rate-of-exchange figures.

Consignment Laws

Theoretically, consigned goods remain the property of the seller until they are sold to the retail customer, and in normal situations, there are no problems. According to the Uniform Commercial Code (which has been adopted by most states), if an establishment goes bankrupt, consigned goods may be subject to the claims of creditors, and be seized by such creditors unless certain protective steps have been taken by consignors. (A standard consignment contract is not enough to protect one in this instance.) It's a good rule of thumb to never consign more than a few items to a new or unknown shop until you have developed a satisfactory relationship with the owner or manager (based on prompt payment after the first merchandise has been sold) and see other indications that the shop is being well managed.

Several states now have consignment laws designed to protect artists and craftspeople. Those known to the author include Alaska, Arizona, Arkansas, California, Colorado, Connecticut, Florida, Idaho, Illinois, Iowa, Kentucky, Maryland, Massachusetts, Michigan, Minnesota, Missouri, Montana, New Hampshire, New Mexico, New York, North Carolina, Ohio, Oregon, Pennsylvania, Tennessee, Texas, Washington, and Wisconsin. Some state laws protect "art" only, excluding protection to items that fall outside the area of painting, sculpture, drawing, graphic arts, pottery, weaving, batik, macrame, quilting, "or other commonly recognized art forms." Since each state's law offers varying degrees of protection—and since other states may now have such a consignment law on the books—all sellers interested in consignment should obtain complete details from their state legislature.

▢ Smart Tip

Never consign merchandise without a consignment agreement that includes the name of the owner and addresses such things as insurance, pricing and commission, payment dates, how merchandise is to be displayed and maintained, and how and when unsold merchandise will be returned.

Consumer Safety Laws

(See also *Insurance/Product Liability Insurance; State Bedding Laws*)

All levels of the government are concerned about consumer protection and, as a consumer yourself, you no doubt are pleased by this concern. As a business owner, however, you must look at consumer safety in a different light. Following are specific consumer safety laws affecting homebased manufacturers of toys, wearing apparel, and other textile household furnishings.

Consumer Safety Laws

Toys and Other Goods for Children

The Consumer Product Safety Act of 1972 created The Consumer Product Safety Commission, which establishes and enforces mandatory safety standards for consumer products sold in the United States. One of the Commission's most active regulatory programs has been in the area of products designed for children. If you make toys of any kind, avoid problems by making sure your toys are (1) too large to be swallowed; (2) not apt to break easily or leave jagged edges; (3) free of sharp edges or points; (4) not put together with easily exposed pins, wires, or nails; and (5) nontoxic, nonflammable, and nonpoisonous. (The latter requirement explains why most toymakers do not paint or varnish wooden toys.) For more information, contact the CPSC's toll-free hotline, 1-800-638-2772 or check the Web at www.CPSC.gov. (The site features a special "Talk To Us" department where you can ask questions and get a reply by e-mail.)

If the toys you make happen to be stuffed, see also "State Bedding Laws/Stuffed Toys" for other labels that may have to be added to your products.)

Textiles

"Textiles" includes garments, quilts, stuffed toys, knitting, rugs, yarn, piece goods, etc. Manufacturers (including individual craftspeople) who are involved with textiles and wearing apparel must affix special labels to their products, as follows:

- **Content Labeling Law.** *The Textile Fiber Products Identification Act,* monitored by both the Bureau of Consumer Protection and the FTC, requires a label or hang tag that shows: (a) the name of the manufacturer or person marketing the textile fiber product, and (b) the generic names and percentages of all fibers in the product in amounts of 5 percent or more, listed in order by predominance by weight. Examples: "100% combed cotton," and "50% cotton, 50% polyester." (If the item contains wool, it falls under the *Wool Products Labeling Act of 1939,* and thus requires additional identification.)

- **Country of Origin Labels.** The FTC requires that all wool or textile products bear information on labels that clearly indicates when imported ingredients are used, even if the product is made in the United States. (Example: a tie made from imported silk must indicate that fact with such wording as "Made in the USA from imported products," or your own variation of that information. Items made from materials obtained

261

in the United States need only state "Made in the USA" or "Handcrafted in the USA," or whatever similar words you like. Furthermore, similar information must be passed on to the consumer whenever such products are described in mail order catalogs.

- **Textile Wearing Apparel and Household Furnishings.** In connection with its *Fabric Care Labeling Rule*, the FTC also requires a permanently affixed "care label" on all textile wearing apparel and household furnishings. Manufacturers can design and make their own labels or use standard ones available from a variety of sources, so long as such labels give care and maintenance instructions for the item, such as "Wash in warm water; use cool iron" or "Dry clean only." (Note that a recent change to this rule now places emphasis on being specific about the temperature of the water that must be used to wash a particular item. More specific information will be found on www.FTC.gov.)

- **Flammability of Fabrics.** In addition to labels, the textiles manufacturer must also be concerned with the flammability of fabrics and fibers used in the production of wearing apparel and home furnishings. Handwoven, hand-dyed items, as well as fabrics of all kinds, must conform to the standard of *The Flammable Fabrics Act*, which is policed by the Consumer Product Safety Commission.

Smart Tip

The tags and labels supplied by the following companies (and others you will find advertised in craft magazines) will satisfy most of the tag and label requirements of the government agencies mentioned above. Free samples will be sent on request to: Sterling Name Tape Co., 1-888-312-0113, www.sterlingtape.com and Widby Fabric Label Co., 1-888-522-2458, www.widbylabel.com.

Contracts

(*See also* Attorney/Lawyer)

A written contract is a lot easier to prove in court than a verbal one, but a verbal contract is just as legal and binding—unless it is for the sale of goods over a certain amount. (This varies from state to state but is usually around $500.) Any written agreement, dated and signed by the parties involved, can serve as a legal document, and legal language is not required. Complicated agreements, however, should at least be approved by a lawyer, and certain contracts and agreements should never be signed without advice of counsel, as mentioned earlier.

Companies often have standard contracts filled with unacceptable clauses, but remember that nothing is written in stone. Through negotiation, clauses may be amended to the satisfaction of both parties. In some cases, such as when you are selling a book to a publisher or trying to arrange a licensing agreement with a manufacturer, an agent with good negotiating skills is likely to give you greater power in making contractual changes while also increasing your profits from the deal.

Note: Since electronic signatures now have the same legal weight as a signature written in pen and ink, contracts (and other legal documents) bearing an electronic signature now have the same legal force as a contract written on paper.

Copyrights

(*See also* Trademarks)

You will recall my earlier discussion of copyright law in Chapter Two, which explained how to avoid violating the rights of others. Here, the focus is on how to protect your own intellectual property through copyright registration:

What Copyright Protects

The U.S. Copyright Law (enacted in 1790 and amended a number of times, most recently by Acts in 1978 and 1989) protects the rights of creators of intellectual property in seven broad categories that include literary, musical ,and dramatic works; pantomimes and choreographic works; pictorial, graphic, and sculptural works; motion pictures and other audiovisual works; and sound recordings. The *five* main categories of interest to home-business owners are:

1. **Form SE** is used to register a copyright for a SERIAL, which includes periodicals, newspapers, magazines, bulletins, newsletters, annuals, journals, and proceedings of societies.

2. **Form TX** is used to register TEXT of any kind—books, directories, and other work written in words, such as the how-to instructions for a crafts project.

3. **Form VA** is used to register a work of the VISUAL ARTS, which includes pictorial, graphic, or sculptural works, including fine, graphic and applied, photographs, charts, technical drawings, diagrams, and models.

4. **Form PA** is used for works of the PERFORMING ARTS, including musical works and accompanying words, dramatic works, pantomimes, choreographic works, motion pictures, and other audiovisual works.

5. **Form SR** is used to register SOUND RECORDINGS, including musical, spoken, or other sounds.

You cannot copyright names, titles, and short phrases, but brand names, trade names, slogans, and phrases may be entitled to protection under the provisions of trademark laws discussed later in this section. Inventions cannot be copyrighted, but may be patented. (The "drawing" or written description of an invention, however, could be copyrighted.)

Although ideas themselves may not be protected, a copyright does protect the *expression* of an idea. For example, four people could paint a picture of the same scene (the idea), and all four could copyright their original creations (their individual expression of the idea). Procedures for doing, making, or building something cannot be copyrighted, either, but the expression of those ideas, fixed in tangible form (in a book or product insert, for example) can be copyrighted.

Short sayings cannot be copyrighted, which explains why many manufacturers create products using the same common sayings. Although all of these products bear a copyright notice, what is really being protected here are not the words themselves, but the overall design of the work—how the words are actually arranged or displayed along with artwork.

You can have fun doing your own original adaptations of public domain sayings, but do not copy the quotes of famous people for your own profit. "This may be viewed as unfairly affecting the livelihood of the author," warns a copyright expert with whom I've consulted.

Here is an example to help you remember the difference between copyrights, trademarks, and patents: The *artwork* on a can of cola can be copyrighted. The *name—and the way it is expressed on that can*—can be trademarked. The *formula* for the cola itself can be patented.

Smart Tip

Check the recorded messages on the Copyright Office's automated message system by calling (212) 707-3000, or get the same information online at www.loc.gov/copyright. For free publications by mail, write to The Copyright Office, Register of Copyrights, Library of Congress, Washington, DC 20559.

Copyright Searches

To investigate the copyright status of a work today (to see if something has already been copyrighted), you can (1) examine a copy of the work to see if a copyright notice is present, (2) make a search of the Copyright Office catalogs and other records, or (3) ask the Copyright Office to make a search (for which there will be a fee).

Since a notice of copyright is no longer required by law, you cannot automatically assume that a work is unprotected by copyright simply because a copyright notice is absent. In fact, under current law, copyright protection exists from the moment a work is created. To illustrate: If you give a speech, you own your words the moment they fall from your lips, and you're the only one who has the right to put those words into written form or on an audiotape for purpose of profit. Everything you draw or put on paper or express in an e-mail—even a letter to your mother—is your property the moment it is written, and no one else has the right to use or sell it without your permission. That is one reason why you need not be concerned about sending articles or book manuscripts to magazine editors and book publishers without registering the copyright first. In addition to the fact that editors and publishers usually are ethical people who do not steal from writers, it is automatically understood that you are the owner of that material *until such time as you decide to sell or convey its copyright to someone else.* (Refer back to point 3 in "Ten Moneymaking Ideas That Violate Copyright Law" in Chapter Two.)

Note: In the past, there has been a movement in Congress to abolish the requirement that one must register a copyright in order to be able to sue for infringement. Though much discussed, this had not become law as of August, 2002 and whether Congress will succumb remains to be seen. If this does become law, it will be almost impossible for anyone to investigate the copyright status of a work, and we will all have to presume everything is copyrighted.

Application Forms

Application forms may be ordered by mail, by phone, or on the Web. The completed application form must be returned to the Copyright Office with the required fee (currently $30) plus two copies of the "best edition" of the work (and the Copyright Office has a list of criteria that determine exactly what the "best edition" is in each case). In printed matter, for example, it would mean a hard-cover book instead of the paperback edition; for other graphic matter, the best edition would be the one in color, instead of black and white. In the case of three-dimensional works, photographs or accurate drawings may be accepted in lieu of actual copies, etc. Note that it takes the Copyright Office six to eight weeks to process an application and return the registered copy. Be patient.

Smart Tip

If you're a designer interested in protecting your work through registration, you need not copyright each individual design. The Copyright Office will accept collections of designs that are bound together in any fashion. Similarly, a collection of articles could also be bound as a book and registered as a single work.

Length of Copyright

Copyright protection for works created after January 1, 1978 lasts for the life of the author or creator plus 70 years after his death. If the work is created anonymously, pseudonymously, or done for hire, copyright protection lasts 95 years from year of first publication, or 120 years from creation, whichever ends first. For works of two or more authors, it is extended for the life of the last to survive, plus 70 years. For works created before 1978, there are different terms, which a copyright lawyer can give you.

Note: Sometime in its 2002–2003 term, the U.S. Supreme Court will hear a case that makes a significant constitutional challenge to the length-of-copyright extensions mentioned above. Some statutory adjustment may occur as a result. If length of copyright is important to you, consult with an attorney for the latest information on this topic.

Copyright Notice

Failure to place a notice of copyright on copies of protected material can no longer result in the loss of copyright, but the lack of a notice only makes it more inviting to others to steal your creativity. When this happens, people may claim "innocent infringement" saying they didn't see a notice. *Because the remedies against innocent infringers are limited, the Copyright Office still strongly recommends the use of a copyright notice.* Thus, if you make or manufacture items of any kind, always include a proper copyright notice on each item offered for sale:

1   the word "copyright" or its abbreviation, "copr.," or the copyright symbol, ©

2   the year of first publication of the work (when it was first shown or sold to the public)

3   the name of the copyright owner. Sometimes the words, "All Rights Reserved" will also appear, which means that copyright protection has been extended to include all of the Western Hemisphere. *Example:* Copyright © 2003 by Barbara Brabec. All Rights Reserved.

Such a notice notifies the public that you own the copyright, and warns them against using your work for their own profit. The copyright notice can be affixed in a number of ways, including handwriting, printing, stamping, burning, etching, sewing, etc.

Now here's the real trick to the whole copyright business. You can place a formal copyright notice on anything you create and thereby announce your claim to copyright . . . *but* formal registration is optional. On the other hand, if you do not file this official claim, you cannot sue anyone who copies, or infringes upon, your copyright. In any case, in each copyright situation, you must decide how important your work is to you in terms of dollars and cents, and ask yourself (1) whether you value it enough to formally register it, and (2) whether you would be willing to pay court costs to defend your copyright, should someone steal it from you. If you never intend to go to court to protect your work, there is little use in registering it officially. But since it costs you nothing to add the copyright notice to your work, you would be foolish not to do this.

> **Note:** Although it is not necessary to formally register a copyright claim, there is a "Mandatory Deposit Requirement" for all work bearing a copyright notice. There is no charge for this, and no forms to complete. Simply mail two copies of the work to the Library of Congress.

Computer Software

If you create software for sale, be aware that you have added protection in *The Software Rental Amendments Act*. Passed by Congress in 1990, this law prohibits the commercial rental, leasing, or lending of software without written permission of the creator. In response to the growing concern over software piracy, a 1992 amendment to this Act instituted criminal penalties for copyright infringement of software that include imprisonment up to five years and/or fines of up to $250,000. Thus all computer users must be particularly careful about reading the licensing terms on software they have purchased.

Using Copyrighted Material of Others

Never post to your Web site (or use in any other way) content from someone else's Web site or published work. You may think it's "fair use" to use the writing of others if you simply give them credit, but if legal action were taken against you, the case of "fair use" would be decided on four factors: (1) the purpose and character of the use; (2) the nature of the copyrighted work; (3) the amount and substantiality of the portion used; and (4) the effect your use of the material would have on the market for the protected work.

Copyright Information on the Web

There is a wealth of free copyright information on the Web, but you must be cautious about accepting as gospel all the information you will find there from well-meaning individuals. However, many insightful articles have been published by attorneys and other small business professionals who are well versed in copyright law, and you can also get your information straight from the Copyright Office's Web site (see above). Note that the Copyright Office is prohibited from giving legal advice or opinions about your rights in connection with cases of alleged copyright infringement, "or the sufficiency, extent, or scope of compliance with the copyright law." Thus, if you have a copyright problem that is costing you money, consult a copyright attorney for advice.

Credit/Credit Cards

(*See also* Business Loans and Other Money Sources)

If you do not have a personal credit history, this should be an immediate goal. (Married women: be sure to read the special tip under "Business Checking Account.") In addition to having your own business checking account, you should apply for a bank charge card whether you need it or not, and use this card to charge as many business expenses as possible. This will give you an excellent paper trail of all transactions and build a credit history in your name. The more you use the card, the higher the credit limit can be set, and the more useful the card is in obtaining emergency cash.

Beware of credit card companies that urge you to buy insurance to protect you against illegal use of your card in the event it is lost or stolen. By federal law, you are liable only for $50 worth of unauthorized charges but, in checking my credit card companies, I was told I would not be held liable for *any* unauthorized charges so long as I notified them promptly in accordance with their reporting rules and procedures.

Caution: After several years of using credit cards and having your credit limit automatically increased, you may someday find yourself with more credit than is good for you. If you were to apply for a mortgage or business loan, for example, and had available credit of $10,000 or more on several charge cards, the lending institution could count this against you because it suggests that you might actually incur that much debt and become a financial risk. To avoid this problem, write to credit card companies and ask them to lower your credit limit figure.

☑ *Smart Tip*

Even though credit card companies ask you to write your account number on your check when you make monthly payments, this is not a good idea because other people will be handling those checks. If merchants request a credit card number to validate a purchase made by check, refuse to give it as this could leave you open to fraud. Since merchants cannot cover a bounced check by charging the amount to your credit card, you should merely *show* them your card to prove you have credit—not let them *copy* your account number. You have rights of privacy, and this is one of them.

Checking Your Credit Rating

There are over nine hundred credit bureaus in the United States, but only three major credit rating firms:

Equifax, 1-800-685-1111, www.equifax.com
Trans Union, 1-800-888-4213, www.tuc.com
Experian, 1-888-397-3742, www.experian.com
For information about all three, check www.creditbase.com

Credit bureaus used to serve local areas only, but thanks to computer technology, each now has credit information on everyone across the country. The above three major bureaus all have the same information, but each may process it differently, which means errors might slip into your record from time to time. If you were to apply for a loan, your bank might call any one of the three, so prior to applying for a loan, you might ask your bank which bureau it uses, then check your own credit first. Expect to pay a small fee for your report.

Shopping for Low-Rate Cards

As you probably know, credit card companies frequently offer a card at a very low introductory rate along with a bunch of blank checks you are urged to use to pay off higher interest-bearing cards. Most of these offers are enticing, with high credit lines and no annual fee, but six months to a year later, the interest rate will shoot back up to the usual high 16–18 percent rates.

One lesson I've learned is that *interest rates are negotiable.* When the introductory period on one of our newer accounts expired and the interest rate suddenly shot up to 16 percent, I closed the account. When I just got a call asking why, I said "because the interest rate is too high." And I was told, "*For good customers like you, we often make special arrangements. If you'd like to keep this card, we will give you a permanent interest rate of just 9 percent.*" Since this was a lower rate than I had on other cards, I said sure. Three years later, that low rate is still locked in. If you're tired of paying high interest rates on your credit cards, you might ask for a lower rate and threaten to cancel the card if your request cannot be accommodated. Also be aware of new rules that allow credit card companies to raise your rate if your payments are received late. Some people have fallen into a terrible trap here, being stuck with high rates while they try to pay off their card balance.

● **Using Credit Cards on the Web.** To limit your liability when using a credit card to order merchandise online, get a card with a low credit limit (no more than $1,000) and use this card exclusively for Web-related transactions. If anyone should try to use this card illegally, they won't get much mileage from it.

Environmental Protection Laws

There are several restrictions on the taking and use of protected wildlife and plants. If your business in any way involves such things—particularly feathers, bones, claws, or ivory—obtain additional information from the U.S. Fish and Wildlife Service, Department of the Interior, www.FWS.gov. (The Endangered Species Hotline is 1-800-447-3813.) For general information on environmental laws, check the Web site of the Environmental Protection Agency at www.EPA.gov.

Federal Laws and Regulations

(See also *Consumer Safety Laws; Copyrights; Environmental Protection Laws; Federal Trade Commission; Mail Order Laws; Taxes Businesses Must Pay; Trademarks; Trade Secret*)
For information about current legislation or the status of any federal law, check this Web site: http://thomas.loc.gov.

Federal Trade Commission (FTC)

(See also *Consumer Safety Laws; Scams and Frauds*)

In addition to the laws pertaining to consumer safety and the labeling of certain products, the FTC is also concerned with truth in advertising, use of endorsements and testimonials, warranties and guarantees, and the 30-day Mail Order Rule, topics discussed in this book's business management and marketing companion, *Bringing in the Bucks*. (Basic information on these topics may also be found on the Web at www.FTC.gov.) The FTC also monitors the business community for scams and frauds against both consumers and small business owners and brings legal action against lawbreakers.

Government Agencies (Federal)

(See also *Consumer Safety Laws; Copyrights; Federal Trade Commission; Environmental Protection Laws; Taxes Businesses Must Pay; Trademarks*)
A "quick contact" list for U.S. government agencies. Also check your telephone book for local offices of the various agencies:

Bureau of Consumer Protection, www.FTC.gov/ftc/consumer.htm
Census Bureau, www.Census.gov
Consumer Product Safety Commission, 1-800-638-2772; www.CPSC.gov
Cooperative Extension Service, www.reeusda.gov
The Copyright Office,1-202-707-3000; www.loc.gov/copyright
Department of Commerce, www.DOC.gov
Department of the Interior, www.FWS.gov
Department of Labor, www.DOL.gov
Work-at-Home Statistics, www. stats.bls.gov/cpshome.htm
Environmental Protection Agency, www.EPA.gov
Fish and Wildlife Service, www.FWS.gov.
Federal Trade Commission, 1-877-FTC-HELP; www.FTC.gov
Food and Drug Administration,1-888-INFO-FDA; www.FDA.gov
Internal Revenue Service, 1-800-829-1040; www.IRS.gov
Patent & Trademark Office, 1-703-308-9000; www.USPTO.gov
Service Corps of Retired Executives (SCORE), 1-800-634-0245; www.SCORE.org

Small Business Administration (SBA), 1-800-827-5722; www.SBA.gov
Social Security Administration, www.SSA.gov
United States Postal Service, www.USPS.com
Postal Inspection Service, www.USPS.gov/postalinspectors
Identity Theft, www.consumer.gov/idtheft/index.html

Hobby Business

(*See also* Business Expenses/Tax Deductions)

The IRS says you are in business if you (1) are sincerely trying to make a profit, (2) are making regular business transactions, and (3) have made a profit at least three years out of five. (There have been exceptions to the last rule. In the end, the most important factors are the amount of time you devote to your activity, plus the way you present yourself to the public as being engaged in the sale of products or services; also the way you keep records of your business.) If you do not meet IRS criteria, your business will be ruled a "hobby" and any loss you deducted will be disallowed. (You *can* show a loss on a business, but not on a hobby.)

If you decide you want to work at home only as a hobby, you are still required to report your hobby income on Schedule C of Form 1040, and list all the expenses you incurred to earn this income. If you end up with a profit, you'll have to pay taxes on it. If you end up with a loss, however, you are not entitled to a deduction, but you can deduct expenses up to the amount of your hobby income.

Insurance

Half of us are probably insurance poor from paying on several necessary insurance policies while the other half is so underinsured we're worried to death about what will occur if "the worst" should happen. Some of us have both problems. Insurance is one of the most important considerations for self-employed individuals because lack of the right coverage can put you out of business overnight. Following, in order of importance to the self-employed individual, is a discussion of the various types of insurance you may need, with special alerts to financially dangerous situations you might have overlooked. This information will help you ask the right questions the next time you meet with an insurance agent.

In analyzing your various insurance needs and discussing them with various insurance providers, be sure to lay all the details in front of the agent so proper coverage can be provided. Withholding information can only lead to problems in the event of a claim.

Smart Tip

Before you purchase a new policy, be sure to check the stability of the insurance company in question. With so many insurance companies going belly-up, you can't afford to take out a policy with any company that doesn't have a superior rating. (The A. M. Best Company is one of the best sources for insurance ratings of U.S. companies. 1-908-439-2200; www.AMBest.com.)

Hospitalization/Major Medical Insurance

Nearly 3 million self-employed Americans are currently uninsured. Some people have preexisting conditions that severely limit their ability to get adequate coverage or make them totally uninsurable, while others simply can't afford today's high premium costs. Most people seem to be stuck with HMO programs whether they like them or not, but you must decide how important it is for you to be able to choose your doctors. In shopping for a new medical plan, look for:

(a) A choice of deductibles;
(b) A stop-loss feature that limits your financial risk;
(c) A plan that doesn't charge for children if you don't have them;
(d) Sufficient outpatient coverage for such things as cancer treatment;
(e) Benefits that cover organ transplants/implants.

Most policies do not cover the latter item and may severely limit the dollar amount of outpatient treatment benefits, so check these points carefully as they are the ones that could bankrupt you. If you already have coverage, take a moment to double-check the cancellation/conversion clauses in your policy. By law, one is always entitled to some kind of conversion policy, but the benefits are never as good for an individual policy as they are for one obtained through a group, and the premiums are higher as well. The only good thing about insurance premiums—besides the peace of mind a good policy brings—is that they are now tax deductible in part, and will soon be deductible in full.

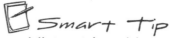 Smart Tip

Before you quit your full-time job and lose its accompanying medical insurance, make sure you can get adequate coverage elsewhere. One secret to cutting health insurance costs is to join a large professional organization that offers a group plan. For starters, check out the insurance programs of Home Business Institute, Inc., National Association for the Self-Employed, Small Business Service Bureau, and Support Services Alliance listed under "Organizations" in "Other Resources." Good insurance is also available to Chamber of Commerce members, some of whom have been able to cut their insurance premiums in half by joining their local Chamber and getting into its United Chambers group insurance program.

Homeowner's or Renter's Insurance Policies

In 1999, Terri Lonier (WorkingSolo.com) did a survey of more than 900 home-business owners to gain some insight on the kind of insurance they had. Surprisingly, 60 percent of those surveyed said they didn't own any form of business insurance. *This is a very dangerous way to operate.* When you run a business at home, you stand to lose *twice* as much as the ordinary homeowner in times of tragedy—both home and business. To ensure the survival of your business, make sure you're covered for all possible disasters, including fire, flood, tornado, hurricane, or earthquake. An insurance agent once laughed when I said we wanted earthquake insurance on our home in Illinois, but it costs less than $100 a year and gives me great peace of mind every time I think of the major quake possibilities in Missouri that may also affect my state. Remember that regular homeowner policies do not cover such things as cracks in the foundation due to earth movement (including sinkholes), sewer problems, water damage from hurricanes (unless, for example, a tree first knocks a hole in your roof or wall so the water can get in), and so on. (Most people in flood-prone areas do not have flood insurance, but those who are running businesses at home should give careful consideration to this potential problem.) If you have a sump pump, make sure appliances and furniture on that level are covered in the event of flooding due to a power outage.

Also, if you have special collections of any kind (antiques, diamonds, silver, furs, guns, cameras, artwork, etc.), be sure to have them appraised and insured by a separate, all-risk endorsement. (The typical homeowner's policy limits loss on such items to no more than $1,500.)

- **Replacement-Value Insurance.** For about 15 percent more a year, you can obtain "replacement-value insurance" on all your personal possessions. If your insurance agent does not bring this to your attention, be sure to ask about it. With a regular homeowner's/renter's policy, what you get in the event of loss is figured on the current value *after depreciation*. This often brings dollar amounts down to little or nothing. A replacement-value policy, on the other hand, will pay you whatever it costs to replace any item that's been damaged or destroyed, regardless of its age at time of loss, up to the limits of your policy. Note that this coverage is applicable only to *personal* possessions; loss of furnishings and equipment in your office or studio would be figured on a depreciable basis, and be limited to the amounts shown on your special business rider.

Smart Tip

No policy will be worth much if you can't prove what you owned prior to total destruction by fire or other disaster, so be sure to make a comprehensive list or photographic record of your possessions. Keep this information in a safe place outside the home, such as a safe deposit box. Also, in the event of theft, you should have a handy record of all the model and serial numbers of all your electronic and computer equipment.

- **Business Pursuits Endorsement.** It's important to tell your insurance agent that you run a business at home because your regular homeowner's or renter's policy will *not* cover business equipment, supplies, or inventory nor, in all probability, any losses due to fires that may be caused by such things. Note that "goods for sale" are considered business property that must be separately insured, either with an individual policy or a special rider.

A Business Pursuits Endorsement to your homeowner's policy is a good answer for many small businesses since it offers some liability coverage for people in your home for business purposes as well as materials and products you are storing. If you are storing over $3,000 of inventory, however, you should probably obtain a separate fire, vandalism, and theft policy. Note that a business rider on your home insurance carries no personal liability coverage for your business.

● **Studio Policy.** If you sell art or handcrafts, normally taking them to fairs or shows, you might want to investigate special studio insurance policies designed to protect such property at home, in your studio, or in transit to and from exhibitions and shows. Two organizations that offer this type of insurance to members are the American Craft Council and the National Craft Association (see "Other Resources").

● **Computer Insurance.** Personal computers used for business will not be covered by your regular homeowner's policy, except possibly against loss by fire or theft. But that leaves you with possible risks related to damage caused by water, high humidity, or power surges. The latter can cause extensive damage to circuits, although a voltage surge suppressor can prevent this. (See a discussion of surge protectors in Chapter Eleven.) The insurance problem can be solved simply by insuring your computer system separately with a company that specializes in this kind of coverage. (I use Safeware, The Insurance Agency, Inc., 1-800-848-3469; www.Safeware.com.) Such coverage would also protect your computer while it's in transit to and from the repair shop, or whenever you travel with it.

Home-Office Policies

When a Business Pursuits Endorsement to your homeowner's policy is insufficient (see below), you may need one of the special home office/home business policies now being offered by most of the major insurance companies, including Aetna, Liberty Mutual, and Firemen Insurance Co. One company I've investigated is RLI Insurance Company (1-800-221-7917; www.RLICorp.com). For as little as $150 a year with a standard $100 deductible, you can get up to $50,000 all-risk protection, $5,000 per person medical payments, and a million dollars in general liability insurance (both product and professional).

 Smart Tip

To protect your home and office from fire, consider spraying drapes, furniture, carpeting, and storage cartons with No Burn, a nontoxic, nonstaining formula that retards smoke and flames. It is colorless, odorless, and harmless to pets. Comes in a trigger-spray bottle.

Personal Liability Insurance

Each of us can be held liable for a lot of things, and when you have a business at home you need to be doubly careful. *Personal liability insurance* protects you against claims made by people who have suffered bodily injury while on your premises, while *product liability insurance* (see below) protects you against lawsuits by consumers who have been injured while using your product. My insurance agent emphasizes that personal and business liability should not be intertwined since claims will be treated differently because of the different pursuits.

Ask your insurance agent if, as a sole proprietor working at home, you would be covered in these cases: A delivery person (maybe the UPS driver) slips on the ice on your steps while delivering a business package, breaks his or her back, and can never work again. Big lawsuit! Or a customer or client suffers bodily injury while in your home on business and sues for hospitalization costs and loss of job income. *Why* these people are on your property will determine the coverage your insurance policy provides. *Read the fine print and talk to your insurance agent.*

If you perform services for clients in their homes, offices, or plants, you may wish to obtain general liability coverage to protect you against such things as your causing injury to someone, or accidental damage of another's property or equipment. Such insurance should be substantial enough to cover costs that would be incurred in a lawsuit against you.

Smart Tip

To decrease your personal risk, inquire about a "personal umbrella policy" that will take over where your present coverage stops. You might be able to buy $1 worth of liability insurance for as little as $100 per year. The same kind of umbrella policy is available on your automobile policy as well. Here, the difference in premium costs for $1 million vs. $5 million of insurance may be ridiculously small. As my insurance agent confirms: "Personal umbrella programs are excellent vehicles for providing broader coverage, and they are especially important today where judges and juries are awarding some unbelievable numbers in lawsuits. Business umbrellas are also important but they are a little more expensive than the personal umbrella."

Insurance

Product Liability Insurance

For many businesses, product liability insurance is simply too expensive to buy, yet it can sometimes be critical to the sale of merchandise. For example, a garment maker had to cancel a large order because the store she was doing business with insisted she have product liability insurance on her products—gifts for babies and children, a touchy area. National mail order catalog houses often insist that their suppliers have product liability insurance, too.

Many small business owners are thus faced with a hard decision: should they continue to operate without liability insurance, or cease operation? Before you give up on obtaining insurance, investigate help that may be available to you through a trade association. Some groups are able to negotiate policies for their members.

Historically, few craft manufacturers have carried product liability insurance because most handcrafted/handmade items are considered relatively safe. But ceramic pots have been known to break and spill hot contents on the owner's lap, doll's eyes have been swallowed by children, and stained glass windows have shattered while being hung. According to Lee Wilson, author of Making It Legal (out of print), the legal rule of product liability is this: "*Defective product plus injury arising from customary or foreseen use equals maker or seller pays.*" Here are four ways to guard against product liability suits:

1. Set high quality control standards to avoid possible injury.

2. "Idiot-proof" your products, and try to design away any potential harm. If the latter isn't possible, at least warn the public of possible harm by including detailed instructions on the proper use of your products to avoid that harm.

3. In advertising your products, don't make any claims or promises you cannot meet.

4. Include a questionnaire with your products, asking for customers' input. Their comments might alert you to potential problems.

In seeking insurance coverage, first check the policies offered by the home business/small business organizations listed in "Other Resources." Most offer $1 million worth of liability insurance. If more is needed, look for a nearby agency that sells business or commercial insurance, such as American Family, Allstate, or State Farm. One insurance agent told me product liability insurance rates vary greatly from state to state, depending on your annual gross sales (or anticipated sales), the number of products you sell, and the possible risks associated with each of them. An insurance company will look closely at what your products are made of and consider possible side effects you'd never imagine. If your income is low and your product line small, you may be able to buy an affordable policy. In your desire to save insurance premium money, however, don't overlook the fact that you do need high limits of coverage.

An Idea to Consider: The owners of a party-plan business told me product liability was a major consideration and obstacle in the establishment of their business, but insurance was not available in their area at a reasonable premium because they had no storefront. Their solution was to incorporate under Subchapter S (see "Legal Forms of Business"). Although this didn't give them the product liability coverage they sought, it did work to protect their personal and family properties. Their insurance agent advised that, given the relative safety of their inventory, this type of protection should be adequate for them.

Smart Tip

A product liability policy should be written so that limits apply on a "per claim" basis instead of a "per occurrence" basis. For example, a flaw in the manufacturing process that causes hundreds of defective products is a "single occurrence" to the court, and a "per occurrence" limit in a policy might not cover the several "per claim" lawsuits that could result.

Vehicle Insurance

If you plan to use your car, van, truck, or trailer for business, be sure to tell your insurance agent exactly *how* it will be used. Otherwise, if you insure the vehicle for personal use only and have an accident while "doing business" in that vehicle, you might not be covered. (*See also* "Checklist of Home-Related Tax-Deductible Expenses for Home-Business Owners.")

Invoicing Terms

- **Freight Charges (FOB).** "F.O.B." means "Freight or free, on board." These initials with the name of a city immediately after them indicate the point to which the seller will pay the freight. If the customer is to pay freight, the notation would read "F.O.B. (your city)"; if you are paying the freight, it would read "F.O.B. (buyer's city)." This F.O.B. notation could be important in the event goods are lost or damaged in transit since, legally, title of the goods changes hands at the F.O.B. point.

- **Pro Forma.** If you are uncertain about the credit worthiness of a new outlet, do not ship and bill, but sell your first order to them on a *pro forma* basis, which means you want your money in advance. Simply send a Pro Forma Invoice for the merchandise that has been ordered and ship the goods when payment has been received.

- **Terms of Sale.** When full payment is desired within ten or thirty days, simply include the appropriate terms on your invoice: either "Net 10 days" or "Net 30 days." If you wish to offer your customers a discount for prompt payment, you would state the terms of sale as "2%/10/30" or "2% 10 days, net 30." Either term indicates to a buyer that you will give a 2 percent discount if payment is made within 10 days, and full payment is expected within 30 days.

When an invoice includes sales tax, you should state the exact amount a customer may deduct, and this deduction should be based on cost of merchandise before tax is added. (If you do not state this figure, your customer may calculate the 2 percent on the total invoice. Over time, this could add up to a sizable amount of lost dollars.)

Some buyers pay an invoice a month late and still take the discount, in which case they should be invoiced for the difference. Although they may ignore such a small invoice, such action will show them that you mean business.

- **Statement.** A statement shows an account's balance at month's end. If an account does not pay your invoice, send another invoice, not a statement. Unless you are making several shipments to major accounts each month, statements should not be necessary.

Legal Forms of Business

Following are the pluses and minuses of each of the four basic forms a business can take: sole proprietorship, partnership, corporation, and limited liability company.

Sole Proprietorship

Most small businesses are sole proprietorships simply because this is the easiest kind of business to start, operate, and end. Controlled by the owner, all profits from the business go directly to the owner. There is little regulation, and earnings are personally taxed. The main disadvantage of this form of business is that liability is unlimited; that is, the owner is fully liable for all business debts and actions, with personal assets unprotected from lawsuits.

Partnerships

Many small businesses elect to form a partnership so the workload and responsibility for the management of the business can be shared. General partners run both types of partnership and, like sole proprietors, their earnings are personally taxed and they have unlimited liability in the event of a lawsuit. A "limited partnership" (almost never used for small businesses) would include silent partners who have no say in the business, and no liability beyond the money they've invested.

Smart Tip

It's important to have a contract in any kind of business partnership and advice from legal counsel. You also need *partnership insurance*. It is necessary to establish a Buy-Sell Agreement, funded by life insurance. By law, at the death of a partner, your business is dissolved and can no longer operate until it is either liquidated or reorganized. The agreement, prepared by an attorney, establishes the price the survivor will pay for his share of the business, and that the heirs will sell for, and the insurance provides the money to complete the transfer.

Be cautious about entering into a partnership with a close friend because many friendships have been destroyed in the name of business. In a chapter she contributed to the book *Word Processing Plus*, Colleen Perri said that the number of failed partnerships rival those of failed marriages. "Just as in a marriage, innumerable things can happen to confuse, to hurt, and to horrify." She identified eight reasons for why partnerships can go wrong: different priorities (the race horse vs. the turtle), different skills and equipment (overequipped vs. underequipped), different personalities (overachiever vs. underachiever), different attitudes (long-term vs. short-term thinking); different goals; different philosophies; lack of communication; and the failure to "put it in writing." For more perspective on partnerships, consider these stories shared by readers.

- **Unmarried Partners.** The following e-mail from a reader illustrates the worst that can happen in the event one unmarried partner dies: "I lost everything when my longtime companion and partner passed away," she wrote. "We had been together for more than eight years. He was the sole proprietor, and because there is no common law in my state, the company passed to his mother who was legally the next of kin. Although she now owns the business name, she will not be able to do anything with the company because she knows nothing about the business, and I am not about to help her. I have not decided whether to try to continue under another name or not. I am still too numb. Fortunately, this was not my main source of income."

"Always have a written, notarized agreement before doing business with a friend, or starting a partnership with someone other than your spouse," cautions one woman who lives and partners with a man not her husband. "It may sound hard and cold to some, but there are certain things that must be spelled out in any partnership, even an informal one. The agreement doesn't have to be written by an attorney, but both parties need this kind of legal protection."

Corporation

A corporation is the most complicated form a business can take. While it offers special advantages, such as protection for one's personal assets in the event of a lawsuit, it involves a lot of paperwork, plus legal and accounting services. One must pay corporate income tax plus tax on personal salary and/or dividends.

Since a corporation is a legal entity unto itself, it does not die with the retirement or death of its officers. Investments may be transferred from one party to another without affecting the operation of the company. Some small business owners incorporate their businesses merely to obtain legal protection for personal assets in the event of bankruptcy.

While incorporation does afford a certain degree of protection, it is not the complete answer. As attorney Leonard D. DuBoff explains, "Individuals who are actually responsible for wrongful acts will remain liable for those acts. The corporation will protect your personal assets from being exposed only when your employees or agents are responsible for the business's liability."

In some cases, it may be easier and less expensive simply to purchase liability insurance. Other times, however, a homebased business needs to be incorporated because it involves individuals from two or three families, and this is the best way to protect everyone's interests. An interesting reason to incorporate came to my attention when a senior entrepreneur told me he was incorporating after seventeen years as a sole proprietor because this was the only way he could avoid giving much of his social security income back to the government at the end of the year. Something to think about, at least.

"The decision on whether to incorporate a business is not as simple as it was a few years ago," says Judith H. McQuown, author of *Inc Yourself—How to Profit by Setting Up Your Own Corporation*. "Nearly every year of the past decade has produced major tax legislation that has impacted the small corporation," she says, "yet there are still many compelling business and tax reasons to incorporate." Some experts have said that incorporation does not justify its additional costs unless one's business profits have reached five figures and exceed personal income needs. However, only you and your lawyer or accountant can determine what's best for your particular business and personal tax situation.

Subchapter S Corporation

This is a corporate structure for new or low-income businesses, and even a one-person business can operate in this fashion. Yvonne Conway, who provides mobile beauty services, incorporated as an S Corporation. "I am the only employee of the corporation," she says. "It pays my wages and pays into the State Unemployment Insurance program. One benefit of a Subchapter S Corporation is that income taxes and Social Security taxes are compiled on your wages, not on the total income your business produces."

Unlike the usual type of corporation, profits or losses of a Subchapter S are reported on a shareholder's Form 1040, as in a partnership, meaning you're taxed at the lower personal rate. Since this legal form of business offers the advantages of a corporation without double taxation, it's often a good choice for entrepreneurs.

Limited Liability Company (LLC)

LLCs, first introduced in 1992, combine the best attributes of other business forms, but tax and regulatory requirements vary from state to state. "This form of business is similar to an S Corporation, with limited liability for the stockholders, and pass-through profits taxable to the owners but not to the business," says CPA Bernard Kamoroff. "LLCs offer more generous loss deductions than S Corporations, offer more classes of stock, and are not limited to the S Corporation's maximum of 35 individual shareholders. The IRS does not recognize LLCs for federal income tax purposes, and will tax them either as partnerships or corporations, depending on how they are legally structured."

For more complete information on all the legal forms of business mentioned above, see the book, *Small Time Operator* by Bernard Kamoroff, available in bookstores or on the Web at www.bellsprings.com.

Licenses and Permits

(See also *Business or Trade Name*)

Many home business owners have never bothered to get a local (municipal or county) license or permit, even when this is required by law. Fortunately, no one goes around checking to see who has a license and who doesn't, which probably accounts for the lack of attention new business owners sometimes pay to this detail. However, authorities may discover such unlicensed businesses by checking state sales tax returns and resale licenses.

Local Registration

Contact local authorities (city or county clerk or local council) to learn if you need any special permits or licenses to legally operate a business in your area (in addition to the registration of your business name). It's a good idea to find out how solid the ground is under any unlicensed business you already may be operating. Take a trip to the city or county clerk's office under the guise of "just wondering about starting a business" and get the facts. If you operate without a required license, you run the risk of discovery, at which point you might be fined or ordered to cease business. You may find it a simple and inexpensive matter to legally establish your business, and then you won't have to worry about it anymore. If you're truly concerned by what you learn on your research trip, ask a lawyer for advice on what to do next.

Homemade Money

Some communities, now realizing that homebased entrepreneurs represent a terrific source for extra revenue, have begun charging extra fees of from $15 to $200 for what they're calling a "home occupation permit"—sort of a "taxation without representation" situation in that such permits offer no real benefits to the homebased entrepreneur but do add to city coffers. When Sylvia Landman (Marin, California) questioned what this money was for, she was told it was to "police and control the nature of new home businesses" in her city. "I then asked who comes out to check on this, and was told that no one ever does this. All this seems to be a case of 'just pay and obey.'"

In *Legal Barriers to Home-Based Work* (a report for the National Center for Policy Analysis), Joann Pratt pointed out that ". . . cities both want to cash in on the home-business boom by levying additional taxes without voting on them first, and that these fees are but one of the systematic methods used nationwide to discourage homebased business. The question is, will this issue slow the tremendous surge in the home business boom, or just irritate it?" (Joann's Web site, JoannPratt.com, includes several reports of interest to home-business owners and researchers that can be downloaded free of charge.)

Whether you get a license or permit for your business may depend on zoning regulations in your area. For example, in Santa Fe, New Mexico, a plumber who wanted to launch a business from home couldn't get a business license because city officials required him to have handicap parking at his own house—even though he wasn't actually doing business out of his own house.

In some towns and cities, all homebased businesses are outlawed by archaic zoning laws, but this hasn't stopped thousands of individuals from operating businesses anyway. Such illegal businesses simply never ask city officials if they need a license, because this would only draw attention to themselves. (See "Zoning Laws" for more on this topic.)

 Smart Tip

A mail order seller in New York who uses her home address for her business had to obtain a "special use permit" to operate. On the other hand, a homebased publisher in California was advised by the license bureau to obtain a post office box number for his address because "the post office is in a commercial zone," and that eliminated the need for any "special use permit." Check this out, because it may work in your area, too.

Licenses and Permits

Other Licensing Agencies

Depending on the type of business you plan to operate, you may need to get a permit from other municipal or county agencies. In general, food-related businesses will be subject to special restrictions and inspections by both local and state health departments, and day care centers will have to conform to local and state regulations as well. The fire department may have to give some kind of permit or official OK if you work with flammable or dangerous materials. If your business causes the release of any materials into the air or water (even a ceramic kiln), you may need approval from the local environmental protection agency. If you work with animals or agricultural products, check with your local Department of Agriculture; if you work with the handicapped or elderly, contact the social services department of your local or state government.

Certain business professionals, such as accountants, auto mechanics, photographers, cosmetologists, TV repairers, and others, will need occupational licenses issued by the state agency that administers consumer affairs. Contact your state capitol to connect with this particular agency to see if you need an occupational license of any kind.

Commercial Kitchen Laws

The person who decides to launch a homebased food-related business must be concerned not just with permits and zoning ordinances, but with local health officials and state regulations as well. (Local health authorities reportedly comb newspaper ads to spot unlicensed food/catering services.) In fact, the "commercial kitchen" law in your state may make it almost impossible to set up a food-related business in your home.

Thumbs up to the state of Iowa, which has a "home bakery provision" that draws a line between commercial food businesses and small operations like bake sales and farmer's markets. (It is possible that other states have similar home-bakery provisions in their food laws, so ask about this.) Iowa's law allows home bakers to operate without a license if they earn less than $2,000 per year and agree not to advertise their products. (All business must come from word-of-mouth advertising).

One way around commercial kitchen laws in your state is to rent an outside kitchen in a commercial building. A reader in California said it was popular there to rent bakeries in the evening hours, and pizza parlor kitchens in the early A.M. One woman met her state's requirement by buying a storage building, then put in the required sinks, two Coleman stoves, etc. to make her jams and jellies in her backyard. Another reader reported that she solved her cake-baking problem by using the commercial kitchen in her church.

Mail Order Laws

(See also *Federal Trade Commission*)

The U.S. Postal Service is the watchdog of the mail order industry, and anyone who uses the mail to sell products and services must always be careful to accurately represent themselves and their products to their mail order customers. In discussed in Chapter Two, postal authorities actively pursue promoters of chain letters and pyramid schemes, as well as anyone else who runs a scam that involves the mail. Many companies have been put out of business because they have engaged in a scheme or device for obtaining money or property through the mails by means of false representation, a phrase that packs a powerful punch.

For instance, consider the case of a man who was put out of business because he was selling herbs and herbal formulas through a catalog. In itself, this would have been okay; but this seller maintained that the advertised products had certain curative powers that dissolved malignant tumors, among other things. To say that certain herbs are believed by some to have curative powers is one thing; to claim they will cure anything is selling by means of false representation. Remember this story whenever you make claims of any kind about your products or services.

Merchant Account Providers (MAPS)

Many homebased business owners have complained about the difficulty they've encountered in trying to get a merchant account so they could offer their customers a charge card service. In one of her small business seminars in California, Sylvia Landman (Sylvias-Studio.com) invited her banker and the bank's merchant sales rep to be guests in her class. In fielding questions from her class, she learned why so many fledgling business owners fail to qualify.

"Banks prefer storefronts to homebased businesses," she says, "and they also prefer to deal with clients with whom they have a long-term banking relationship. A business must be legal within the community, be at least one-year old, and be prepared to provide the various documents a bank wants to see: credit and bank references, resumes, sales figures, proof of the legal structure of your business, tax returns, your promotional printed materials, and more."

Smart Tip

If you belong to a business organization of any kind, you can probably get better discount rates through the program they offer than what you can get on your own. See "Organizations" in Other Resources and check out the merchant account services offered by the Home Business Institute, Inc., and the National Craft Association.

Comparing Costs

Because all merchant accounts are expensive, it's important to do some comparison shopping to make sure you're getting the best deal. In her book, *The Complete Idiot's Guide to Making Money with Your Hobby*, Barbara Arena, Managing Director of the National Craft Association, urges sellers to gather at least five price quotes from prospective merchant account providers and suggests visiting Merchant Workz (www.MerchantWorkz.com). "Here you'll find a free and impartial listing of MAPs and their primary rates and fees," she says. "These rates and fees are negotiable," she says, "so don't hesitate to push MAPs into a bidding war."

To help you decide which provider might be best for your needs, work up an estimation of what you think your monthly sales might be over a period of three months (number of orders, dollar amounts, etc.), then estimate what it would cost to use each provider's services to handle your estimated order volume. In all cases, *be sure to read the fine print in any contract* to make sure you understand each company's charges, payment methods, and cancellation options. Pay attention to the one-time application or setup fee, the discount rate (always higher for mail order sales), transaction and chargeback fees, statement fee, gateway access fee (for doing business on the Web), and monthly minimum (payable whether you have any business or not). If you need a mobile setup for shows, find out what hardware or software you'll need. *Avoid leasing agreements if at all possible because once you sign up for a four-year lease, you can't get out of it, even if you decide you no longer want or need the service.*

Note that it's one thing to have merchant account status when you sell products at a show, and another if you also want to sell them online. "One drawback most Internet people will find is that banks will not carry their merchant account unless they have a shopping cart that automatically bills the credit card for the purchase," says Cheri Marsh (SoapMeister.com). "Banks do not want the vendor to have the ability to intervene. Due to the custom features of my business, I could not utilize my bank's program. I went instead with Costco because they have great rates and outstanding merchant assistance round the clock, seven days a week. The initial setup costs are expensive (printer/transmission hardware), but I recommend having your own equipment—not the software. The biggest benefit of the hardware is that you can take it with you if you go offsite to market. You can process cards immediately, which is imperative if you are selling product and the customer leaves with it. You know the card has cleared before they take the merchandise. With software, you take all the information, go home and process the charge. Only then do you know whether the card is good or not, and if not, it's too late to get the merchandise back."

"MasterCard and Visa are extra concerned about who they give merchant status to when you're online," confirms Barbara Arena. "Each association cuts their own deal with these companies. Sixty percent of NCA's new members now take our MC/Visa services. They can do it either on a software basis only (software in their PC), hardware (swipe machine), or a totally mobile unit (laptop/cell phone at shows). NCA members can have an online site as well as sell at shows, but the discount rate varies. It's based on average ticket sales, rather than volume. For our members, we negotiated with both companies to set up an average ticket price—the higher the average, the lower the rate."

☑ Smart Tip

Membership in Sam's Club (www.SamsClub.com) or Costo (www.Costco.com) could be your solution for getting a merchant account at a good rate. As a member of such organizations (check your local telephone book), you can also save money on office supplies and business services.

Merchant Account Providers

Novus Services, Inc.

Another option you might explore is offered by Novus Services, Inc., the umbrella company for the Discover and Bravo credit cards. The only information Novus requires is your social security number or federal tax identification number or EIN (Employee Identification Number) so they can run a credit check on you. When you apply to Novus, they can also get you set up to take Visa, MasterCard, and American Express as well. However, although Novus automatically accepts brand new businesses with a good credit rating, some Visa and MasterCard processors won't grant acceptance unless one has been in business for at least two years. For more information, call this toll-free number: 1-800-347-6673.

Independent Sales Organizations (ISOs)

Merchant status can be obtained through an ISO, but this is the most expensive route you can go, and some companies in this field have questionable business ethics. Since hucksters everywhere are preying on home-based entrepreneurs today, you must be particularly cautious when dealing with an ISO. Some may take your application fee and disappear. Others just don't deliver the terminal and forms that have been paid for. One of the best known and most stable ISOs is Cardservice International, founded in 1988 and sold through individual sales representatives (network marketing). Their service and leasing fees are very high, however, and from personal experience, I do not recommend them. Again, you can probably save a great deal of money by joining a business organization that offers merchant card services as a benefit of membership.

MAPs on the Web

If most of your selling will be done on the Web, you'll find many merchant account options simply by surfing the Internet. Many Web hosting companies now offer free hosting when you take the merchant account program they offer, and shopping carts are also offered with many of the electronic credit card options now available. (You'll need to do your homework here. When I did a search on Google.com for "merchant account," I turned up half a million pages.) You might begin by checking out the following companies, which some of my readers have recommended:

- **www.ClickBank.com.** This company will handle the processing of credit card orders but only one item can be purchased at a time, which is why it is often used by electronic publishers selling reports or books. Currently, the charge is $1 per transaction, plus 7.5 percent of the sale. This program also includes an affiliate program, in case you want to sell your publications through other dealers on the Web.

- **www.CCnow.com.** This quick-and-easy shopping cart solution for new Web site owners offers secure transaction processing for all major credit cards with no extra charge for international orders. No startup costs or monthly fees; just a straight 9 percent commission on sales.

- **www.GoEmerchant.com.** Another e-commerce solution, but the $49.95 monthly fee makes this service too costly for most beginners. Probably best for established/growing Web sites with sales of $1,000 a month or more.

- **www.PayPal.com.** Now allied with eBay, this service provider is often the choice of beginners who have no sales track record yet. Fees occur only when sales are actually made. Currently, the cost is 30 cents per transaction for sales under $15; for items $15 and more, the cost is 30 cents plus 2.2 percent of the sale. The downside of PayPal is that some shoppers who aren't already registered with PayPal may not take the time to open their own account there (which is necessary before they can buy on a PayPal site).

- **www.ProPay.com.** Similar to PayPal, except that shoppers do not have to register before making a purchase. This service provider claims to be 55 percent less expensive than other merchant account providers and is easy to set up. Currently, the fee is 3.5 percent of the sale, plus 35 cents per transaction.

For more information on doing business on the Web, read this book's companion marketing guide, *HOMEMADE MONEY: Bringing in the Bucks.*

Occupational and Health Hazards

"100 million Americans may be using dangerous materials without knowing it," says The Center for Safety in the Arts, a national clearinghouse for information on this topic. If you have an undiagnosed illness, it could be related to your improper use of certain materials related to your work. Particularly harmful when not properly used are paints, paint thinners, plastics, photo chemicals, dyes, lead, asbestos, and dozens of other materials or substances.

Smart Tip

Two or three live plants in your office will improve the oxygen supply and help combat the pollutants you're adding to the air with your laser printer and other office machines.

In addition to occupational hazards related to your health, there may be hazards relating to your safety as well, particularly if strangers ordinarily come to your door in the normal course of business. Take these sensible steps to ensure your personal safety:

1 If you don't know your customer, don't advertise the fact that you are alone in the house. There is much you can do to create the impression someone else is at home.

2 Never tell anyone except trusted neighbors and your mail carrier that you're going to be out of town. Casually dropped information like this can easily be overheard by the wrong person, making you a prime burglary candidate.

3 Don't tell people on the phone that you'll "be gone until 4:30" for the same reason; and when recording a message for your answering machine, don't say "I'm not at home now." Instead, word your message to suggest that you are merely away from your desk, or on another line.

4 A course in self-defense might make you feel safer. So would a guard dog.

Post Office Box Address

(*See also* Licenses and Permits)

Although the U.S. Postal Service will deliver business mail to a home address, a post office box address is the best way I know to keep a low profile in the community and discourage drop-in customers. As mentioned in the "Licenses and Permits" section, it can also be a helpful way to get around local zoning laws that prohibit businesses at home.

Smart Tip

Some states require the inclusion of a street address along with a post office box address on business stationery and other printed materials, so check to see if this applies to you.

Some people wonder whether they should use a box number as their business address since prospective customers might be suspicious of it. In nearly 30 years of selling by mail from my P.O. box address, I never saw any indication of concern from buyers, and I routinely received a huge volume of mail from publicity mentions. Given some people's reluctance to deal with homebased businesses, I believe the use of an easily recognized residential street address might actually deter more buyers than a P. O. box number.

Moving does present a problem for many mail order businesses because mail is normally forwarded for one year only, after which time it is stamped, "Moved, not forwardable," and returned to sender. Since ads and publicity in books and magazines often pull for several years, this is a great way to lose orders and prospective customers. If you don't want to lose your mail when you move, use the strategy that worked for me as Harry and I moved about the country in the 1970s and 1980s. Instead of entering a change-of-address card when we moved, I simply retained the post office box as long as sufficient mail was received to warrant its cost, and hired someone locally to pick up and forward the mail each week. I gave this person a rubber stamp with my new address ("Please forward to . . ."), and he stamped all first class mail and dropped it into the nearest mailbox. (The post office will forward this kind of mail indefinitely at no extra cost. Other classes of mail, however, must be repackaged and forwarded at regular postage costs.)

At the point when you wish to discontinue the use of the box and hiring of an individual to forward your mail, then enter a change-of-address card, at which point the post office will continue to forward your mail for another year. Remember to guarantee forwarding postage on second class mail (periodicals) that you may have forgotten to change, and keep in mind that bulk mail will not be forwarded even if you guarantee postage.

Resale Tax Number

(*See also* Taxes Businesses Must Pay)

Resale tax numbers are required by sellers in most states. Anyone who sells a product (goods) in a state that collects tax must obtain a tax number from the state even if they do not sell directly to the ultimate user. This resale number may be called different things in different states, but the idea is the same everywhere. You collect sales tax on sales *to the final user in your state,* then send this money to the state with the appropriate form.

Small businesses may be able to file annual sales tax reports; others will have to file quarterly or monthly, depending on total sales and amount of taxes normally collected. When you apply for a tax number, your state will send you information and instructions on how much tax to collect, when to file, and so on.

Some people think their tax number entitles them to avoid sales tax on business-related purchases; not so. *This number applies only to merchandise purchased for resale.* The suppliers you deal with will want your number for their files, and whenever you sell to dealers, be sure to get their number for yours. This documents to the state why you haven't collected tax on a sale. (If you sell wholesale to dealers who do not have a tax number, you have to charge them sales tax on their purchases.) Another misconception about a sales tax number is that it automatically entitles one to buy goods at wholesale prices. This is not true. Each manufacturer and wholesaler has its own terms and conditions of sale. In addition to establishing certain minimum quantities, these suppliers may also have strict policies against selling to anyone who is not a retailer (owner of a shop or store).

● **Sales to Buyers in Other States.** In the past, many states have tried to force businesses to collect use taxes on sales made to buyers in states other than their own. Mail order businesses everywhere heaved a sigh of relief in the fall of 1992 when the U.S. Supreme Court ruled that states could not legally do this, but there has been much debate of this topic ever since. States have long been trying (with little success) to get consumers to voluntarily pay tax on items purchased out-of-state, but this law is not uniformly enforced. *If your state has a sales tax, however, and you have a business in that state, you do need to collect sales taxes on all taxable products or services sold online, just as you do when you sell to consumers off the Net.* Your state will give a list of the specific items that are taxable in your state.

295

Scams and Frauds

Among the top ten Internet scams of 2001—in addition to chain letters discussed in Chapter Two—were e-mails offering information on how to investigate people or spy on them, how to repair bad credit, and virus e-mails with deceptive subject lines and hidden code that causes one to spread them to friends. Several sites on the Web are devoted to educating consumers about both spam and scams. With a little research on the following sites, you can learn how to cut down the number of spam e-mails you receive and also learn whether certain business opportunities are for real or just another scam.

- **www.BadBusinessBureau.com** (The "Rip-Off Report")—This is a good place to start if you're trying to decide whether a certain opportunity on the Web is legitimate or a scam that has brought consumer complaints. The site has a search area where you can type in the name of the company or other information you may have about it, and turn up any bad reports people may have filed on this site. You are also encouraged to file your own scam reports here.

- **www.Consumer.gov/idtheft**—The U.S. government's central Web site for identity theft information.

- **www.Fraud.org**—The National Fraud Center/Internet Fraud Watch site features fraud alerts and information about Internet fraud and scams against businesses. 1-800-876-7060.

- **www.FTC.gov**—The Federal Trade Commission's site includes information on phony business opportunities, identity theft, and chain letters and e-mail scams. (Report scams to the FTC by e-mail to uce@ftc.gov or call toll free 1-877-FTC-HELP.)

- **www.MomsWorkAtHomeSite.com**—Has a good page of tips for avoiding scams.

- **www.Scambusters.org**—For information on Internet fraud, sign up for Audri and Jim Lanford's ezine, *Internet ScamBusters*.

● **www.USPS.com/postalinspectors**—Information on the U.S. Postal Inspection Service and press releases about latest scams. (You can get additional information on scams by visiting www.USPS.gov and typing "scams" into the search box on that page.)

State Bedding Laws

(*See also* Consumer Safety Laws)

The Bedding and Upholstered Furniture Law is an aggravating, frustrating state law that affects everyone in the United States who manufactures items with concealed stuffing, including dolls, quilts, pillows, soft picture frames, and so on. The law not only requires yet another label to be permanently affixed to each item, but a license ($100 or more) for each state in which goods are sold.

The frustrating thing about this law is that it makes no distinction between the manufacturer of pillows and mattresses and the craftsperson who sells a few dolls in the local craft shop. Especially upsetting to some people is the fact that this law is being arbitrarily enforced. In one state, makers of such items and the shops who sell them are "getting away with it," while those in another state are having their merchandise removed from shop shelves and show exhibits. (Some unhappy people in the latter group have been known to seek revenge by turning in other people who haven't yet been caught.)

Smart Tip

If you happen to sell decorator pillows, the "raw pillow" should come with label already affixed. Crafters who need only a few labels might visit a large fabric store to see if they might obtain the extra labels that normally come with the bolts of fabric the shop buys.

● **Stuffed Toys.** Similar to state bedding laws are acts some states have on their books about the manufacture of stuffed toys. I don't know how many states have such laws but a note about Pennsylvania's "stuffed toys act" was brought to my attention by a reader in that state. Here, state officials often visit craft shows and inspect merchandise to make sure it is both safe for children and properly labeled. Regardless of what Pennsylvania sellers might call their products, this state's stuffed toy law says a product is a "toy" if it looks like a toy and contains any fiber, chemical, or other stuffing.

If you wish to pursue this topic, contact your state's Department of Health and try to connect with "the bedding official." (In some states, you may have to call or write State Tagging Law Enforcement Officials, usually listed under bedding, milk or food, product safety, health, home furnishing, sanitation or Department of Health and Environment.) Ask for samples of the required tag and a source where labels can be bought.

Note: The only penalty that appears to be connected with a violation of either state bedding or stuffed toy laws is removal of merchandise from store shelves or a fine if the seller refuses to comply with the law after being notified of it. For that reason, most sellers ignore this law until they are challenged by authorities.

State Laws

(See *Commercial Kitchen Laws; Consignment Laws; Post Office Box Address; Resale Tax Number; State Bedding Laws; Taxes Businesses Must Pay; Telephone*)

To get information about laws and regulations in your state, along with contact information for the various government agencies in your state, go to www.businesslaw.gov and, under "Laws and Regulations" click "State/Select Your Jurisdiction."

Taxes Businesses Must Pay

(*See also* Resale Tax Number)

As a business owner, you must pay the following taxes:

Local Taxes

In addition to certain local taxes, your state or local governments may impose an inventory tax—a property tax, actually—on business equipment and inventory, such as the for-sale goods you're holding, or the large supply of books you've just self-published. You'll have to investigate this point on your own.

Taxes Businesses Must Pay

State and Sales Taxes

These include income tax, unemployment tax (if you have employees), and sales tax. Most states have an income tax. Like the federal income tax, it's calculated on your net income or profit and is generally due at the same time you file your annual federal tax return. In addition to state sales tax, there may be local sales tax as well. All are calculated together and paid to the state on a regular basis. (See also "Resale Tax Number" for information on collecting and paying sales taxes to your state.)

For links to state tax departments across the country, type the name of your state and "state tax deparments" into your browser's search engine.

Federal Taxes

These include owner-manager's income tax or corporation income tax, and employee income tax and unemployment tax (if you have employees). Estimated tax payments, which are due from self-employed individuals, must be made quarterly, on the 15th of April, June, September, and January. Naturally, there's a penalty for not paying taxes when due, as well as for underestimating them. An accountant will help you figure out the amount you need to pay each quarter.

To get tax forms, the latest information about tax laws, or IRS publications in PDF format, visit www.TaxPlanet.com, one of the best tax sites I've found on the Web. (You can also connect directly to www.IRS.gov, if you prefer.)

Self-Employment Taxes

When the profit on your Schedule C tax report reaches $400 or more, you must file a Self-Employment Tax Form along with your regular income tax form and pay into your personal social security account at a rate and wage base that is continually being increased. However, self-employed individuals now have some relief in the form of a page one tax deduction currently equal to half the amount of self-employment. Keep tabs on the money you're putting in your account by periodically requesting a statement of earnings posted to your social security record. To get it, request a "Statement of Earnings" by sending your social security number and date of birth to the Department of Health & Human Services, Social Security Administration, Baltimore, MD 21235. You can also request this information on the Web at www.SSA.gov.

If you are now collecting social security and want to start a business, be aware that, until you are 65, you are limited in the amount you can earn without losing any of your benefits. This dollar amount (available from your local social security office) has been rising slowing through the years, and someday it is hoped that Congress will allow senior citizens to work and earn unlimited income without losing benefits. After the age of 70, there is no earnings limit, but by then we may be too tired to work that hard.

Smart Tip

Self-employment taxes take a big chunk of an entrepreneur's profits. To keep them as low as possible, you must "get smart" about tax deductions. A good place to start is the author's eBook, *Money-Saving Tax Strategies for Homebased Entrepreneurs.* (See "Other Resources.")

Telephone

(See also *Checklist of Home-Related Tax-Deductible Expenses for Home-Business Owners*)

Many home-business owners use their personal telephone for business, then list this number on their business cards and stationery not realizing this may be a violation of local telephone company regulations. Each state has a separate commission that determines the usage of a residential phone, so you need to check on this. In some instances, a fine may be imposed for improper use; in others, you may only be asked to stop doing this. Still others may simply start charging you business rates.

Although you cannot legally advertise a personal phone number in connection with a homebased business, you can receive business phone calls on it and make outgoing calls, deducting expenses for long-distance business calls. (The IRS now limits deductions of other portions of a personal phone bill, and since they may question your long-distance business charges, it would be a good idea to keep a telephone log to substantiate your business deductions.)

Until you have a separate business line or other approved arrangement, do not answer your residential phone with your business name. Instead, answer with your name. For example, "This is Barbara Brabec. May I help you?"

Contact your local telephone company to see what special literature they may be able to send you about extra lines or numbers for business, special phone equipment, voice mail, electronic mail, availability of toll-free numbers, and so on. Getting an extra line for business may be easier and less expensive than you think. Some phone companies offer special "Remote Relay Services" or "phantom phones." Here, you keep your personal line and the phone company sets up a separate business number for you. Calls to the business number are relayed through your personal phone line and charged separately. Such approved business numbers can then be legally advertised.

When arranging her telephone hookup, Martha Oskvig learned that a separate phone line into her home (used exclusively as her business toll-free and message line) could officially be classified as a second personal line. "Of course, the rates are cheaper this way," she says. "Since my name is part of my business name (Martha Oskvig & Associates), the listing appears in the white pages as "Martha Oskvig" with my street address directly beneath our family phone line, which includes both my husband's and my name."

Martha suggests that this type of phone listing will work best when you personally know your customers and you have an uncommon surname. "Another Smith or Johnson who *isn't* in business might get your calls if clients don't know your street address," she points out. "Because of safety and privacy concerns, many women use only their surname and first initial in public directories. Also, a personal line does not qualify for a Yellow Pages listing nor for most phone-directory display ads."

Smart Tip

In selecting a business phone for your office, you might look for such special features as two lines (one for home and business), a hold button, speaker button, conference call button, preprogrammed memory buttons, and auto redial. One entrepreneurial mom suggests you get a mute button, too, because it allows one to "hiss at the children while listening."

● **Answering Machines vs. Voice Mail.** Using an answering machine, you can leave only one message and take one call at a time, which may be all many businesses need. But most business owners prefer voice mail because it allows them to leave a variety of messages for callers while taking several calls at once. Many phone companies and outside service bureaus offer voice mail services at affordable fees. Those who receive many calls or those who spend a lot of time providing the same information to many callers should find it most advantageous.

Note: *The FCC's Telephone Consumer Protection Act* strictly prohibits the sending of unsolicited fax advertising or prerecorded telemarketing calls unless a prior business relationship exists, or the sender has granted permission for such messages.

Trademarks

A U.S. trademark "includes any word, name, symbol, or device, or any combination thereof adopted and used by a manufacturer or merchant to identify his goods and distinguish them from those manufactured or sold by others," according to the Trademark Act of 1946. The primary function of a trademark is to indicate origin, but in some cases it also serves as a guarantee of quality.

To protect your business name on the national level, design a logo that incorporates both your business name and a related graphic. Note that generic and descriptive names in the public domain cannot be trademarked, nor can you adopt any trademark that is so similar to another that it is likely to confuse buyers. Trademarks thus prevent one company from trading on the good name and reputation of another.

If you have access to the Web, you can do a preliminary search at http://tess.uspto.gov to see if the business name you've chosen has been trademarked. As the site cautions, this is no guarantee that the name is clear, but it's a good starting place. In large city libraries, also look for the annual *Trademark Register of the United States*, which includes all registered trademarks in use.

To establish a trademark in the United States, you first decide which mark you want to use, then do preliminary research to be reasonably sure no one else is using that mark. Then you take steps to prevent others from also using it on the same or related goods by filing an application for trademark with the Patent and Trademark Office in Washington. (Get more information online at www.uspto.gov.)

"A trademark cannot be registered until proof has been furnished of use in commerce," says Mary Helen Sears, "which means *interstate* commerce (not intrastate commerce). If one advertises mail order trademarked goods in national magazines or in newspapers sold in an interstate area and gets at least some out-of-state orders, that's considered interstate sales. Note that U.S.–Canada or U.S.–Mexico sales and promotions, even in a cross-border town, are considered 'intercountry' and will qualify as well as interstate sales and promos for 'use in commerce' of the United States."

Although you can *reserve* a trademark by filing an intent-to-use application, this is not recommended for home-business owners. "Such applications can be very expensive and extremely tricky to maintain without the help of a lawyer who understands how they work," says Ms. Sears.

Once a trademark registration has been confirmed, one places the notice of trademark ® (an R with a circle around it), after every use of the trademark word or symbol. (The words, "Registered in U.S. Patent and Trademark Office" or "Reg. U.S. Pat. and Tm. Off." may also be used.) Trademarks must be renewed every ten years, and if you do not renew in a timely manner, renewal will be barred and you'll have to file a new application.

On the surface, it sounds simple enough to get a trademark, but the process could take as long as two years if you do it yourself. Study some of the self-help legal guides available in any library to lessen the chances of your application being rejected, causing you to lose your application fee. In this event, you would be wise to hire an attorney to help you resolve any problems. Since the use of an attorney (whose rates may be as high as $300 an hour) could bring your total costs for filing up to $2,000 or more, you will have to do some soul searching to decide whether the benefits are worth the cost.

Smart Tip

U.S. companies generally use a "TM" symbol (or "SM" for a service mark) to indicate they are claiming a particular mark and may also be in the process of filing a trademark application. Although this symbol offers no statutory legal benefits, it does tend to deter others from using the mark. Since use of the TM symbol does not obligate you to actually file for trademark, you have nothing to lose by tacking it on to anything you're trying to protect.

Trade Secret

A "trade secret" is something a business owns that gives it a competitive advantage over others who do not know it. The Department of Labor provides this legal definition of trade secret: "Any confidential formula, pattern, process, device, information or compilation of information that is used in an employer's business, and that gives the employer an advantage over competitors who do not know or use it." More specifically, a trade secret might be the secret recipe that makes your catering service special, a VIP contacts list you've spent years developing, a foreign source of supply for a product much in demand, etc.

"If you invent a small device for cutting fingernails that can be easily copied, get a patent," says inventor Jeremy W. Gorman. "If you have a complex formula that will be essentially impossible to copy, keep it as a trade secret. Colors, flavors, perfumes and shampoos are commonly trade secrets."

Common law trade secret protection exists, and if anyone were to steal your trade secret, you might have grounds for a lawsuit.

United Parcel Service

You don't need an introduction to UPS, the most economical and dependable shipping service in the country, so this is just a reminder that UPS packages are rarely lost or damaged, and delivery halfway across the country takes only a few days. ("Red Label" and "Blue Label" service is available at extra cost for packages that need even faster delivery.) UPS will pick up packages anywhere with just one day's notice—and that includes your residence. There is a modest weekly pickup charge that applies to the first pickup of the week and covers all other packages and pickups in that same week. Packages must be weighed beforehand by the mailer, who then calls the nearest UPS office (toll-free numbers provided) for postage applicable to each package. A simple form, plus a check for total postage completes the process. Packages are automatically insured for up to $100 and additional insurance may be purchased if desired. Call your nearest UPS office and ask for information about their "Ready Customer Pickup Service." (Get more information online at www.ups.com.)

Smart Tip

Do not use UPS when shipping items into Canada that could just as easily be mailed. All UPS packages must go through Customs, causing delays and extra charges to customers who must pick up packages themselves. Standard mail (formerly fourth-class mail), however, is free from Customs inspection, and is delivered right to the customer's door.

- **C.O.D Shipments.** If a customer asks you to send a UPS shipment C.O.D., and there is more than one carton or box per shipment, be sure to put a C.O.D. tag on each carton. One reader reported that a customer who ordered five cases of products returned the one case bearing her C.O.D. tag marked "delivery refused," but kept the other four cases and never paid for them.

Zoning Laws

If you haven't done it already, learn where you stand by reading a copy of your community's zoning regulations, either at city hall or in your city library. Find out what zone you're in and read the section that pertains to home occupations. If you're already in business and think you may be operating illegally, do *not* use your home or business phone number to get this information from City Hall because many municipal numbers now have Caller ID. (The city of Tacoma, Washington, reportedly has a zoning bounty hunter who tracks down zoning violators and fines them retroactively, and this may well be happening in other communities as well.)

If you rent, or live in a condominium or town house, be sure to check your lease, apartment regulations, or condominium covenants for any clause that may prohibit a homebased business. A business in one unit of a co-op apartment, for example, can affect the tax-deductibility aspects of others in the building. So even if local zoning ordinances aren't a problem, this sort of thing could stop you dead in your tracks if your business activity involves the sale of products or people coming and going. On the other hand . . . if you are operating an "electronic business," who is to know unless you tell them? I believe many people running computer-related businesses from home are ignoring such restrictive clauses. As one of my readers puts it, "I live in a condominium association that forbids any work at home, but my writing and Webmaster duties bother no one, so I continue to work and I am not telling anyone what I do. I have a Mail Boxes Etc. account and I use that address for all business, including my business license (even though my state says you shouldn't do this)."

Regardless of laws to the contrary, I and many others believe we all have a right to do whatever we wish in our own home *so long as we do not bother any of our neighbors or do anything to change the nature of our neighborhood.* If you are earning money from an electronic business, I suggest you continue to do what you feel you must do and don't discuss your work with anyone in your building. Most homes have computers these days and what you do on *your* computer should be nobody's business but your own.

Common Zoning Restrictions

Although the detailed aspects of zoning laws can vary considerably from one city to the next, most communities have restrictions on:

- The number of customers or clients allowed in the home (often none)

- The amount of space the business occupies in the home (often severely limited)

- The sale of merchandise (often, sales of all kind are prohibited)

- The number of employees (often, no outside employees are allowed)

- The posting of signs (small or none)

- The type and size of vehicles used for business

- The number of businesses per residence

- The use of machinery (nothing that disturbs neighbors)

- The storage of hazardous materials

- The type and number of deliveries that may be received

- The number of businesses in a home

The following reports from my readers on some of the above mentioned restrictions will give you an idea of how zoning laws sometimes restrict an individual's ability to earn a living at home. As you will learn, many business owners are either forced to do business in a different way than desired or operate illegally and hope for the best.

Zoning Laws

- **Customers or Clients in Your Home.** If your city's zoning ordinance prohibits customers or clients coming to your home, you're surely going to get into trouble if you try to present regular home parties to sell merchandise, and it probably means no teaching of any kind either. A quilting teacher in Herndon, Virginia, who decided to be aboveboard obtained the required personal service license and zoning permit, which prohibits the following: signs, accessory buildings, displays, sales, consultation visits from clients for commissions, employees, and more than four students at a time, or more than eight in a day (which certainly limits this teacher's financial prospects). "What's especially irritating," she said, "is that I know at least ten people who flagrantly violate the ordinance, either with students or sales."

It's this kind of situation that often prompts people to enter complaints against neighbors and friends. And if your neighbors don't get you, the competition might. (As soon as you give your illegal homebased business visibility with a shot of publicity or an ad in the paper, people can find you and turn you in.) In most cases, home-business owners don't want total strangers coming to their home anyway because this is a disruption to normal family life and an easy way for would-be thieves to "case the joint." None of us who work at home want people dropping in unannounced. On the other hand, in some cases where zoning laws aren't prohibitive, some business owners have figured out a way to totally isolate the business area in their home from personal living quarters, and also have separate entrances for each. If you're going to do this, however, you would be wise to install a good burglar alarm system.

- **Amount of Space the Business Occupies.** Zoning laws in many communities often set severe restrictions on the amount of space a homebased business may occupy, sometimes as little as 10 or 15 percent of the total space, *including the garage and detached accessory buildings.* Sometimes the law will also state that no additions, alterations, or remodeling of the dwelling, garage, or accessory structures may be made as a result of the home occupation.

- **Sale of Merchandise.** Holiday boutiques and open house sales are common across the country, but many of these events may be in violation of local zoning laws and some people are just fortunate not to get caught. On the other hand, even when a community's zoning laws prohibit a business from selling products in the home, exceptions may be allowed for a one- or two-day "home boutique" because it may be perceived in the same light as a garage sale. Before spending time and money to market this way, however, make sure it's okay not only with local authorities but with your neighbors as well, since this kind of event can certainly create traffic and parking problems.

Home parties are likely to be a problem in many areas where customers or clients are restricted in one's home business. (Although who is to say these aren't just friends coming over for coffee and cake?) When zoning laws expressly forbid the actual sale of products in the home, however, some people get around this by simply taking payment for merchandise they deliver to customers' homes the next day.

I used to think that if you lived in the country, you were probably home free where zoning laws were concerned. But that was before I heard this story from Joan, a quilter and dollmaker in Tucson, Arizona. After holding a small "country barn craft show" on her five-acre property several miles outside Tucson's city limits, Joan learned she had been reported to zoning officials. (She later learned that she had been turned in by a craft mall owner in the city who didn't want this kind of sales competition.) She was informed that she had "created a public nuisance with traffic." She protested by saying that fewer people had come to this sale than had come to her last Christmas party for friends, and everyone parked on her own property so none of her neighbors could have been inconvenienced. (Besides, the nearest one lived five acres away.) Nonetheless, she was told she could never again sell quilts or dolls (or any other crafts) from her property again without risking a fine of $600 a day for the offense.

In addition, she was required to buy a county license that did nothing more than entitle her to *make things* in her own home. All her arguments to the zoning official were ignored, including the fact that she was just one of a thousand or more artists and crafters in this particular community being cited, and the only one who had ever been told a county license was needed. In addition, all of Joan's neighbors had homebased businesses, including a bed-and-breakfast, a dog-breeding kennel, a tax accounting business, and an assisted living facility. Ah, said the zoning official, all these occupations were included on the "approved list." But there was no designation for selling quilts, dolls, or other craft items, so that activity had to be prohibited. (Joan, could, however, sell tomatoes in a stand at the end of her lane.)

"I used to have a sizeable number of people who I met at shows, who came, one by one, to my house to order custom quilts, to have old quilts repaired, or quilt tops finished into quilts. I no longer do this, however. Now I have to meet these people elsewhere and make arrangements to do the job they require."

- **Employees.** Although some of the more enlightened communities now allow one outside employee in a homebased business, most prohibit employees of any kind, except for people who live in the dwelling (spouse, kids, etc.). One angry business owner said her city's zoning law prohibited her from even *meeting* with an outside employee in her home. "This means that, to be 100 percent legal, I couldn't invite an employee to dinner!" To me and others, this kind of restrictive law is infringing on our constitutional rights.

- **Use of Signs.** Most communities prohibit business signs of any kind on one's property. In some places, this also means you cannot have the name of your business painted on your vehicle if you park it in your driveway.

- **Vehicles Used for Business.** In most communities, there will be restrictions on the type and number of vehicles that can be used for business, and where they are parked. In Roseville, California, this restriction has caused serious problems for Velda, the owner of a scissors sharpening business. Her zoning law reads, *"Not more than one vehicle specifically designated to be used for a home occupation shall be parked at the subject residence at any time. Such allowed vehicle shall not be larger than a standard pickup or van. No commercial vehicles, equipment or trailers shall be parked at the residence at any time."*

"We purchased a van similar to that used by UPS that is actually smaller than many motor homes that are legally parked in our neighborhood," says Velda. "We were in the process of converting the van for later use in mobile sharpening because it is impractical to move equipment back and forth. We were notified that we must stop sharpening in the van, however, even though this did not cause any noise or traffic. We were told we could keep the van if we took the sharpening equipment out of it, but what good does a sharpening van do if we have to move massive amounts of equipment in an out daily? None, so we had to quit using the van and sell it at a loss."

- **Number of Businesses Per Residence.** As if Velda doesn't have enough troubles, her city has added to it by restricting to *one* the number of businesses that can be housed in her home. Her son wants to start a business maintaining and restoring residential ponds. All he needs is a phone to make and return calls, but because the city code says only one permit per residence, he cannot do business legally, even though his business would not in any way change the character of the residential neighborhood. "What this means," says Velda, "is that we must have one business wide enough in scope to cover all we each do, *or* one of us must run our business illegally, *or* one of us must rent space outside the home."

- **Use of Machinery.** Remember that annoying your neighbors is probably the quickest way to get caught by zoning officials. When an artist began to do woodworking in her garage, the neighbors objected to the noise, called the authorities, and she was slapped with a zoning violation. To continue her business, she had to move to a new location.

- **Storing Hazardous Substances.** Zoning laws everywhere have rules about storing hazardous substances, which is good. Certainly none of us wants to live next door to someone whose garage could explode at any moment. But what's ridiculous is that, as a homeowner, we can have paint thinners, bug poison, herbicides, BBQ lighter fluid, gas for the lawn mower, etc., but if we have a business in our home and are inspected, and the inspector thinks any of those substances are being used in our business, we could be fined if we do not have a fire department permit for each of them.

- **Type and Number of Deliveries.** Although a homeowner can receive UPS packages every day if necessary, business owners who work at home may be limited to no more than two deliveries of "materials" a month, and the size of the delivery vehicle may be limited to nothing larger than a standard van. No shipments at all by truck. (It's okay to have the Sears truck deliver a washer and dryer, but if you were a book publisher, you couldn't accept a shipment of books from the printer.)

Zoning Laws

Changing Outdated Zoning Laws

If you decide that your business is violating local zoning laws, but isn't going to create any problems for your neighbors or the community at large, you can either keep working as quietly as possible and hope no one ever notices what you're doing, or you could go out on a limb and consider asking for a variance or some kind of "conditional use," "special use," or "special exemption" permit. This is generally issued following a public hearing about which your neighbors must be informed. If you can get support from neighbors, the special permit may be easy to obtain.

In many communities across the country, zoning officials who are well aware of the number of home businesses in their area simply "look the other way" because this is easier to do than changing the law. Velda tried to get the one-business-per-home ruling changed in her city when the city planning person agreed it was ridiculous, but he told her that citizens must take on the task of researching, writing the proposal, and presenting it to the city council because they are not allowed to do that. "Seems pretty dumb that the city's own planning department cannot propose change," says Velda.

If, in the end, you choose to operate illegally until things change, you do need to plan on the possibility that you might someday be caught and forced to cease business operations. Although there have been exceptions, people are rarely fined for zoning violations unless they persist in the operation of a business after they've been warned to stop.

Two Possible Solutions to Zoning Problems

If local zoning laws prohibit or limit the activities of your homebased business, doing business out of a post office box could be one way to get around this problem. (Refer back to the special tip in the "Licenses and Permits" area.) Although most homebased entrepreneurs prefer to work in their homes, supplementary use of outside facilities known as business centers or incubators is one way to avoid zoning problems because a business would have a legal presence at the center itself.

A "business incubator" is a physical facility used to "hatch" small businesses by providing under one roof all the resources and facilities needed for their survival. Some entrepreneurs house their entire operation in such centers, while others simply use their "business identity package" service, which may include a business address; telephone answering service; secretarial, word processing; and copying services; and the use of fax machines. Often, such business centers are started in small business development centers or by individual entrepreneurs in a position to acquire a building for such purposes.

Smart Tip

The incubator industry is represented by the National Business Incubation Association. Association members have links to NBIA's site on the Web. Visit this site's Resource Center to download a list of all the incubators in your area: www.nbia.org

Some business owners rent office space on an occasional basis. For example, a woman in one of my workshops said this had been the perfect solution for her business, not because of zoning problems, but because it was impossible for her to meet with clients with a baby underfoot. So each time she needed to confer with a client, she would grab her "office box" and set up temporary shop in the business center, just for an hour. In the box was an assortment of things one might normally expect to see in an office: a desk pad, pen set, calendar, pictures, etc. When she was finished, she packed up and went home with the client thinking this was her regular office. All her business calls were forwarded to her home phone through the business center, with only one small problem: there was an automatic cutoff after fifteen minutes, so every time the phone rang, she had to set a timer and if the call ran long, she sometimes had to get creative in making excuses for why she had to hang up and call back.

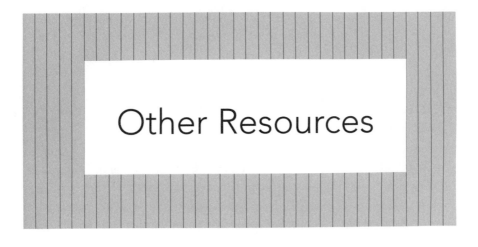

Other Resources

Books

Books will always be one of your best sources for reliable business information, and never before has there been such a wealth of how-to titles on every aspect of business. Nearly 50,000 books are published every year as countless others go out of print, some only a year or two after publication. Whether a book lives or dies depends not only on the value of its content, but on how hard a publisher or author works to promote it. Even when good books go out of print, however, they often survive on library shelves. In trying to wade through the many titles of interest to you, always consider the author's experience and background, and trust most the advice of authors who do for a living the thing they are writing about.

The books listed in this section are recently published or long-established books by leading authors or business experts whose knowledge I respect. Note that many recommended titles have gone into new or revised editions, a signal not only of a book's sales popularity, but an indication of its quality of content. A book that survives into a second or later edition is often on its way to becoming a classic in its field (if not already there).

For more titles on any given topic, browse bookstores, visit your local library, or do an online search at an online bookstore such as Amazon.com or BarnesandNoble.com.

Homebased Business and Entrepreneurship—General

The Best Home Businesses for the 21st Century by Paul and Sarah Edwards (J. P. Tarcher).

The Best Home Business Opportunities for Women by Liz Folger (Prima).

Business Savvy for Today's New Entrepreneur! by Marilyn M. Burns and Cathy Bolton McCullough (New Forums Press).

E-Money! The Complete Guide to Using the Internet to Profit at Home NOW! An eBook by Jeffrey Lant available from www.WorldProfit.com.

The Entrepreneurial Parent: How to Earn Your Living at Home & Still Enjoy Your Family, Your Work and Your Life by Paul and Sarah Edwards and Lisa Roberts (Putnam/Tarcher).

Finding Your Perfect Work The New Career Guide to Making a Living, Creating a Life by Paul and Sarah Edwards (J. P. Tarcher).

The Home Office and Small Business Answer Book, 2nd ed., by Janet Attard (Owl Books)

How to Raise a Family and Career Under One Roof—A Parent's Guide by Lisa M. Roberts (Bookhaven Press).

Let's Go Into Business Together—8 Secrets to Successful Business Partnering by Azriela Jaffe (Career Press).

Living in an RV—How to Get a Life Living Full-time in a Recreational Vehicle, an eBook by Coleen Sykora (www.WorkersonWheels.com).

101 Best Home-Based Businesses for Women: Everything You Need to Know About Getting Started on the Road to Success, 3rd ed., by Priscilla Huff (Prima Pub.).

The Shoestring Entrepreneur's Guide to the Best Home-Based Businesses by Rob Spiegel (Griffin).

The Shoestring Entrepreneur's Guide to the Best Home-Based Franchises by Rob Spiegel (Griffin).

The Shoestring Entrepreneur's Guide to Internet Start-ups by Rob Spiegel (St. Martin's Press).

The Stay-at-Home Mom's Guide To Making Money From Home, by Liz Folger (Prima).

Working Solo: The Real Guide to Freedom & Financial Success with Your Own Business, 2nd ed., by Terri Lonier (Wiley & Sons).

How-to Business Start-Up Guides

The Birthday Party Business: How to Make a Living As a Children's Entertainer by Bruce Fife (Piccadilly Books).

Bizy's Guide to Building a Successful Network Marketing Business, an eBook by Jackie Ulmer, available from www.Bizymoms.com.

Bizy's Guide to Starting Your Own Child Care Service, an eBook by Karen M. Potter, available from www.Bizymoms.com.

Cleaning Up For a Living—Everything You Need to Know to Become a Successful Building Service Contractor, 2nd ed., by Don Aslett (Betterway Books).

The Complete Guide to Self Publishing—Everything You Need to Know to Write, Publish, Promote, and Sell Your Own Book, 4th ed., by Marilyn and Tom Ross (F&W Pub.).

Complete Idiot's Guide to Making Money with Your Hobby by Barbara Arena (Alpha Books).

Crafting for Dollars—How to Establish & Profit from a Career in Crafts by Sylvia Landman (Prima).

The Crafts Business Answer Book & Resource Guide by Barbara Brabec (M. Evans).

Creative Cash: How to Profit from Your Special Artistry, Creativity, Hand Skills and Related Know-How, 6th ed., by Barbara Brabec (Prima).

Flowers for Sale: Growing and Marketing Cut Flowers Backyard to Small Acreage; A Bootstrap Guide by Lee Sturdivant (San Juan Naturals).

From Kitchen to Market: Selling Your Gourmet Food Specialty, 3rd ed., by Stephen F. Hall (Dearborn Trade).

Getting Started as a Freelance Illustrator or Designer by Michael Fleischman (North Light Books).

Handmade for Profit—Hundreds of Secrets to Success in Selling Arts & Crafts, 2nd ed., by Barbara Brabec (M. Evans).

How to Be a Literary Agent—An Introductory Guide to Literary Representation by Richard Mariotti and Bruce Fife (Piccadilly Books).

How to Get Happily Published, 5th ed., by Judith Appelbaum (HarperPerennial).

How to Make at Least $100,000 Every Year As a Successful Consultant in Your Own Field: The Complete Guide to Succeeding in the Advice Business by Jeffrey Lant (Jeffrey Lant Associates).

How to Make a Whole Lot More Than $1,000,000 Writing, Commissioning, Publishing, and Selling How to Information by Jeffrey Lant (Jeffrey Lant Associates).

How to Open a Profitable Child Care Center: Everything You Need to Know to Plan, Organize and Implement a Successful Program by Patricia C. Gallagher (Mosby).

How to Set Your Fees and Get Them by Kate Kelly (Visibility Enterprises).

How to Start a Home-Based Catering Business, 3rd ed., by Denise Vivaldo (Globe Pequot Pr.).

How to Start a Home-Based Landscaping Business, 3rd ed., by Owen E. Dell (Globe Pequot Pr.).

How to Start and Operate Your Own Bed-And-Breakfast—Down-To-Earth Advice from an Award-Winning B&B Owner by Martha Watson Murphy (Owlet).

How to Start and Operate Your Own Homebased Teaching Studio, an eBook by Sylvia Landman, available from www.Bizymoms.com.

How to Start Your Own Virtual Assistant Biz, an eBook by Dianne Ennen and Kelly Poelker, available from www.Bizymoms.com.

Make Money Reading Books! How to Start and Operate Your Own Home-Based Freelance Reading Service by Bruce Fife (Piccadilly Books).

Making a Living Without a Job by Barbara Winter (Bantam).

Making $$$ at Home—Over 1,000 Editors Who Want Your Ideas, Know-How & Experience by Darla Sims (Sunstar Pub.).

Making Money Teaching Music by David R. Newsam and Barbara Sprague Newsam (Writer's Digest Books).

Making Money With Your Computer at Home by Paul and Sarah Edwards (Putnam).

Money Talks: The Complete Guide to Creating a Profitable Workshop or Seminar in Any Field by Jeffrey Lant (Jeffrey Lant Publications).

Net Strategy: Charting the Digital Course for Your Company's Growth by Rob Spiegel (Dearborn).

Network Marketer's Guide to Success by Jeffrey A. Babener (Forum for Network Marketing).

The New Professionals—The Rise of Network Marketing As the Next Major Profession by Charles W. King, Ph.D. and James W. Robinson (Prima).

Other Resources

101 Great Mail-Order Businesses, 2nd ed., by Tyler G. Hicks (Prima).

1-2-3-Guide to Medical Billing: Start and Market Your Own Medical Billing Business, an eBook by Beth Coats, available from www.Bizymoms.com.

Open Your Own Bed & Breakfast, 4th ed., by Barbara Notarius and Gail Sforza Brewer (Wiley & Sons).

Profitable Email Publishing: How to Publish a Profitable Emag, an eBook by Angela Adair-Hoy, available from www.WritersWeekly.com.

The Self-Publishing Manual—How to Write, Print and Sell Your Own Book, 13th ed., by Dan Poynter (Para Publishing).

Sell & Resell Your Photos by Ron Engh (North Light Books).

Speak and Grow Rich by Lily Walters (Prentice Hall).

Web Design Made Easy by Dennis Gaskill (Morton Publishing).

Your Guide to EBook Publishing Success by James Dillehay, an eBook available from www.00ebooks.com.

Business Planning and Management

Back to the Basics: Running Your Homebased Business for Profit, an eBook by Russ Schultz, available from www.WriteandReap.com.

The Business Planning Guide: Creating a Plan for success in Your Own Business, 8th ed., by David H. Bangs (Upstart).

Homemade Money: Bringing in the Bucks by Barbara Brabec (M. Evans).

Home Office Know-How by Jeffrey D. Zbar (Upstart).

Home Office Life: Making a Space to Work at Home by Lisa Kanarek (Rockport).

Make It Profitable—How to Make Your Art, Craft, Design, Writing, or Publishing Business More Efficient, More Satisfying, and More Profitable by Barbara Brabec (M. Evans).

101 Home Office Secrets by Lisa Kanarek (Career Press).

Organizing Your Home Office for Success, 2nd ed., by Lisa Kanarek (Blakely Press).

Safe@Home: Seven Keys to Home Office Security by Jeffrey D. Zbar, available online at www.GoinSOHO.com.

Legal and Financial

Directory of Grants for Crafts—And How to Write a Winning Proposal by James Dillehay (Warm Snow Publishers).

422 Tax Deductions for Businesses and Self-Employed Individuals by Bernard Kamoroff (Bell Springs Pub.).

Government Giveaways for Entrepreneurs, 4th ed., by Matthew Lesko (InfoUSA, Inc.).

Inc Yourself—How to Profit by Setting Up Your Own Corporation, 9th ed., by Judith H. McQuown (Bantam).

Invasion of Privacy—How to Protect Yourself in the Digital Age by Michael Hyatt (Regnery).

Money-Saving Tax Strategies for Homebased Entrepreneurs, an eBook by Barbara Brabec, available from www.Bizymoms.com.

Online Operator: Business, Legal, and Guide to the Internet by Bernard Kamoroff, CPA (Bell Springs Pub.)

Pricing Guidelines for Arts and Crafts by Sylvia Landman (Writers Club Press).

The Small Business Money Guide: How to Get It, Use It, Keep It by Terri Lonier (Wiley & Sons).

Small Time Operator—How to Start Your Own Business, Keep Your Books, Pay Your Taxes, and Stay Out of Trouble by Bernard Kamoroff, CPA. Revised annually (Bell Springs Pub.).

Motivational Guides

Invest in Yourself—Six Secrets to a Rich Life by Marc Eisensen, Nancy Castleman, and Gerri Detweiler (Wiley).

Living Your Life Out Loud—How to Unlock Your Creativity and Unleash Your Joy, by Salli Raspberry and Padi Selwyn (Pocket Books).

A Whack on the Side of the Head, rev. ed., by Roger Von Oech (Warner Books).

What Are Your Goals? Powerful Questions to Discover What You Want Out of Life by Gary R. Blair (Blair Pub. House).

What to Say When You Talk to Yourself by Shad Helmstetter (Pocket Books).

Home Business/Small Business Organizations

● American Craft Council (ACC), 72 Spring St., New York, NY 10012. 1-800-724-0859 www.CraftCouncil.org

● Association of Business Support Services, Inc. (ABSSI), 5852 Oak Meadow Drive, Yorba Linda, CA 92886-5930, (714) 695-9398; www.abssi.org

● Home Business Institute, Inc., P.O. Box 301, White Plains, NY 10605-0301. 1-888-DIAL HBI; www.HBIweb.com

● National Association for the Self-Employed, P.O. Box 612067, DFW Airport, TX 75261. 1-800-232-6273; www.Nase.com

● National Craft Association (NCA), 2012 E. Ridge Rd., #120, Rochester, NY 14622. 1-800-715-9594; www.craftassoc.com

● National Mail Order Association, 2807 Polk St. NE, Minneapolis, MN 55418-2954. 612-788-1673; www.NMOA.org

● Small Business Service Bureau, 554 Main St., Worcester, MA 01608. 1-800-222-5678; www.SBSB.com

● Society of Craft Designers (SCD), Box 3388, Zanesville, OH 43702-3388. 1-740-452-4541; www.CraftDesigners.org

● Support Services Alliance, P.O. Box 130, Schoharie, NY 12157. 1-800-322-3920; www.SSAinfo.com

● Volunteer Lawyers for the Arts, 1E. 53rd St., 6th Fl., New York, NY 10022. 212-319-ARTS, ext. 1; www.vlany.org

Support Networks on the Web

- Assist University—www.Assistu.com. The premier virtual training program for virtual assistants.

- At-Home Dads—www.AtHomeDad.com. Peter Baylies turned his print newsletter into an online network he calls a "loose-knit grassroots organization for at-home dads." It now sponsors the annual At-Home Dad Convention in Chicago.

- BizyMoms.com—www.bizymoms.com. This online network, founded by Liz Folger, offers eBooks and eClasses on home business topics, message boards, chat rooms, a large archive of home-business articles, a newsletter and more.

- Home-Based Working Moms—www.HBWM.com. Founded by Lesley Spencer to help bring working moms closer to their children. Offers support, networking, information, PR and work opportunities, a monthly print newsletter, a weekly ezine and more.

- The National Association of Entrepreneurial Parents—www.EN-Parent.com. Created by Lisa Roberts for parents who work at home. Serves as a vehicle for connecting local entrepreneurial parents.

- Virtual Assistants Network—www.VirtualAssistantsNetwork.com. Founded by Sherry Huff Carnahan to supply motivation, resources, friendship, and knowledge so that people with service skills can get out of the rat race and into a take-charge, professional business of their own. Two free e-mail newsletters are available on this site. Also includes a forum for networking with other VAs.

Selected Web Sites with Good Content

The following list is merely a sampling of recommended Web sites the author has personally visited and used in her own research. You can turn up thousands more by typing appropriate keywords into your browser's search engine.

Computer and Web Technology

- www.BigNoseBird.com. Over 300 pages of tutorials, reference materials, and other free resources located on this site—everything you need to built a great Web site, including HTML tricks, free graphics, scripts, software tools, and more.

- www.Ibiz-Tools.com. A collection of business management, Web site, and promotional tools for small and big business alike designed by Michael R. Harvey. Some programs are free, including a site statistics package and site-mapper software that allows you to list all links in your Web site so you can find the broken ones.

- www.JohnDilbeck.com. John Dilbeck's site is a good information resource for artists, crafters, and others who want to market products on the Web.

- http://download.cnet.com. When looking for inexpensive software to do a particular job, just type "free computer software" in your browser's search box, or visit this link to find specific programs you may be searching for.

- www.NewbieClub.com. The Newbie Club is a great source of help and information for Internet beginners, offering inexpensive resources to help one learn, such as a "First Website Builder Course," a guide to using Windows, and an eBook on computer key shortcuts. Sign up for the free newsletter, and check out the low-cost Newbie Club membership where you can get answers to technical questions from experts.

- http://RustySmith.com/computer.html. Computer tutorials offered by Rusty Smith, plus troubleshooting tips, reinstall guidance, virus info, advice on buying equipment, tutorial quizzes on Windows, and links to many helpful computer resources.

- www.shortcourses.com. Information and articles on buying and using digital cameras.

- www.SmallBizTechtalk.com/index.html. Computer technical info and support.

- www.Steve.Maurer.net. Steve Maurer offers several free online e-mail and software tutorials, computer tips, a free ezine, and *Email Primer*, a free eBook you can download in your choice of formats.

- www.WebMonkey.com. Excellent Web developer's resource, with a library of how-to articles, a JavaScript library, "HTML Cheatsheet," color codes and much more.

- www.WilsonWeb.com. The Web's largest source of key information about doing business on the Net, with hundreds of articles and thousands of links to resources on e-commerce and Web marketing. This site also offers three free e-mail newsletters on Web marketing, eBiz, and eCommerce.

- www.WorldProfit.com/ezines. Visit this site to sign up for a variety of ezines on different topics related to designing and developing a profitable Web site, with heavy emphasis on how to market products and services on a Web site.

Arts and Crafts Business

- www.About.com. A large network of rich content sites on specific topics, including arts, crafts and needlework. All sites feature articles, forums, chats, and a free newsletter.

- www.CraftAssoc.com. Maintained by the National Craft Association, this site is a primary information and resource center for the professional crafter. The site includes a message board, free e-mail discussion list, free NCA newsletter, and a collection of valuable business articles, and Web links.

- www.Craftmarketer.com. This site features the books of crafts author James Dillehay and includes many valuable business resources, articles, and links. A special "Toolbox" department also lists free software programs and business aids James has personally checked out.

- www.CraftsReport.com. Check this site's archives of crafts business articles from back issues of the magazine, and use the search engine on the site to turn up several articles by Barbara Brabec.

- www.Procrafter.com. This site contains business articles, crafting tips, and a bulletin board for professional crafters.

Home Office/Home Business

- www.About.com. About.com is a large network of rich content sites dedicated to specific topics, including homebased business. All sites feature articles, forums, chats, and a free newsletter.
- www.BarbaraBrabec.com. The author's personal domain features all of her books with a table of contents, reviews, and reader feedback for each title, plus a variety of articles on homebased business, "Computertalk," writing, publishing, and personal reflections. Previously published issues of *The Brabec Bulletin*, the author's free ezine, are also archived here.

- www.HomeOfficeLife. Lisa Kanarek's site offers a good collection of home office organizational tips, Q&A pages, and online seminars.

Industry Research

- www.Bizjournals.com. From this site, you can track what is going on in your business in your neck of the woods. As a registered user, you would have access to a searchable archive of a half-million local business articles from across the nation; the ability to set up your own personalized Industry Journal (with over 45 industries to choose from); and access to industry-specific updates by e-mail. You can also track your customers, prospects, and competitors and receive an e-mail whenever they are mentioned in an article.

- www.Business.com. A directory of business industries, with dozens of subindustries, all linking to articles and related Web sites. (A good place to research an industry you're trying to break into.)

- www.JoannePratt.com. This site contains several reports by Joanne Pratt of interest to home-business researchers that can be downloaded free of charge in PDF format.

Internet Hoaxes and Scams

- htttp://hoaxbusters.ciac.org/HBHoaxCategories.html. Here you can explore all categories of Internet hoaxes, scams, and myths.

- www.vmyths.com. Check whether a virus alert is genuine or not.

Legal Information

- www.FreeAdvice.com. You'll find answers to many of your legal questions here, including information about your state's laws, business law questions, and answers to questions about the use of employees and independent contractors.

- www.IvanHoffman.com. The Web site of attorney Ivan Hoffman contains many articles related to law for writers and publishers, entrepreneurs, Web site designers and owners, trademarks and domain names, Internet and electronic rights.

- www.LawGuru.com. A network of over 2,000 attorneys and law firms in over 35 countries. Various attorneys answer questions online free of charge, and the Web site's database now includes answers to 35,000 FAQs in 45 legal categories.

Speaking Professionally

- www.VoicePower.com. June Johnson's site contains a collection of articles and guidelines to help you develop a winning voice.

- www.Walters-Intl.com. Dottie Walters's site is *the* source for information on speakers and speaking, seminar leaders, humorists, and experts. Here you'll find products on how to market yourself as a speaker and articles from *Sharing Ideas*, the largest newsmagazine in the world for professional speakers with all the issues, tips, news, and trends.

Other Resources

Trends

- www.BrainReserve.com. The Web site of trendmaster Faith Popcorn includes a collection of fascinating articles on current trends relative to business and marketing.

- www.HermanGroup.com. Strategic business futurists Roger Herman and Joyce Gioia issue an e-mail "Trend Alert" every week and their site includes a collection of their articles.

Writing and Publishing

- www.BarbaraBrabec.com. The author's Web site includes articles on her experiences in writing and publishing.

- www.Freelancewrite.about.com. Includes links to hundreds of other sites of interest to writers.

- http://marketing-internet.getcash.ws. From this site you can download several free e-mail courses and eBooks on Internet marketing and electronic publishing.

- www.ParaPublishing.com. The Web site of publishing guru Dan Poynter, includes hundreds of pages of information and free documents on self-publishing, with links to many self-publishing resources.

- www.WritersWeekly.com. The Web site of Angela Hoy, who offers a wealth of info for freelance writers, with links to paying markets and an excellent collection of articles by Angela and other pros in her network. Hoy publishes the highest circulation freelance writing ezine in the world and her site links to many eBooks on the topics of freelance writing and electronic publishing.

- www.WritersWrite.com. A good one-stop resource for information about books, writing, and publishing.

Book Contributors

(Home Business Owners, Web Entrepreneurs, Authors, Attorneys, and Other Professionals)

Angela Allen, www.CumberlanDunes.com

Barbara Arena, www.CraftAssoc.com

Jeffrey A. Babener, www.MLMlegal.com

Jeanne Baratta, www.KitchenElf.com

Peter Baylies, www.AtHomeDad.com

Ilise Benun, www.SelfPromotionOnline.com

Karen Booy, www.KarenBooy.com

Barbara Brabec, www.BarbaraBrabec.com

Pamela Burns, www.Injeanious.com

Silvana Clark, www.SilvanaClark.com

Malcolm and Sandy Dell, www.LewisClarkGifts.com

Dodie Eisenhauer, www.VillageDesigns.com

Bruce Fife, www.PiccadillyBooks.com

Georganne Fiumara, www.HomeWorking Mom.com

Liz Folger, www.BizyMoms.com

Lesley Fountain, www.FriendsinBusiness.com

Pat Fountain, www.Hearts-Delight.com

Dennis Gaskill, www.BoogieJack.com

Myrna Giesbrecht, www.Press4Success.com

Donna L. Gunter, www.SohoBizSolutions.com

Tammy Harrison, www.HBWM.com

Michael R. Harvey, www.Ibiz-Tools.com

Alberta S. Johnson, www.K6ArtLessonPlans.com

Bernard Kamoroff, www.BellSprings.com

Lisa Kanarek, www.HomeOfficeLife.com

Patricia Katz, www.PatKatz.com

Kate Kelly, www.KateKelly.com

Terri Kralik, www.MooseCountryQuilts.com

Sylvia Landman, www.Sylvias-Studio.com

Jeffrey Lant, www.JeffreyLant.com

Tim and Connie Long, www.NorthStarToys.com

JoAnna Lund, www.HealthyExchanges.com

Cheri Marsh, www.SoapMeister.com

Other Resources

Gary Maxwell, www.GaryMaxwell.com
Martha Oskvig, www.Beautipage.com/here4u
Leila Peltosaari, www.TikkaBooks.com
Faith Popcorn, www.BrainReserve.com
Joanne Pratt, www.JoannePratt.com
Diana Ratliff, www.BusinessCardDesigns.com
Lisa Roberts, www.EN-Parent.com
John Schulte, www.NMOA.org
Russ Schultz, www.WriteandReap.com
Shirley Sigmund, www.Marrak.com
Donna M. Snow, www.SnowWrite.com
Cindy Thomas, www.JCTublishing.com
Richard Tuttle, CalliDesign.com
Jackie Ulmer, www.StreetSmartWealth.com
Dottie Walters, www.Walters-Intl.com
Philip White, www.RigelEngineering.com.
Barbara Winter, www.BarbaraWinter.com
Michelle Winterhalter, AtHome.com/Shelle
Susan Young, www.PeachKittyStudio.com

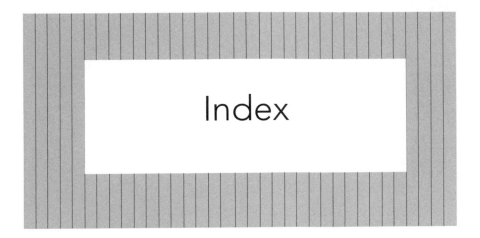

Index

Index

Index

Index

More great advice from Barbara and her readers!

Once your business is up and running, turn to this book's companion guide, *HOMEMADE MONEY: Bringing in the Bucks*, to find the information you need to maximize sales and profits from your homebased business. Topics include how to:

- Improve business management skills
- Slash business expenses and maximize tax deductions
- Get higher prices for everything you sell
- Develop new marketing strategies
- Scout for new customers or clients
- Resell established accounts
- Expand a product line or add new services
- Diversify into totally new business areas
- Save money on paid advertising
- Build word-of-mouth advertising
- Get free publicity
- Do business on the Web
- Manage time, cope with stress, and fight burnout

Continuing the type of information found in *HOMEMADE MONEY: Starting Smart*'s A-to-Z "Crash Course" in Business Basics, *HOMEMADE MONEY: Bringing in the Bucks* also includes an invaluable collection of A-to-Z tax, legal, and financial information needed by small business owners:

- Money-saving tax tips and the Home Office Deduction
- Changing your legal form of business
- Getting a business loan or line of credit
- Protecting your intellectual property
- Credit/trade references and collection techniques
- Employees, independent contractors, and labor laws
- Licensing arrangements
- Patent and trademark insight
- Trade practice rules and regulations

. . . and much more!

Published by M. Evans and Company, Inc.
Available in bookstores everywhere, as well as on the Internet.